P9-CZV-026

DATE DUE

DEC 0 1 1998	
OCT 0 9 2000	
DEC 1 6 2013	

BRODART.   Cat. No. 23-221

Endangered Children

Dependency, Neglect, and Abuse
in American History

Twayne's History of American Childhood Series

Series Editors
Joseph M. Hawes, University of Memphis
N. Ray Hiner, University of Kansas

Endangered Children

Dependency, Neglect, and Abuse
in American History

LeRoy Ashby

Twayne Publishers

An Imprint of Simon & Schuster Macmillan
New York
Prentice Hall International
London Mexico City New Delhi Singapore Sydney Toronto

Endangered Children: Dependency, Neglect, and Abuse in American History
LeRoy Ashby

Twayne Publishers
An Imprint of Simon & Schuster Macmillan
1633 Broadway
New York, NY 10019

Library of Congress Cataloging-in-Publication Data

Ashby, LeRoy,
    Endangered Children : dependency, neglect, and abuse in American history / LeRoy Ashby.
        p.   cm. — (Twayne's history of American childhood series)
    Includes bibliographical references and index.
    ISBN 0–8057–4100–3 (alk. paper)
    1. Abandoned children—United States—History. 2. Orphans—United
States—History. 3. Abused children—United States—History.
4. Child welfare—United States—History. 5. Children—
Institutional care—United States—History. I. Title.
II. Series.
    HV881.A78 1997
        362.7'6'0973—dc20   96–36013
                                                                                    CIP

The paper used in this publication meets the minimum requirements of American National Standard for Information Sciences—Permanence of Paper for Printed Library Materials. ANSI Z39.48–1984. ∞™

10 9 8 7 6 5 4 3 2 1

Printed in the United States of America

In memory of our son, Eric
1967–1977

Contents

Illustrations

Series Editors' Note

The history of children is coming of age. What began in the 1960s as a spontaneous response by some historians to the highly visible and sometimes unsettling effects of the baby boom has emerged as a vigorous and broad-based inquiry into the lives of American children in all generations. As this series on American childhood attests, this new field is robust and includes the work of scholars from a variety of disciplines.

Our goal for this series is to introduce this rich and expanding field to undergraduate students as well as to nonspecialists in related fields. Thus, books in this series are more synthetic than monographic in nature, although some areas are so little known that original research was necessary. All of the books provide important insight into the changing shape and character of children's lives in America. Finally, this series demonstrates very clearly that children are and always have been influential historical actors in their own right. Children play an essential role in the American story that this series is designed to illuminate.

This volume by LeRoy Ashby focuses on dependent, neglected, and abused children who as a group have been virtually invisible to most American historians. Professor Ashby argues convincingly that these children nevertheless have a compelling and important story to tell to those who are willing to listen, not only concerning their own remarkable experiences but also about the adults who alternately discovered and ignored them and who too often used them as symbols or surrogates for their own personal concerns, especially during periods of great social stress. At times, writes Ashby, the history of dependent, neglected, and abused children seems "to be circling back upon itself," and harmful conditions that were once thought ameliorated or eliminated appear once again to plague children. Lessons that society should have learned are too often lessons forgotten, and it is children who must pay the price for this social amnesia. Professor Ashby gives his readers a valuable opportunity to learn these lessons again.

N. Ray Hiner   Joseph M. Hawes
University of Kansas   University of Memphis

Acknowledgments

I am grateful to Joe Hawes and Ray Hiner for inviting me to contribute this volume to the Twayne series on the History of American Childhood. It has been a pleasure to work with them. They have been encouraging, helpful, and understanding.

As always, I owe an unpayable debt to my wife, Mary. Her own work with victims of neglect, abuse, and dependency is a source of inspiration to me and to others. She read the entire manuscript and offered indispensable suggestions. I am delighted once again to acknowledge how dependent I have long been on her love, support, and advice.

As usual, I also relied on my longtime friend, Bob Zieger, of the University of Florida history department, who also read the complete manuscript. His critical talents are superb, and any scholarly effort is the better for the shrewd attention he gives it. Thanks as well to Gay Zieger, who read several chapters. She, too, is an invaluable friend, and I hope that her fine work on the Boys' Republic outside Detroit will soon be in print.

Thanks also to Krista Undeberg and Julie Sandri for helping me gather library materials, and to Pat Hawkins for her time and effort in preparing the final manuscript. Once again I received support and encouragement from my department heads, Richard Hume and, more recently, Roger Schlesinger, as well as from John Pierce, the dean of the College of Liberal Arts. Laurie McGee, Mary Ray Worley, Mary Boss and Laura Van Toll at Impressions Book & Journal Services did an excellent job of copyediting and getting the manuscript ready for print.

I am deeply indebted to the many scholars from whose writings I have drawn information and interpretations. While I researched this book I was reminded once again of what fine work many scholars in history and related disciplines, as well as journalists, have done and are doing.

Introduction

Who speaks for Joshua? In 1989 a frustrated and angry Supreme Court Justice Harry Blackmun implicitly raised that question when he discussed the plight of three-year-old Joshua DeShaney, who had been permanently disabled by a parental beating. Blackmun could have asked that question about any of the children in American history who, like Joshua, were dependent, neglected, or abused.

For example, who spoke in 1807 for five-year-old James Jones, living in the Philadelphia Almshouse because his mother was dead and his father too ill to care for him? Who spoke in 1854 for Edmund Davis, homeless at age 10, whom the New York Children's Aid Society put on a train for Iowa so that he could live with a farm family? Who spoke in 1874 for 10-year-old Mary Ellen Connolly, scarred from whippings she had received at the hands of the couple with whom local charity officials had placed her? Who spoke in the early 1900s for the boy, orphaned at age four, who lived in a farm bunkhouse for several years doing chores for room and board until a reform-minded organization took him to Allendale Farm, a home for dependent boys? Who spoke for Sarah Sander Wirpel, living at that time with around four hundred other children in the Cleveland Jewish Orphan Asylum? Who spoke in the 1960s for grade-schooler Ruthie Bolton, whose grandfather beat her time and again while she "was screaming, screaming, screaming," as she recalled? Who spoke for Tony Godby Johnson, born in 1977 to parents he soon "feared more than anything in the world"—parents who brutalized him so unmercifully that doctors found he had 54 badly healed fractures—and whose mother forced him to have sex with one of her male friends, who infected him with AIDS? Who spoke in the early 1990s for Richard, almost four, caught in a custody battle between his adoptive parents, who had cared for him since birth, and his biological parents, a mother who had relinquished him and a father who thought he was dead?[1]

Adults spoke for them, of course, but historically with many voices and changing agendas. Those responses invariably told far more about adult needs,

1

expectations, anxieties, status, and ideologies than about the children themselves. Over time, parents, experts, philanthropists, advocates, and policymakers have argued about how best to deal with and define the interests of children. Dependent, neglected, and abused children especially have figured in that debate as powerful symbols for dominant groups in pursuit of various versions of the good society. Increasingly in the nineteenth and twentieth centuries, the victimized, endangered child provided a potent ideological weapon. The perceived nature of that victimization reflected shifting social demands and issues. Influential groups thus "discovered" problems such as physical abuse or, later, emotional and sexual abuse. But, in most instances, the formulation of those problems, the claims about what children needed, and the proposed solutions avoided confronting the issue of poverty, a basic contributor to dependency, neglect, and abuse.

I

Concerns about endangered and needy children have been particularly evident during times of social stress and among groups especially anxious about the future. The nineteenth-century "inventors" of the orphanage and modern foster care, just like the "discoverers" of cruelty to children, worried about the growing disorder and squalor of burgeoning cities. A century later, as worries mounted in the late 1900s about the nation's economic and social health, contending ideological groups agreed that children were imperiled but differed over the nature of the threat. Some people pointed to the collapse of the family, which they blamed on social permissiveness, pornography, the women's movement, and big government. Their opponents countered that children were indeed in jeopardy but partly because of attacks on government programs such as Aid to Families of Dependent Children (AFDC), which since 1935 had been a major component of the welfare system.

At different times in the history of child dependency, neglect, and abuse, a changing combination of factors directed the attention of particular adults to particular problems: homeless street children, or "battered children," or sexually abused children, for instance. The "discoveries" of problems and their proposed solutions were typically products of a complex blend of idealism, self-interest, and impulses that shaped the culture as a whole—a complicated mixture of elements, varying from religious convictions to concerns about social status and alarm about family and country.

Usually a small number of people or organizations were instrumental in pushing an issue before the larger public. To publicize an issue, a shocking event or compelling image was often crucial. Sometimes reformers looked hard for an event to seize upon; in other instances, they stumbled on it. In the

1870s the anticruelty movement rallied to the brutalized Mary Ellen Connolly; and in the 1960s the concept of the "battered child" struck a public chord. Not surprisingly, people with wealth, social status, established reputations, influential contacts, and close ties with authorities were at an advantage when they championed a particular concern. Once an issue gained public attention, the challenge was to keep popular interest from fading. Advocates characteristically broadened the issue, making it more comprehensive. Indeed, matters related to dependent, neglected, or abused children often served as wedges for larger causes. Sometimes the enlargement of an issue followed a kind of bureaucratic imperative, as experts and policymakers solidified their positions, enhanced their roles, and increased their influence. But the process usually also reflected an evolving awareness; the effort to understand one problem moved attention to others—from, say, physical to emotional abuse. Invariably, however, efforts to identify children's problems and shape policies spurred reactions and backlashes. At stake, ultimately, was not simply the matter of protecting children but who did the protecting, and on whose terms, at whose expense, and at what level of public obligation.[2]

II

Debates about child dependency, neglect, and abuse faltered over definitions, numbers, and interpretations. In 1971 historian Robert Bremner perhaps offered the best definition of "dependent" children. They were, he said, children "who, because of the death, incapacity or poverty of natural guardians, had to look to the community for support, protection and guidance." Within even that framework, different kinds of dependency existed. There were true orphans, children who had no parents. But many children in orphanages actually had one or even both parents living; the children resided in the asylums, sometimes briefly, to enable their families to weather economic or medical crises. Some children were "virtual orphans," according to various child rescue groups, because of "morally dead" mothers and fathers given to lives of drink, debauchery, and crime. Half-orphans usually qualified as dependent children, particularly if they lived with their widowed mothers. In the early 1900s, in fact, many states provided a number of single mothers with small pensions so they could keep their children at home rather than in an orphanage or in foster care; in the 1930s, such pensions evolved into Aid to Dependent Children, and later into AFDC.[3]

"Neglected" children typically were at risk because they lacked care that met their basic needs. Historically, because of deeply rooted assumptions that poverty was a consequence of moral failings, policymakers tended to judge the parents of impoverished children as neglectful. As the twentieth century progressed, notable reformers rejected such traditional wisdom and argued that poverty itself was the culprit, producing neglectful situations despite the best efforts of many beleaguered families. The lack of a consensus on the causes of poverty became abundantly clear in the late 1900s, however, when a powerful backlash against welfare gathered momentum. Strongly punitive in tone, the backlash ended AFDC and other forms of income supplements, leaving in question the fate of an estimated five to six million poor children.[4]

Just as the extent and causes of child neglect were debatable, efforts to define and identify "abuse" proved equally controversial. Most people agreed that abuse generally involved aggressive acts against a child. Still, for years, reformers and child welfare policies concentrated on problems of physical abuse. Not until the 1970s did emotional and especially sexual abuse emerge as major issues. A backlash again resulted as debates raged over false accusations, government intervention, and the rights of parents and families.

In this context, child welfare statistics stirred disputes. Disagreements over numbers plagued discussions of child abuse, for example. In 1981 Richard Gelles, one of the top researchers on family violence, conceded in frustration that "we don't know a *damn* thing about whether child abuse is increasing, decreasing, or staying the same." Some people concluded that child abuse existed primarily in the minds of overexcited zealots. "We never used to have this kind of stuff—this child abuse, this incest, and stuff—when I was younger," complained one individual. "You never heard a thing about it, now it's all you *do* hear." Other individuals were certain that unreported abuse was one of the nation's great family secrets.[5]

If agreeing on the information presented a challenge, interpreting it was even more difficult. In 1994, for example, social welfare scholar Duncan Lindsey said that "more children are reported for child abuse and neglect in the United States than [in] all the other industrialized nations combined." From one angle, that news was staggeringly bad, a bleak commentary on violence in the United States. From another angle, the news was reassuring in that it suggested Americans were at least reporting abuse, rather than ignoring it. And from yet another perspective, the large number of reports was suspect, evidence mainly of hysteria, poor judgment, and a disregard for basic family privacy.[6]

Interpretations differed as well regarding the growth of child protection agencies and laws. One view was that such agencies and laws often did more harm than good. The "child savers," from this perspective, too often pursued their own agendas at the expense of children. They "took a problem and created a tragedy," as one advocate of children's legal rights said. Another interpretation judged the emergence of child protection as an indication of progress, however slow and uneven. Social psychologist Murray Straus, for example, referred optimistically to the nation's "moral passage," a journey that gradually expanded "human rights and humanitarian values," and whose proud history included the abolition of slavery, the gains in civil rights and, Straus hoped, the end someday of corporal punishment in American families. Historian John Demos, on the other hand, took a more skeptical view. "It is now fashionable, in family history," he said, "to believe that things have been getting better. . . . I doubt it."[7]

III

Sometimes the history of dependent, neglected, and abused children has seemed to be circling back upon itself. As the twentieth century wound down, debates over the plight of such children in the United States sounded eerily like those of more than a hundred years before. Once again, there were horrifying reports of neglect and abuse. Discussions of a moral crisis in the American family fueled proposals to "save" children from parents, especially parents who were poor. Several prominent writers and politicians looked to orphanages to house children of "undeserving," "immoral," neglectful, and abusive parents. Others advocated "anti-institutional institutions" (such as cottage-style homes), an idea that had been popular at the turn of the twentieth century. And, as in that earlier era, foster care, adoption, and the sanctity of the home were again heated subjects.

As usual, too, while adults debated, children waited. Some children— Rachel Carver, for example—ran out of time. Born in 1986, she lived in a world of domestic violence and neglect, her smile belying the danger around her. Her father sexually abused her. In 1994, when child welfare workers in California suspected that her divorced mother's fiancé was also abusing her, they sent her to live with her aunt and uncle in Spokane, Washington. There, in June 1995, her uncle, free on bail pending sentencing for the attempted rape of a teenager, beat the third grader to death with a blunt weapon and hid her in a cardboard box beneath some bushes. Awaiting trial, the uncle reported that Rachel's last, desperate words to him were, "Why are you doing this to me?" That question has echoed throughout the history of dependent, neglected, and abused children.[8]

1

Old Solutions, New Circumstances, 1607–1800

Dependent children were among the first English colonists in North America. Some were homeless even before they departed England. Others were orphaned on the arduous voyage across the Atlantic. Others lost their parents in the colonies where, for example, the Chesapeake Bay area's high death rates constituted a killing field.

When dealing with child dependency, the colonists—as well as their late-eighteenth-century successors—drew upon familiar solutions embedded in English law and custom. In an age that was virtually without children's institutions, adults relied heavily on the traditional indenture system. Within that system masters were supposed to provide children with food, clothing, shelter, a general education, and work skills; the children, in return, were obligated to serve the masters. Indenture agreements typically included protections against cruelty.

Although the indenture system reflected concerns for children's welfare, it also suggested the limits of those concerns and manifested a fundamental truth: The priorities, needs, and expectations of adults determined policies concerning children. Adults, on their own terms, defined children's needs. Indenture, for example, reflected both a desire to keep tax loads down, by avoiding public expenses, and the assumption that children were economic assets—not as property under common law but as valuable sources of labor. Policies regarding children were laced with economic imperatives. Moreover, given the prevailing respect for parental rights, determinations of child neglect and cruelty were infrequent. "A man's home is his castle," said the famed seventeenth-century English jurist Sir Edward Coke. No less important was the view that children needed strong disciplinary measures; short of causing permanent injury, correction was not abuse. "If one beats a child until it bleeds," according to a common-law rule of thumb, "then it will remember the words of its master. But if one beats it to death, then the law applies." As legal concepts, the "abused" or "neglected" child did not exist. What was best for the children depended, in sum, on considerations quite apart from the children themselves.[1]

I

Colonial responses to child welfare matters owed much to long-developing English poor laws, as well as the principle of *parens patriae* and the structure and authority of household government. The 1601 Elizabethan Poor Law consolidated a series of earlier measures that dealt with poverty and economic stress in England. In one comprehensive statute, the Poor Law spelled out public obligations and types of assistance to needy citizens such as the infirm, the elderly, and the poor. The Elizabethan system endorsed both "outdoor" and "indoor" relief. "Outdoor" assistance provided the "worthy" poor with such basics as food and fuel in their own homes. "Indoor" (or institutional) relief included poorhouses for the impoverished who were not employable, and houses of correction for employable individuals who refused to work. Able-bodied citizens who shunned labor were also subject to corporal and even capital punishment. Administration of the system was local. Officials, typically known as overseers of the poor, had the authority to apprentice orphaned, pauper, and illegitimate children to artisans and farmers who were to provide care and training. Because the terms of apprenticeship usually took the form of legally enforceable indenture contracts, "indenturing" and "apprenticing" were virtually synonymous.[2]

As a demonstration of society's obligations to poor and needy children especially, indenture affirmed the doctrine of *parens patriae*—the doctrine by which, in the words of historian Joseph Hawes, "the state is the ultimate parent of every child." Although the common law recognized parents as "natural protectors" of children, the state had the power to remove children from their parents if the children's safety or morals, or the community's interests, demanded such intervention. Poor parents, whose children might become public charges, were particularly vulnerable to having authorities remove and indenture their children. In 1646 a Virginia statute thus empowered officials to remove children from parents who, "either through fond indulgence or perverse obstinacy, are most averse and unwilling to part with their children."[3]

For most Anglo-Americans throughout the seventeenth and eighteenth centuries, however, the household was the immediate source of authority. Household government, as historian Carole Shammas has argued, was patriarchal and allowed dependents—wives, children, servants, and slaves—"little *direct* relationship with the rest of the state." Given the embryonic nature of government institutions in the colonies, the authority of the household head was enhanced. Although community concerns about family orderliness required the policing of family governance, outside intervention on behalf of dependents was rare and occurred only in extreme circumstances. In that regard, indenture provided a form of correction and welfare and reduced public responsibility for colonial dependents, including children who were orphaned or whose parents were unfit.[4]

II

Indentured children were a familiar sight in the colonies, but their circumstances were often shrouded in mystery, especially in the early seventeenth century. Few details existed, for example, regarding the children who reportedly had been kidnapped, or "spirited," from England to the colonies. In 1618 officials rounded up one hundred impoverished, vagrant children from the streets of London and sent them as apprentices to Virginia. Some of the youths died en route. When the Virginia Company told the king that a number of the youths had resisted the move, the English Privy Council gave permission to find more of them and "to imprison, punish, and dispose any of those children" in order to ship them to Virginia as quickly and conveniently as possible. During the next several decades, thousands of homeless, poor, and orphaned children, some without indentures, journeyed to the colonies. "There are many ships going to Virginia," read one report, "and with them fourteen or fifteen hundred children w'ch they have gathered up in divers places." Most of these and other youths were apparently in their teens; a number of them undoubtedly suffered considerable mistreatment. Rumors that some children went to the colonies against their will motivated at least one English father, who was convinced that his 11-year-old son had been kidnapped, to obtain a warrant to search a ship.[5]

While indenture provided a means by which to bring youths from England to the colonies, it also helped to solve problems within the colonies regarding poor, neglected, and orphaned children. And those problems were substantial, particularly in the Chesapeake Bay region, where staggering death rates made the challenge of child dependency especially urgent. Perhaps one-third of the male infants in Maryland died before age 1; and around half failed to live 20 years. Death claimed many young parents as well. Between 1650 and 1689 in Middlesex County, Virginia, virtually half of the children by age 9, and 61 percent by age 13, had lost one or both parents. By age 13, 20 percent were full orphans. Over the next 60 years, the figures dropped only slightly. The county court, which assumed general oversight of the children, dutifully tried to honor parental wishes regarding the disposition of children and property. Other family members and friends, aware that their own children might someday need similar attention, shouldered what responsibilities they could. In the Chesapeake region, more than in New England, families were in constant flux as aunts, uncles, stepparents, and older siblings assumed parental duties. For the children, life was often a series of tragedies and disruption. Remembering his childhood, one Virginia planter wrote, "Before I was ten years old . . . I look'd upon this life here as but going to an Inn, no permanent being."[6]

Kinship networks in the Chesapeake area were not often available for dependent children, however, because so many seventeenth-century immigrants had left their families behind. Until the 1700s, when such networks became more extensive, Virginia and Maryland thus relied heavily upon "orphans' courts" to protect children and their property. Typically, justices of the county courts held special sessions to examine the estates of orphans. If the estate was large enough, a court-appointed guardian could use it to care for the child; elaborate legal procedures were supposed to protect as much of the estate as possible until the child came of age and took possession of it. If the estate provided insufficient income, and if no one volunteered to care for the child, the court would indenture the child. As "a father to us poor Orphans," in one person's words, the courts attempted with some diligence to oversee the system, although they were apparently concerned mainly with ensuring the rights of property.[7]

Against that backdrop, the indenture system had a number of strengths. It squared with the traditional commitment to household government by keeping children within family settings and ensuring that they received food, shelter, and instruction in reading, writing, and usually religion. It added to the labor supply and trained children in skills so they would not place a burden on the community. It allowed officials to remove children from neglectful families that failed to supply, according to one law, "Competent and convenient food and raiment for theire children." And it helped the community meet its obligations without requiring public expenditures. Indeed, apprenticeship was so widespread that many parents voluntarily indentured their children to ease financial pressures at home or to allow their sons and daughters to learn a trade.[8]

Although indenture generally protected dependent children from homelessness and vagrancy, it was a faulty system nonetheless. For the most part it did not serve small children well. Officials apprenticed some infants—for example, two-year-old Moses Love in 1747 when his parents in Massachusetts could not support him. More commonly, indenture applied to children who were six or older. Very young, poor children typically stayed at home through some form of "outdoor" relief, or with relatives (including godparents). If the children had no relatives, they lived with private families at public expense.[9]

Although indenture hardly suited small children, it was a chancy proposition for other youngsters as well because, at bottom, it was always a business deal. In exchange for support, the child was supposed to work. Some masters were kindly and even affectionate, but others were terribly cruel. "The inevitable tendency of the system," as social welfare scholar Henry Thurston wrote in his classic work on dependent children, "was to stimulate the employer to exact the pound of flesh from the indentured child."[10]

In 1655 in Plymouth, Massachusetts, 12-year-old John Walker paid with his life. When the boy, already suffering from inadequate care, fell while carrying a heavy log, his master gave him yet another thrashing. Several days later, after viewing Walker's "blackish and blue" corpse, "the skin broken in divers places" and several toes frozen, a jury convicted the master of manslaughter. In Boston, authorities executed a master, William Franklin, for killing his apprentice with "sundry cruel stripes and other kinds of cruel usage."[11]

In some abuse cases, officials transferred indentures to another master. John Ward, for example, in 1660 finally won his freedom from the oppressive Arthur Turner. As an orphan, around age nine, Ward had been indentured to Turner. Ultimately, Turner's mistreatment became so bad that, according to the court record, "the people crieth shame thereat." By then the boy was in abysmal shape, his clothing torn, his hair seemingly "rotted off with ashes," and his "most rotten filthy, stinking, ulcerated leg" a dreadful sight. The court freed Ward from Turner and bound him over to another man with whom he was supposed to complete the remaining three years of his indenture. In the meantime, however, young Ward had endured eight years of Turner's cruelty.[12]

III

For colonial children, the legal and informal systems of care and protection had decidedly mixed consequences. Officials, neighbors, and kinship networks in many cases responded to orphan and needy children with sympathy and concern, and they did so despite often severe financial constraints. Still, their natural tendency was to watch out for their own families and affairs first. Within families, indentured youngsters probably enjoyed equal status with biological children only rarely and were presumably subject to harsher discipline. The fact that indentures sometimes passed to several different masters added emotional distance between families and apprentices.[13]

In the Chesapeake and southern areas, orphans' courts protected children more in theory than in practice. In Maryland the judges seldom placed orphans unless someone petitioned in the children's behalf. As a result, poor orphans especially lacked formal court safeguards. In North Carolina, an absence of close supervision allowed legal guardians to pay little attention to orphans and even embezzle their estates. In 1735 Governor Gabriel Johnston complained about "unjust Guardians who rob their Wards, a practise too common in this country." Twenty years later, the colonial assembly attempted to make the orphans' courts more responsive to such mismanagement, but little changed. Between 1757 and 1775, for example, the Edgecomb County orphans' court met only seven times.[14]

Whether in New England or the southern areas, social and economic class very much influenced official responses to issues of dependency, neglect, and abuse. In two Virginia parishes by the mid-1700s, around 38 percent of all child apprentices were orphans. (Over 39 percent of the others were considered poor, 10 percent were illegitimate, and around 12 percent were mulatto.) Orphans of wealthy backgrounds typically received more favorable indenture placements than did those who were poor. Whereas authorities bound out one child as a simple servant, they sent a more fortunate individual to learn the "Office of Clerke" and other "lawfull Imployments" but exempted him from "Common workeing at the house in tending Corne and Tobaccoe." Some indenture contracts allowed masters to ignore educational matters. In Pennsylvania, for example, Thomas Harper was apprenticed for five and three-quarter years, if he learned to read and write; if he did not, his indenture was supposed to end after five years. By law in North Carolina, the courts placed wealthier orphans under guardianships and poor children under apprenticeships. Without the apprenticeships, the counties would have faced the burden of caring for the children.[15]

In Boston by the eighteenth century, authorities were inclined to intervene only in the affairs of poor families. A law in 1722, for instance, required that idle or dissolute parents should have their children "put out into orderly families." Thirteen years later, the legislature provided Boston with 12 Overseers of the Poor whose responsibilities included apprenticing children. Poverty was apparently the only criterion the overseers used.[16]

For a poor, dependent child such as Isaiah Thomas, indenture was an unhappy experience but nevertheless beneficial. Shortly after the boy's birth in 1749 in Massachusetts, his father abandoned him and four siblings. Because his mother was too poor to care for him, Isaiah lived for several gloomy years with family friends on a farm outside Boston. In 1756 Boston's Overseers of the Poor "bound out" the seven-year-old boy to printer and bookseller Zechariah Fowle, who was childless and wanted someone to do chores around the shop and peddle printed items. Fowle was a slow-witted and irritable man whom the boy did not like, but Thomas built upon his experience in the shop and became a celebrated publisher. Unlike a number of indentured children, he did not suffer physical mistreatment.[17]

IV

Throughout the colonial and early national eras, the extent of child neglect and cruelty was impossible to measure, and the laws against such mistreatment were ambiguous at best. In 1641, for example, the Massachusetts Puritans produced a remarkable document, the *Body of Liberties*, whose provisions included protecting "the liberties of children." Although the law prescribed the death penalty for youths over 16 who cursed or struck their natural parents, it at the same time allowed a defense that the parents had "so provoked them by extreme and cruel correction, that they have been forced . . . to preserve themselves from death or maiming." That law, and a "stubborn child" statute five years later, placed the power of the state behind parental authority and at the same time protected the children from "unnatural severitie" and provided them with the right "to complaine to Authorities for redresse." As significant as these laws were, they actually had little effect. No "stubborn child" was in fact put to death, nor did any child win a case in court against abusive parents. And although the Massachusetts colony indeed executed William Franklin, whose cruelty resulted in his apprentice's death, it generally dealt more leniently with severe treatment of indentured children. In Salem, Massachusetts, a court confirmed the master's right to discipline a servant, but decided that Phillip Fowler had gone too far by hanging a boy "up by the heels as butchers do beasts for slaughter." The court nevertheless settled for reprimanding and fining Fowler.[18]

Child neglect, from the colonists' perspective, indicated primarily a failure to instill proper values concerning religion, labor, and family order. This viewpoint was particularly apparent in New England, where authorities sometimes removed children when biological families or masters did not provide instruction in religion or work. In 1675 the General Court of Massachusetts established a group of officials, the tithingmen, to monitor parental instruction and to bolster good household government by reporting unruly children and adults. Each tithingman was supposed to "diligently inspect" a dozen or so families in his neighborhood and to report unacceptable behavior to the courts. As community guardians who policed parental effectiveness in raising obedient children, the tithingmen implicitly symbolized the doctrine of *parens patriae*.[19]

Colonists typically disparaged Native American parents as "neglectful." In Indian culture, as the colonists viewed it, husbands were not sufficiently involved in their households, wives enjoyed too much authority over household property, and parents generally avoided physical punishment of their children. To the colonists, such family relationships, with their limited male authority and "permissive" standards, were inherently unstable, disorderly, and negligent.[20]

Colonial families viewed the physical "correction" of dependents as a right and a duty. Vigorous discipline fit, moreover, with the era's reliance on corporal punishment, such as whipping, to deal generally with aberrant behavior. In Puritan Massachusetts, justifications of physical punishment squared with scriptural interpretations that emphasized parental responsibilities for children's souls. Although the aphorism "Spare the rod and spoil the child" was not in the Bible, it summed up various scriptural passages: "He that spareth his rod hateth his son: but he that loveth him chasteneth him betimes," or, "Withhold not correction from the child: for if thou beatest him with the rod, he shall not die. Thou shalt beat him with the rod, and shalt deliver his soul from hell." Controlling and breaking the wills of stubborn children was thus the obligation of caring, responsible parents; corporal punishment was a concerned act of last resort, not of abuse. Excessive cruelty to children may nevertheless have been infrequent, according to historian John Demos, in light of "the twin principles of mutual support and mutual surveillance" in Puritan communities. Still, most forms of discipline were acceptable unless they produced permanent injury. In such a setting, consideration of the rights of the child was an anachronism. Between 1633 and 1802, for example, none of the complaints about abuse in the Plymouth, Massachusetts, courts concerned children.[21]

In all of colonial New England's courts, in fact, only one natural father faced child abuse charges. The Essex County court convicted Michael Emerson of "cruel and excessive beating of his daughter." He had kicked the 11-year-old girl and beaten her with a stick used to thresh grain. Even then, the court reduced his fine six months later and settled for a bond of good behavior.[22]

Slave children had even fewer protections against maltreatment than did youngsters like Emerson's daughter or those who were indentured. Some slave children were working in the tobacco fields by ages five or six. When one girl accidentally failed to pick several worms off a leaf, the master forced her to eat them. Elsewhere, a boy had to choose between biting worms he overlooked or receiving a whipping. Ironically, some slaveholders criticized slave parents for treating the children too brutally. "What the Lord Almighty make trees for if they ain't for lick boy chillen?" asked one slave woman. Yet harsh parental discipline was considered, as the writer Ralph Ellison later said, "an expression of concern, of love." In the treacherous world of slavery, children had to learn quickly how to behave, follow rules, and work hard; their future survival depended on how well they understood the nature of their condition and of race relations. With the stakes so high, parents had little room in which to maneuver. In that regard, the main onus for severe discipline within slave families rested, as historian Eugene Genovese observed, "with the masters, who commanded a social system that introduced extreme provocations and tensions into a family life that would have remained difficult in the best of worlds."[23]

The slaveowners provided a crude social welfare system, which included such basics as food and shelter. However, those basics were usually minimal at best. Moreover, the claims that slave parents had on their children were even more tentative than those that nonslave poor parents had on their offspring. Slave children were unquestionably more vulnerable than other children to neglect and abuse, but the fact that they were property added another barrier to the public's willingness to intervene in their behalf. If prudent citizens in New England were reluctant to get involved in a neighboring family's quarrels and violence "lest they get a broken head for their pains," as one Puritan minister said, the likelihood that people would meddle in situations involving the treatment of slaves was slim indeed. Slavery's harmful legacy even for free African American children proved substantial. As Andrew Billingsley and Jeanne Giovannoni wrote in their pioneering study of race and American child welfare, "the very existence of slavery meant that child welfare institutions could develop in this country without concern for the majority of Black children." White children paid a price as well because the abuses they suffered "could be rationalized by the notion that they were treated better than Black slaves." Indenture reforms thus developed slowly.[24]

Dependent children were occasionally sold at auction. "Public vendue," a poor-law provision by which poor families were auctioned for care, was the legal instrument for such sales. According to this system of "selling the poor," bidders indicated how much they would charge to care for families, family members, or orphans for one year. The lowest bid won, and the Overseers of the Poor paid the money, thereby in effect establishing precedents for foster care. Theoretically, the overseers avoided turning individuals over to bidders who were cruel or not of good character, and children who were "bid off" were supposed to receive some schooling. But the vendue system in actual practice undoubtedly operated in less salutary ways. The auctioning off of nonslave children nevertheless continued into the nineteenth century. In 1801, for example, Elisha James of Shapleigh, Maine, became the master of "Jane Whool's boy set up at vendue . . . till he is twenty-one years old," at a price of $1.50.[25]

V

Although indenture, mixed with outdoor relief, dominated seventeenth- and eighteenth-century policies regarding child dependency, events sometimes encouraged institutional solutions. In Virginia in 1668, for example, a desire to increase the manufacture of woolen and hemp products prompted a law allowing county courts to build workhouses for poor children. Local authorities had the power "to take poore children from indigent parents to place them to worke in those houses."[26]

In the early 1700s several towns built almshouses, as Boston had done several decades earlier, to supplement traditional forms of welfare. These institutions were small, initially served only unusual or emergency cases, and functioned as substitute households. By midcentury around 15 percent of the inhabitants of New York's almshouse were orphaned or deserted children who awaited apprenticeship or boarding out. As the growing population of Boston, New York, and other towns required larger almshouses, dependent children in those institutions ended up under the care of older inmates, most of whom were in deplorable physical or emotional condition.[27]

Not until 1738 did orphan asylums appear in the British colonies of North America. That year the Ebenezer and Bethesda orphanages both opened in Georgia. Nine years earlier, in French-controlled New Orleans, Ursuline nuns had built an orphanage to care for young survivors of Indian attacks. The Catholic institution continued to operate after New Orleans became a part of the United States in the late 1700s; by then the Ebenezer asylum had disappeared.[28]

The Ebenezer orphanage was the creation of a small group of German Lutherans who had founded a community not far from Savannah. The two-story orphanage cared initially for a dozen children whose parents had died or were impoverished. It resembled a famed "ragged school" that Professor August Francke had established in 1695 in Halle, Germany. The children rose at 5 A.M. and attended worship services. For much of the morning and afternoon, they attended school. Before and after school, the boys worked in the garden and the girls in the household. Additional religious services concluded the day. Although the Ebenezer orphanage lasted only 12 years, it very much influenced the celebrated British evangelical preacher George Whitefield, who was the driving force behind the Bethesda Orphan House.[29]

Whitefield was much impressed when he visited the Ebenezer orphanage in July 1738. Shortly after arriving in Savannah a few weeks earlier, he had been appalled to see the "miserable circumstances" of the orphans in that community. "An orphanage is much needed in Savannah," he promptly informed the trustees of the Georgia colony. They granted him five hundred acres on which to build such an institution, about 10 miles outside the town. In March 1740, 40 orphans moved into the newly constructed two-story building.

From the outset, however, the orphanage generated controversy and bad feelings. Some critics objected to the expense of building the institution and the road to get to it. Others resented Whitefield's efforts to remove children from families because he thought Bethesda provided better care. Charges also circulated that Whitefield was benefiting financially from the orphanage. The famed preacher regretted the opposition that he faced but expressed joy in 1741 that the orphanage "had been very beneficial not only to the Bodies, but also to the Souls of the Labourers." According to one contemporary account of the children's schedule, which resembled that at Ebenezer, "no time was allowed for idleness or play which are Satan's darling hours to tempt children to all manner of wickedness as lying, cursing, swearing, and uncleanliness." The discipline was so strict that it generated a public outcry. By the time of Whitefield's death in 1770, 183 orphans and many poor children had been sheltered—and mistreated, if the preacher's adversaries were correct—in the institution.[30]

Twenty years after Whitefield's death, the first public orphanage in the United States was established in Charleston, South Carolina. When the institution opened in 1790, 115 orphans moved in immediately at public expense. At the end of the decade, three private organizations also started caring for dependent children. One started in 1797 in New York City and the second a year later in Philadelphia, where a horrendous yellow fever epidemic had left many children without families. Within a short time, the New York and Philadelphia organizations established orphanages. In 1799 citizens in Baltimore opened an asylum for destitute girls.[31]

VI

The founding of almshouses and orphanages demonstrated that, by the nineteenth century, new responses to child dependency were apparent. They grew in part from an altered view of children that began to emerge in the last half of the 1700s, a view that not only was more sensitive to childhood as a stage of development but that also tended to sentimentalize children as innocents who occupied a "place apart" from adults and deserved special attention and protection. But the seeds of change were inherent also in the binding out and indenture systems, so deeply rooted in the colonial era. Although those systems remained crucial to the nation's rudimentary child welfare strategies, they also contained hints of the shift toward foster care and adoption. Moreover, the few almshouses and orphanages of the seventeenth and eighteenth centuries were harbingers of a trend that greatly influenced the care of dependent children in the 1800s: the rise of congregate institutions.[32]

2

The Rise of Antebellum Congregate Institutions

In 1824, when seven-year-old Jane Calder first crossed the threshold of the Boston Female Asylum, she took a step familiar to thousands of dependent children in the nineteenth century: She entered an orphanage. For her, that step proved beneficial. Tuberculosis had killed her mother and father, and her stepmother had collapsed following the death of one of Jane's five siblings. The orphanage sheltered and educated Jane for 10 years. When she was 18 the managers allowed her to board at the asylum while she learned a sewing trade. After supporting herself for a while with her new trade, she eventually married a plumber and started her own family.[1]

Experiences such as Jane's encouraged antebellum reformers who heralded institutions such as the orphan asylum as a solution to the expanding problem of child dependency. Sensitivity to that problem reflected several trends, one of which was a sentimentalized perception of children within the emerging middle class, and another that grew from anxieties about urban poverty and unrest. Children in the Philadelphia House of Refuge, for example, were supposed to learn about "virtue and piety . . . industry and cleanliness." According to its backers, the institution would provide "the moral machinery by which these poor neglected children were to be fitted for usefulness here, and blessedness hereafter."[2]

For dependent children the institutional legacy was far more ambiguous than Jane Calder's encouraging story suggested, however. By the 1850s orphanages also summoned up images of pathetic waifs huddled in drab uniforms in oppressive barracks where they received blows rather than loving embraces. In reality, the history of antebellum asylums was one of well-meaning but decidedly imperfect efforts that helped some unfortunate children while ignoring and even victimizing many others. Although the institutions

Emblem of the Philadelphia House of Refuge idealizing the transformative role of such institutions, which were popular during the antebellum era. Courtesy Print Collection, Miriam and Ira D. Wallach Division of Art, Prints, and Photographs, The New York Public Library, Astor, Lenox and Tilden Foundations.

varied greatly, they generally shared common features: insufficient funding, overcrowding, and a regard for poor families that was at best ambivalent and sometimes even hostile. They typically wavered between goals of helping or punishing, educating or confining, offering new opportunities or trying to contain disturbing social problems. And they reflected a newly discovered concern for "the best interests of the child," a doctrine that, however haltingly, began to recognize the special needs of children.

I

A constellation of economic, demographic, cultural, and legal forces in the early 1800s shaped a variety of institutions within society, including poorhouses and orphanages. The developing market economy played a profoundly important role. As production shifted more and more from the home to the budding world of textile mills and other small industries, the changing economy forever altered the composition of the family. In urban, middle-class homes, the domestic setting turned rapidly into a sphere particularly for women, whose primary duties were to raise children, provide emotional support for their spouses, and serve as society's moral anchors. As the productive capacity of children in such homes fell, the "value" of offspring was tied increasingly to their affectionate ties with parents.

These trends helped to forge a romanticized ideology in which children were vulnerable innocents and mothers had a special responsibility for protecting them from worldly corruption. According to one popular childrearing manual, "The mother, kneeling by the cradle-bed, hath her hand upon the ark of a nation." The cult of motherhood had tremendous appeal, eroding even the traditional patriarchal control over child custody.[3]

Against this backdrop, judges invoked a new legal doctrine with major social implications: "the best interests of the child." In 1809 a South Carolina court moved tentatively toward that doctrine by awarding custody of a small girl to her mother, a "virtuous woman" in the judges' eyes. The woman's abusive husband, William Prather, had deserted her to live in flagrant adultery. The judges were nevertheless so nervous about undercutting the father's common law position as "natural guardian" that they allowed him to keep his older children. Over the next several decades bolder judges moved beyond the pioneering *Prather* decision, openly considering "the best interests of the child" in custody cases. Northern courts, in particular, showed a willingness to grant custody of children in their "tender years" to good mothers. In 1813 Pennsylvania's chief justice ruled that, in one divided household, the children, "considering their tender years, . . . stand in need of the kind of assistance which can be afforded by none so well as a mother." The law in custody cases was moving, in the words of one scholar, "from fathers' rights to mothers' love." Significantly, however, the antebellum legal definition of the child's best interests was narrow, a product of judges' reactions to private custody cases, not to the overall conditions of poor, orphaned, or mistreated children.[4]

For children, these changing doctrines about their best interests nevertheless contained a notable subtext, one that in the larger society increasingly granted them more recognition as individuals and provided a rationale for state intervention in their behalf. When a Georgia court in 1836 asked in a custody case how the child's "interests and health would be best promoted," it thus articulated larger public concerns. Six years later another Georgia judge announced that the court's "great and paramount duty is, to look to the interest and safety of the child." Indeed, he wrote, "the legal rights of the father will not be enforced, if those rights, in any manner, conflict with these interests, or the *welfare of the child*."[5]

A greater sensitivity to the welfare of children did not mean that they necessarily received kinder treatment, however. To instill values such as discipline, which society considered to be good for children, even loving parents could be cruel. The Reverend Francis Wayland, for example, not only starved his disobedient 15-month-old son into submission in 1831 but also publicized such discipline as exemplary. The nationally known minister and president of Brown University was already worried that society was becoming too permissive. When one morning his toddler son cried violently and threw his food, Wayland feared that the child's temper betokened sinful and socially threatening tendencies. He isolated the child, denying him food until the infant changed his conduct—some 36 hours later. Wayland believed that he exhibited "real kindness" when subduing his son through such "a mild yet firm course of discipline."[6]

Wayland's satisfaction in not using corporal punishment mirrored a growing conviction that individuals must voluntarily act as moral beings. Such voluntary action depended on internalizing the rules of proper conduct. "The child must be made his own disciplinarian," advised Theodore Dwight in his book on childrearing.[7]

But even popular counsels about "gentle measures" did not preclude sterner tactics. "A few smart slaps do good when nothing else will," the mild-mannered Lydia Maria Child told parents in 1831. At least six of nine child-rearing manuals in the early 1800s advocated physical punishment such as spanking. In 1840 a Tennessee court refused to rescue a girl from parents who had been convicted of beating and whipping her. "The right of parents to chastize their refractory and disobedient children is so necessary to the government of families, to the good of society," ruled the judge, "that no moralist or lawgiver has ever thought of interfering with its existence. . . ."[8]

Probably most Americans agreed with the Vermont schoolteacher who said that "moral suasion's my belief but lickin's my practice." In 1831 a New Hampshire minister beat his adopted son almost to death when the youngster had difficulty pronouncing words. Although such fierce whippings were by the early 1800s giving way to milder spankings, protection for children against excessive physical discipline received little attention. The family's sentimentalized place as a refuge from a harshly competitive world implied that the household was, by nature, a gentle, protective place where parents looked out for their children's welfare, and deviations from this model were often ignored. "The corner-stone of our republic is the hearth-stone," William G. Eliot Jr. exulted, as he celebrated "that sweet society of wife and children and friends."[9]

Authorities were so reluctant to intrude on domestic matters that they seemed virtually unable even to admit that something as heinous as sexual abuse could occur. In at least five southern states, a stepfather's intercourse with his stepdaughter was not illegal. In 1849 the Texas Supreme Court seemed more worried about undermining the institution of the family than about protecting a young victim of sexual abuse, in this case a daughter whose father had been indicted for committing incest with her. Unwilling to believe that the father had committed such a crime "in this age and country," the judges granted the man a second trial and demanded "the most indisputable proof" to convict him. Fifteen years earlier the Tennessee Supreme Court had shown no more regard for a girl whose uncle had sexually assaulted her. Although there was no doubt that intercourse had occurred, the court ruled that the uncle deserved a new trial because the exact place in which the act had occurred was not part of the evidence.[10]

Not surprisingly, the poorly monitored indenture system also offered fertile ground for child abuse and exploitation. Indentured children, typically the orphaned or poor, were supposed to receive a basic education and decent treatment; yet enforcement of these expectations was rare. At the turn of the century the territory of Illinois specifically barred children, whom local poor officials had apprenticed, from filing grievances against their masters. A half century later, in 1855, the Kansas territorial legislature legalized the binding out of destitute and orphaned children but included a proviso that homicide when "correcting" an apprentice was no crime.[11]

The system of public vendue, by which authorities auctioned off poor children to individuals who provided the cheapest care, was also fraught with perils. As late as 1820, a skinny orphan around 10 years old was among the impoverished group that officials in Rome, New York, put up for bids. The auctioneer taunted him, called him "brat," and slapped him. When it appeared the boy would end up with a notoriously brutal line boat captain, the terrified youth bolted from the platform before the crowd caught him. Only the intervention of a kindly man, who suddenly took pity on the youngster and bid 80 percent less than the captain had done, saved the orphan from an unenviable fate.[12]

Such conditions within the indenture and public vendue systems clashed with the increasingly popular view of children as tender, innocent, vulnerable, and endearing. "There is in childhood a holy ignorance, a beautiful credulity, a sort of sanctity," extolled a writer in 1832 in the fashionable *Godey's Lady's Magazine*. "The impress of divine nature is, as it were, fresh on the infant spirit—fresh and unsullied by contact with the breathing world." By the eve of the Civil War, popular fiction and serious literature featured a host of angelic children, ranging from Little Eva in *Uncle Tom's Cabin* to the martyred Mary in *Ten Nights in a Barroom*. Indeed, so many of these fictional children died in order to provide moral instruction that one individual subsequently described the authors as "literary Herods who put to death all the young children in their vicinity."[13]

Romantic sentiments about noble children, saintly mothers, and cloistered, loving families provided the cultural impetus for major welfare reforms in the early 1800s. Sometimes the reforms were minor, representing efforts simply to soften the harder edges of the old relief system. Authorities in states such as Illinois, for example, tried to scrutinize somewhat more closely the conditions of indentured children.

More sweeping, intrusive solutions were also in the works, however, as Illinois's 1826 Apprenticeship Law suggested. For some time public authorities throughout the United States had taken children from destitute families on relief, even if the parents protested. The 1826 Illinois law went further: It allowed local poor-law officials to indenture children whose parents were beggars, drunkards, or of "bad character." Such legislation showed an enlarged concern about the fitness of poor parents in particular, as well as a more interventionist disposition.[14]

This interventionist mood betrayed considerable anxieties about the realities of family life, especially in rapidly expanding cities. In 1790 only 6 U.S. cities had more than 8,000 residents; by 1850 at least 26 had in excess of 25,000, including New York City with more than 300,000, and 5 others with more than 100,000. Rochester, New York, a quiet community of 1,500 before the completion of the Erie Canal in the mid-1820s, became the fastest growing city in the nation almost overnight, a place with neighborhoods constantly in flux.

Immigration placed additional pressures on these cities. Four times as many immigrants entered the United States in the 1830s as in the previous decade, and the numbers accelerated during the next 20 years. During the 1830s and 1840s, some 2.5 million immigrants, almost half of them Irish Catholics, surged into the country. The burgeoning slums of New York City's Five Points section symbolized cities in crisis. During his visit in 1842, English writer Charles Dickens found the conditions in Five Points among the worst he had ever seen, full of "poverty, wretchedness, and vice." The area, he wrote, reeked of "all that is loathsome, drooping, and decayed."[15]

Violence provided yet another frightening sign of social stress. Between 1830 and 1865 more than one thousand people died in riots that racked almost three-fourths of American cities. "The state of society is awful," lamented Baltimore editor Hezekiah Niles in 1835. "Brute force has superseded the law . . . and violence become the 'order of the day.' The time predicted seems rapidly approaching when the mob shall rule."[16]

The dramatically altered urban environment, the influx of immigrants, the spreading poverty, and the spiraling violence sent reformers scurrying for answers, a number of which related to the proliferation of street children. Not surprisingly, the American family was often the target of the reformers' attention. Bronson Alcott spoke for many of them when he warned that the country was being "stabbed at the hearth-side. . . . It is injured by family neglect." If families, particularly those in poverty, were stabbing the nation to death, there seemed no alternative but to find ways to intervene in behalf of children to save them and society. Public schools provided one such intervention. Schools not only expanded educational opportunities but also allowed teachers, in loco parentis, to help ensure that youngsters received the instruction that was missing at home. One of the founders of the public education system, Horace Mann, praised the benign influence of teachers whose moral influence could rescue virtually every child from greed, licentiousness, and violence. "Momentous thought," crowed the Boston School Committee in 1850. "Thirty thousand of our fellow beings . . . are to pass through and from the institution we now control . . . with habits formed through our counsel or by our sufferance—habits of industry or indolence—order or confusion—neatness or negligence—virtue or vice."[17]

II

New York's Secretary of State, John V. N. Yates, hailed the almshouse as another institution that could educate poor children and also improve their health and morals. In his influential 1824 report on New York's pauper population, Yates asserted that a system of county almshouses could rescue children who would otherwise "grow up in filth, idleness, ignorance and disease, and . . . become early candidates for prison or the grave." According to Yates, the poorhouse could help the truly needy—the very young, the very old, the sick; at the same time, through work requirements and rules of conduct, it would discourage the able-bodied, unworthy poor from applying for relief. As reformer Charles Burroughs excitedly predicted, "The prohibition against alcohol and mandatory work will deter many intemperate wretches, and lazy vagrants from seeking admission to these walls." Before the nineteenth century, only a few almshouses existed in the United States but, starting in the 1810s, their numbers shot upward. Massachusetts, for example, had 83 in 1824, 180 in 1849, and 219 by 1860.[18]

Poorhouses constituted an explicit challenge to the long-standing system of outdoor relief for needy citizens, a system that had provided various kinds of public assistance to people in their own homes. Indeed, officials such as Yates and Boston mayor Josiah Quincy argued that home relief was expensive and undermined character by subsidizing intemperance, sloth, and immorality. Such arguments gained popularity as the traditional relief system buckled under the multiplying numbers of poor people, many of them uprooted by the market economy. The market's influence was ideological as well as demographic because it required more disciplined work patterns and habits than did the premarket economy. These nascent market values resonated with those of the proliferating antebellum institutions. Public school boards emphasized punctuality and regular attendance, and the new prison and almshouse administrations imposed numerous rules and rigid schedules. "The work ethic," as historian Michael Katz has written, was "what poorhouses were all about."[19]

To reformers, however, an institution such as the poorhouse was ultimately as humane as it was instructive, an improvement so vast over the old home relief system that one leading Bostonian called it "noble." The emphasis on schedules, work, and right values was supposed to build moral character and provide relief for the truly needy, including poor and dependent children. In this context, words such as *orphan* and *waif* were expansive, encompassing even destitute children who had both parents.[20]

Despite the rosy scenarios of Yates, Quincy, and others, the shift from home relief was detrimental to many children. In 1814, for example, outdoor relief allowed 70 percent of the children on Philadelphia's welfare roles to stay at home; two-thirds of them were half-orphans living with widowed mothers. Over time, the reductions in outdoor relief forced many such youngsters into institutions.[21]

Granted, such change was not always regrettable. Even that relentless crusader Dorothea Dix found some decent almshouses. Sometimes they kept impoverished families together, allowing mothers and children to sleep in the same ward. In other instances poorhouses, however inadequate, were places of last resort for children without families. Around half of the children in Philadelphia's almshouse in 1807 were homeless, among them three-year-old Alex Murphy. Young Murphy, whose mother was in jail and whose father had deserted him, received at least basic shelter in the poorhouse.[22]

The quality of that care was too often quite another matter. As poverty rates rocketed upward in Philadelphia following the national economic Panic of 1819, the city's poorhouses increasingly deteriorated into institutional slums—unclean, inadequately funded, terribly overcrowded, sometimes brutal, mixing adult strangers and children without regard to an array of medical and emotional problems. The trend in other cities was no better. In the mid-1850s a study of Charleston's poorhouse discovered foul privies, "surface drains filled with offensive matter," and beds "swarming with vermin." Among the two thousand residents who by 1827 lived miserably in New York City's walled, four-story poorhouse were 425 children, a number of them orphans. Equally pitiful were conditions in 1833 in the Boston House of Industry, a combination almshouse and prison with over 600 residents. More than 130 children, some abandoned, others orphaned, crowded together with infirm, dying, and disabled adults, up to seven people per room. When the New York state legislature investigated county almshouses in the 1850s, it found that "common domestic animals are usually more humanely provided for . . . the children are poorly fed, poorly clothed, and quite untaught." Critics justifiably attacked such places as "living tombs" and "social cemeteries."[23]

Some authorities tried to improve upon these wretched conditions by separating children from adult strangers. These efforts meshed with the growing recognition of children as unique from adults and deserving of special attention. Moreover, for reformers whose battles against poverty too often ended in disillusionment, the prospects of rescuing an innocent child could be galvanizing. In children's distinctiveness and malleability lay either the promise of a better future—or the despair of worsening social problems. A visitor to some of New York State's almshouses in 1855 made this point after finding that the children's teacher was too often "a pauper, generally an old drunkard . . . who spends the school hours in tormenting . . . his pupils." The visitor wondered how children in such environments could themselves become anything but paupers or even criminals. Just as one thistle in a field could produce many weeds, he wrote, so New York's three thousand almshouse children each contained "a seed of pauperism."[24]

To isolate such seeds, authorities in several northeastern cities built a new kind of institution in the 1820s, the house of refuge. There, according to literature from the Philadelphia House of Refuge, "the orphan, deserted or misguided child" would be "shielded from the temptations of a sinful world"—which could include the child's own family. In 1838 the Philadelphia institution won a landmark court decision, *Ex Parte Crouse*, which defended state intervention to protect neglected and delinquent children from "incompetent" parents. When Mary Ann Crouse's mother petitioned authorities that her daughter was incorrigible, officials placed the girl in the Philadelphia House of Refuge. Mary Ann's father protested in court, arguing that authorities had violated her constitutional rights by imprisoning her without trial. The Pennsylvania Supreme Court disagreed, emphasizing that children have needs, not rights; that those needs included custody, not liberty; and that the institution was "not a prison, but a school." According to the court, the state could intervene to protect a child and society from parents who were "unequal to the task of education." In the case of Mary Ann Crouse, the judges believed that the state had saved her "from a course which would have ended in confirmed depravity." Indeed, to remove her from the house of refuge "would be an act of extreme cruelty." *Crouse* was the pivotal ruling on institutional custody.[25]

Although houses of refuge were mainly for delinquent youths, they contained substantial numbers of dependent and neglected children. To broaden the appeal of these new institutions and distinguish them from mere children's prisons, advocates early on stressed the concept of prevention and expanded the houses' legal jurisdiction to include noncriminal youngsters. By accepting neglected, abused, and abandoned youths—"the vagrant and perilled children of the streets," as one official history put it—the houses of refuge were supposed to head off future criminals. This blurring of the lines between dependency and delinquency continued into the twentieth century.[26]

Institutions for delinquent youths thus typically included many youngsters who had never committed a crime. Although 13-year-old Mary McConnell had not broken the law, she ended up in the Massachusetts State Industrial School for Girls (Lancaster) when her parents declared her out of control. Lancaster provided her with a sanctuary from abusive parents who beat her when she failed to beg enough money for the family. Besides providing shelter for mistreated children such as Mary McConnell, juvenile reformatories also kept many homeless children who had done nothing wrong or, at the worst, had committed crimes of survival, such as stealing food. A study in 1858 found that only 38 percent of the children in New York City's House of Refuge had broken the law; 61 percent were simply "bad" or "unfortunate."[27]

Despite descriptions of "the loving, nurturing folds" of the New York refuge, such institutions were seldom kind or generous. Order and method were watchwords because the asylums were supposed to imbue young minds with respect for morality, religion, and hard work. Discipline was crucial. One superintendent favored "the judicious use of the rod. . . . I never yet have seen the time when I thought the rod could be dispensed with." The diary of another superintendent in the mid-1820s recorded numerous applications of "the cat." He whipped youths for such offenses as wetting their beds, talking, making noises, and using profanity. And he chained others up for being "quarrelsome" or "artfully sly."[28]

More than a few unfortunate youths ended up in harsher places, including jails, either because there was nowhere else for them or because they had committed minor infractions. After sleeping on sidewalks for a number of days, one 15-year-old orphan in New York City went in desperation to the Essex Street Prison for food and shelter. Jailers kept him for three days before finding alternative care for him. In 1822 New York's district attorney reported that "a considerable number" of vagrant boys and girls, ages 9 to 16, resided in the city's Bridewell prison, a place for adults awaiting trial or serving terms for nonviolent crimes such as prostitution. These were children, he said, "who profess to have no home, or whose parents have turned them out of doors and take no care of them." Some had been "sleeping in the streets or in stables."[29]

Similarly, the inmates at the Massachusetts State Reform School for Boys were guilty mostly of being poor and living in the streets. Around 43 percent of the residents between 1848, when the institution opened, and 1859 were homeless. Over half had only one parent, and 9 percent had none. The Irish Catholic background of about a third of the inmates hindered their cause: A key backer of the institution was Boston mayor Theodore Lyman, who despised the Irish Catholic immigrants in his city and believed that special measures were essential to teach Catholic children the values of hard work and Protestantism. To implement such measures, he tapped his sizable fortune to help build the state reform school. Ironically, Protestant parents in economic straits sometimes brought charges against their own children so that the youngsters could receive temporary care. By the late 1850s the reformatory held more than double its capacity of three hundred, the inmates chafed at the harsh regimen, and the Irish youths were virtually in rebellion against their Yankee Protestant overseers.[30]

Disappointing results also flowed from attempts in some poorhouses to separate children from adults by establishing children's wards, or nurseries. Most of the wards were terribly overcrowded. In a number of instances, authorities segregated children from their parents. Such separation hardly guaranteed better child care because unpaid female inmates, some of them feeble or emotionally unstable, usually watched over the children. Inadequate care undoubtedly helped to account for the fact that foundlings, or abandoned infants, died in the Massachusetts state almshouses at a staggering rate of up to 97 percent. In 1831 an epidemic at New York's Bellevue almshouse forced the removal of orphan and destitute children to temporary quarters on Long Island. Seven years later, an observer lamented their "melancholy" conditions and "imperfect" nutrition. Despite the late November cold, many youngsters huddled without stockings and shoes "round the stoves with an expression of suffering and discomfort." At night the children slept in dreary, poorly ventilated rooms. Ten years passed before New York City moved a thousand pauper children to a new institution, the "Randall's Island Nurseries." A few months later, in 1849, more than half of the 514 infants died there during a cholera epidemic. Meanwhile, at New York's Blackwell's Island almshouse, children still mixed with adult strangers.[31]

In Philadelphia, criticism of the city's almshouse nurseries mobilized officials to establish a public orphanage, only the second one in the United States. The Philadelphia Children's Asylum, which opened in 1820 and admitted 258 youngsters, was a forbidding place. The children wore uniforms, stood in silence while eating, found almost no meat or vegetables in their diets, marched in single file, and followed a rigid schedule. Still, the asylum was better than the poorhouse. Its staff included some salaried workers, not simply pauper residents in the institution; and it paid more attention at least to the children's educational and medical welfare, if not to their emotional wants.[32]

Yet the Philadelphia Children's Asylum met the needs of only a part of the city's poor and dependent children. It admitted only whites under age 10, and most of them were not from the poorhouse, which always contained more youngsters than did the orphanage. A substantial majority came from parents who were able to stay out of the almshouse themselves but needed temporary shelter for their offspring. When the managers tried to indenture children in order to save money, parents blocked the plan. Furious at these attempts to turn the orphanage into a "house of convenience," officials obtained a law in 1828 requiring parents to pay their children's board. Children for whom there were no payments faced indenture without parental consent. The law helped the asylum economically (by reducing the number of children to 136 in 1829) and also provided authorities with added leverage to remove children from poor families. Some families fought back, imploring officials not to indenture their children. One mother hid in the asylum in a failed effort to rescue her son. When authorities put her back on the street, she shouted and hurled rocks at the building until she was arrested.[33]

After 15 years, the growing tax burden forced the closing of the Philadelphia Children's Asylum. In 1835 nearly three hundred children entered the new Blockley poorhouse with a wing that separated most of them from adults, including their parents. Even then, one report showed that three elderly women and an alcoholic slept in the nursery. Up to the mid-1850s a majority of the children came to the institution with one parent. Although mothers occasionally stayed with infants, children usually saw neither their mothers nor fathers. Strapped for funds, the Blockley Almshouse initially used inmates as nurses. That economizing measure perhaps explained in part why 20 children died within one month after their arrival. Although officials responded to that tragedy by hiring a physician and several professional nurses, they continued to trim expenses in other areas. From 1844 to 1849, for example, the asylum's school had no teacher.[34]

Step by step, cost-conscious Philadelphia officials backed away from direct responsibility for the city's poor and dependent children. From 1820 to 1850 the number of children on the relief rolls fell from 1,736 to 523 (all in the almshouse), and the percentage in public institutions declined from 24 to 11. Significantly, by 1848 officials had returned 51 percent of the children in the Blockley Almshouse to their families even if the families had not, in accordance with the 1828 law, regained custody by paying their youngster's room and board. Equally significant, by 1850 Philadelphia had also ended all outdoor relief to children. As economy-minded Philadelphia scaled back its direct assistance to poor and dependent youngsters, the question of who would help them became more urgent. Officials in that city and elsewhere lost interest in special public children's asylums and looked increasingly to private charity for the answer.[35]

III

Between 1820 and 1860, 150 private orphanages were founded across the country—11 in the 1820s, 36 in the 1830s, 39 in the 1840s, and 64 in the 1850s. They had varying agendas and conditions. Some were responses to epidemics that orphaned many children. Almost all were tied to specific religious groups (75 were Protestant, 59 were Catholic, 3 were Jewish). Most initially indentured the older children. Some received public support; by the 1840s, for example, Cincinnati officials paid for the care of around half of the children in a local orphanage. Most orphanages started out as temporary homes for a few children who had lost one or both parents. As the number of residents grew, asylums became increasingly austere, emphasized discipline, were highly regimented, isolated the children as much as possible, and assumed custodial roles. But some, particularly those whose founders and managers were females, were more flexible and sympathetic to the plight of poor families who sought temporary shelter for children.[36]

A pioneer among these orphanages was the Boston Female Asylum (BFA), established in 1800 by a group of women who took seriously the ideal of "republican motherhood" that grew out of the American Revolution. Hannah Stillman, wife of Boston's leading Baptist minister, first came up with the idea of the orphanage in 1799 after hearing a friend's account about the sexual abuse of a small orphan girl. With thoughts of the little girl still bothering her, she read a newspaper story about a newly formed "female humane society" in Baltimore and concluded that elite Boston women should form a similar organization, one aimed at rescuing victims like abused orphans. With the help of women such as Abigail Adams, Stillman formed the society that sponsored the Boston Female Asylum for legitimate orphan girls, ages 3 to 12. When the girls reached their teens, the BFA placed them as servants with respectable families. Stillman, Adams, and the other BFA founders had lived through the American Revolution and believed deeply that the nation's survival depended on the cultural power of mothers to instruct young people in the republican virtues of self-sacrifice, simplicity, and a commitment to the common good. Even the decision to dress all the BFA orphans alike, in plain blue uniforms, drew upon republican opposition to fashion, luxury, and privilege as much as it did upon matters of economy.[37]

On one level the BFA's founders and managers unquestionably benefited personally from their efforts. They served as models for female charity associations in other communities; they provided well-trained domestic help for women such as themselves; they received a good deal of praise; and they found their good works morally reassuring. "Look at these dear orphans," the Reverend Jedediah Morse said in 1807 during an anniversary sermon as he observed the 30 young girls who were present. "They live on your bounty. . . . You see how happy they are." In numerous rituals, the orphans themselves lauded the women. At annual meetings of the board, for example, the girls sang special "hymns" for the occasion: "No more complaining fills the street, / Of Children who deserted roam, / For here the *houseless vagrants* meet / A benefactor and a home."[38]

Still, much to their credit, the BFA women avoided turning their institution into the bleak custodial environment that characterized all too many orphanages by 1850. Within the first 15 years they came close to adopting the kind of rules and regimen that marked more orderly and rigorously disciplined institutions. By the 1820s, for example, they were isolating the children from surviving parents, thereby placing institutional attachments above those of family, and elevating procedures over sentiments. And the BFA's educational program focused primarily on producing trustworthy and respectable domestic servants. But by the 1830s a new generation of managers moved the institution toward what historian Susan Porter has described as "benevolent maternalism," which exhibited a disposition that was kinder toward poor people than that which characterized most antebellum orphanages.[39]

This shift may have been largely a product of gender. Several orphanages that were primarily the responsibility of women exhibited less punitive attitudes toward the poor than did the highly regulated institutions in the control of male philanthropists such as Josiah Quincy. In New Orleans the Poydras Home for female orphans, which a Quaker woman founded in 1817 in response to a yellow fever epidemic, thus differed from its counterpart, the male-directed Asylum for Destitute Orphan Boys. When financial exigencies beset both institutions, the Poydras managers resisted policies that dismissed girls or pushed financial burdens upon poor families. Moreover, Poydras remained less custodial than did the Asylum for Destitute Orphan Boys and more willingly returned children at parental request. The Boston Female Asylum helped to set the patterns that surfaced in places such as Poydras. In its third decade, the BFA reversed its earlier policy of isolating the girls from surviving parents. A sensitivity to gender injustices may have made the female managers of the BFA (as well as those at the Poydras Home) more attuned to the feelings of helplessness that gripped poor women and children, and more inclined to see destitute people as victims of circumstance than as good-for-nothings.[40]

The BFA's managers even somewhat revised their attitudes toward indenture. Initially, they had assumed that the orphans would be better off working as domestic servants for wealthy people than living with poor parents or relatives. Under the tutelage of "true" women in elite homes, domestic service would supposedly be a kind of "moral apprenticeship," extending the social training the girls had received during their stay in the asylum. Although the BFA managers relied on the indenture system into the 1850s, they increasingly viewed it with skepticism. Their firsthand experiences provided evidence that some wealthy women simply wanted cheap labor. "Some who apply for these children have no other thought than to obtain a selfish convenience," complained one BFA manager in 1841. By then the BFA was more interested in developing ties between girls and surviving relatives than in exposing children to elite environments. Around half of the graduates went to live with relatives.[41]

The BFA was indeed an early model of a "benevolent asylum." During its first half century it remained fairly small, caring for no more than 40 girls at a time. The almost four hundred girls who lived there from 1800 to 1840 were for the most part able to escape poverty as adults and adapt to new opportunities, often showing that they had picked up the habit of independence rather than subservience. A growing number opted to leave domestic service in favor of jobs where they used the artisan skills that the BFA increasingly encouraged. Certainly some of the girls found fresh starts in the asylum. Caroline Sophia Hyde, for example, was supported by the BFA after her mother's suicide in 1829, as were the Henderson sisters, who entered the BFA at ages three and five after their mother had died and their father had lost an arm and a foot in a dock accident. By assisting the Henderson sisters and other girls who came from poor, distressed circumstances, the women of the BFA demonstrated a willingness to see the children as products of misfortune, rather than vice.[42]

IV

For the most part, however, distinctions between misfortune and vice blurred in antebellum America. The era's rising democratic tide buoyed up expectations regarding individual power, opportunity, and responsibility. Successive waves of evangelical enthusiasm strengthened these democratic currents by emphasizing free will (that people choose either sin or salvation, thereby controlling their own fate). Activists in the Sunday School movement fretted that youngsters, particularly those in poor homes, were "moral orphans" who lacked personal compasses regarding correct conduct and values.[43]

This sympathy for endangered children energized benevolent campaigns in their behalf. Unitarian minister Edward Everett Hale implored affluent youths "to think more of the miseries of the less favored, and to endeavor to relieve them." But although evangelical zeal encouraged the kind of voluntarism and missionary efforts that shaped institutions such as orphanages, it also imposed a militantly pious agenda on some children's asylums. By the Civil War, for example, denominational competition very much marked the 15 private asylums for dependent children in Boston. Catholics, worried about the aggressive proselytization that accompanied the Protestant efforts, countered with their own institutions. In 1832 several sisters founded the St. Vincent Female Orphan Asylum to protect the daughters of the Irish.[44]

In some children's asylums, evangelical goals very much influenced the regimen of the young residents. "The God we serve is a God of order, and not of confusion," the American Sunday School Union announced. Not surprisingly, the interest in order, stability, and punctuality influenced the day-to-day operations of orphanages. In the Long Island orphan asylum, youngsters "were daily drilled to military exercises," according to Lydia Child. "I was informed that it was 'beautiful to see them pray; for at the first tip of the whistle, they dropped on their knees.' " The New York Orphan Asylum likewise stressed religion: "The boys have committed to memory 8881 verses of Scripture and 3103 verses of hymns," the managers reported happily in 1821. "The girls have committed 4805 verses of Scripture and 6208 verses of hymns; nearly all the children can repeat the Mother's Catechism, the Creed, and the Lord's prayer."[45]

The concern for order intensified as institutions expanded. Even the Boston Female Asylum faced some of the dilemmas of the larger congregate institutions when it moved in 1857 to a new building for one hundred girls. The New York Orphan Asylum took much less time to increase its numbers, even though it initially sent all half-orphans to the almshouse: In 1806, during its first six months, it housed 12 orphans; within two years the number was 53. By 1821, the 152 boys and girls were so crowded together that the managers started building a new wing, which soon included dozens more. The residents received large doses of religious education and work. Because the institution indentured the older children, it very much emphasized work habits: "*In order to inure the boys to hardship and fatigue,*" read a report in 1821, "they are required to cut all the wood, draw all the water, etc." The girls performed "every variety of housework." Bells marked the daily schedule. The children marched to meals and religious services in single files, girls on one side, boys on the other. They could write to relatives once a month, but the teachers scrutinized letters before mailing them. And the children received numerous reminders of how grateful they should be to their benefactors. In a specially designed hymn, the boys sang, "Our friends are here; / They come to dry the orphan's tear." The girls asked rhetorically, "Oh, brothers, when our parents died, / Who did these faithful friends provide? / Who first their generous hearts inclined / To be to helpless orphans kind?"[46]

The relationship between ballooning institutional populations and strict regimens was widely apparent. In upstate New York, Albany's two-story orphan asylum started out in 1832 resembling a large private residence. Over the next five decades the number of inmates increased to six hundred, and the enlarged institution took on a more prisonlike appearance. Because of the sheer number of children, the orphanage's initial goal of building a carefully structured environment gave way to a custodial obsession.[47]

V

Antebellum congregate institutions proved woefully deficient for dependent and needy white children, but they were virtually nonexistent for African Americans. The Shelter for Colored Orphans, which female members of the Society of Friends established in 1822 as Philadelphia's first private children's charity for blacks, initially housed only 12 children, ranging in age from 18 months to 8 years. Even then, the shelter so angered whites that a mob destroyed it in 1837. Relocated to a different Philadelphia location, the shelter accommodated 67 children, substantially more than before but still a small number compared with the number of white children who were welcome in institutions. Moreover, by that time the Quakers' much larger Philadelphia House of Refuge had closed its doors to black children because, in the superintendent's words, "it would be degrading to the white children to associate with beings given up to public scorn." Quakers had opened the House of Refuge in 1828 as an alternative to placing youthful vagrants and offenders in prison with adults. The cheerless institution, with a strict work-or-punishment regimen and a policy of indenturing inmates to new families within a few months, was hardly a happy setting. Nevertheless, its refusal one year after opening to admit blacks forced some African American youths into adult jails.[48]

Unlike the House of Refuge, Philadelphia's public almshouse was racially integrated. Between 1835 and 1850, a quarter of the children in the new poorhouse at Blockley were African Americans. The city nevertheless barred blacks from its short-lived Children's Asylum, a far more hospitable setting than the almshouse. And after Philadelphia officials decided to reduce Blockley's population and end outdoor relief, dependent African American children received virtually no help outside of traditional kinship circles.[49]

In 1850 Philadelphia Quakers, increasingly anxious about "the vicious and neglected children of the coloured population," opened a division in their House of Refuge for around a hundred African American boys and girls. The youths perhaps found their stay in the House of Refuge for Colored Children (usually a year, before indenture) a better alternative than what they otherwise faced. Certainly the institution's sponsors believed so. They looked upon the asylum's creation as an act "of simple justice" to help the downtrodden and make amends for racial prejudice. But their own unrecognized biases and the nature of their mission hardly augured well for the youthful black residents. The overseers of the institution believed, as one of their pamphlets made clear, that African Americans had only "extremely limited" chances of improving their morals or engaging in "useful learning of any kind." They believed also that "in the habits and associations of the lowest grades there is an assimilation to the irrational animals—which, if seen among whites, would excite universal commiseration." When eight of the African American children died in 1858, the managers referred to a "tendency to scrofulous and pulmonary diseases in so many of them" and spoke of relocating the institution in the country. Over the next several years, the managers looked for a small Pennsylvania farm where the youngsters might receive instruction in agriculture that would prepare them for immigration to Liberia. However, nothing came of the plan to remove the children from Pennsylvania, where the climate was reportedly "unfavorable to the African constitution." Instead, fiscal restraints forced the asylum managers to concentrate on reducing expenditures and achieving "greater efficiency" in all of their programs.[50]

In New York City as well, dependent black children received little institutional help. The two white women who organized the city's Colored Orphan Asylum in the 1830s battled incredible odds. They had difficulty raising funds, finding a building to lease, and dealing with horribly overcrowded conditions. In 1863 draft rioters burned the institution down. For several years, the children lived in temporary quarters, including the Randall's Island almshouse. At the end of the decade, 273 youngsters resided in a large brick institution that was barely afloat economically. "Of all the asylums in the city," according to one student of nineteenth-century orphanages, the Colored Orphan Asylum "was and would always remain the poorest, an orphaned institution struggling to survive."[51]

VI

Race was not the only area in which children's asylums were faltering badly by midcentury. The status of foundlings reached crisis proportions. Baby desertion threatened to become an epidemic, particularly in cities, where despairing mothers could abandon their newborn more easily than in small towns. In New York City alone, for example, infanticide resulted each month in the discovery of 100 to 150 bodies in places such as empty barrels or the rivers.[52]

Evidence abounded that America's children's asylums, always insufficient, were not even keeping pace with escalating demands. In New York City at the end of the 1860s, around 12,000 needy children were in the care of private and charitable societies. According to some estimates, that figure was only half the number of the city's homeless and dependent youths. In Chicago, officials had complained almost two decades earlier of growing numbers of "children who are destitute of proper parental care, wandering the streets."[53]

Congregate institutions that only a few years earlier had been jewels in the nation's welfare crown were losing their luster. An 1855 report to the New York state legislature chastised county almshouses for the outrageous conditions in which they sheltered some three thousand youngsters under age 16. Complaints grew as well that houses of refuge were everywhere abandoning even the pretense of rehabilitation. Orphanages, already crowded, faced a desperate situation that would only worsen as the Civil War claimed large numbers of fathers and as immigration pushed the population upward.

Still, despite their imperfections, congregate asylums for dependent and needy children continued to spread rapidly throughout the rest of the nineteenth century. By then, however, they faced mounting opposition from anti-institutional adversaries with competing agendas and strategies.

3

"Placing Out": Orphan Trains,
Foster Homes, and Adoption

To the three forlorn waifs who huddled miserably under a streetlight on a drab city street corner, the friendly, well-dressed stranger was a godsend, rescuing them from despairing conditions. He picked up the small girl, took the hand of one of her brothers, and placed the siblings in the care of an organization that gave them a new start. Soon they gathered with other dependent children at the train station, ready to head westward under the watchful eyes of adults. Dressed neatly and displaying good manners, the grateful trio found a new home with a caring farm family. The oldest brother, perhaps 12, raised his hat in a cheer as he stood happily behind a horse-drawn plow in a field.[1]

This uplifting tale, in which downcast youngsters swapped their hapless condition for opportunity and friendship, unfolded courtesy of the New York Children's Aid Society (NYCAS). Five sketches in the frontispiece of the society's 1873 annual report traced how the three children had moved from homelessness to happiness. By the time of that report, the organization had existed for two decades and stood, along with its founder, Charles Loring Brace, at the center of an increasingly contentious debate over how society should deal with dependent children.

Throughout the latter half of nineteenth-century America, Brace led the discussion over policies regarding dependent children, a discussion that spun out of fears of the growing urban underclass. Like child rescue workers generally at midcentury, he did not differentiate at-risk children according to the particular kinds of danger they faced—homelessness, neglect, or abuse. But he became the chief critic of congregate institutions, and the NYCAS placed thousands of dependent youths in private homes. Throughout the last decades of the 1800s and into the 1900s, the famous "orphan trains" bore

RESCUED.

HOMELESS.

OFF FOR THE WEST.

THE YOUNG FARMER.

ADOPTED.

THE WORK OF THE CHILDREN'S AID SOCIETY.

Frontispiece from the 1873 annual report of the New York Children's Aid Society romanticizing the system by which dependent children were rescued from urban streets and placed with farm families. Courtesy The Children's Aid Society.

carloads of youngsters from the NYCAS and other aid societies to the countryside to live with farm families, especially in the Midwestern and Plains states. The "placing-out" movement did not originate with Brace, but he popularized and reshaped it by seizing upon apprehensions of the urban poor, the decline of indenture, and laws that for the first time in the United States formalized the adoption process.

I

Although the placing-out movement affected the lives of perhaps as many as two hundred thousand youngsters over some 75 years, its burst of popularity in the mid-1800s revealed less about the children themselves than about shifting ideology and a rapidly escalating panic over changing conditions in the nation's economy and cities. In that regard, "childhood" served as a fulcrum that reformers hoped to use as leverage for change. As urbanization and industrialization widened social class divisions, worried reformers looked to

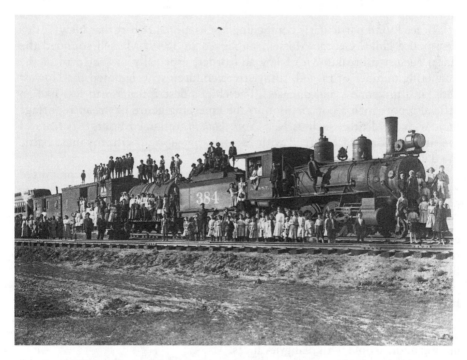

An "orphan train" on the Atchison, Topeka & Santa Fe Railroad line. Courtesy The Kansas State Historical Society, Topeka, Kansas.

children as the material out of which to construct a more stable society, one that was safe from what Brace described as "the dangerous classes."[2]

Brace's tendency to blame the problems of needy children on the depravity of slum parents grew from his evangelical outlook and his revulsion for New York City's teeming shanty and tenement areas, a world in startling contrast with what he had known in his youth. Born in 1826 in the rural community of Litchfield, Connecticut, he had enjoyed the comforts of a respectable middle-class minister's family. When he was seven, his family had moved to the outskirts of Hartford so that his father could direct a prestigious female seminary. Young Charles learned from the sermons of Hartford's famed Congregational minister, Horace Bushnell, about the power of the family to form character through love and example rather than coercion. Bushnell, one of the era's childrearing experts, also advocated placing children of failed parents with another family, one that was "virtuous and Christian." When Brace attended Yale University he particularly missed "Mr. Bushnell's sermons." In 1847 he decided to study for the ministry himself and entered Yale Divinity School. A year later he moved to New York City to enter Union Theological Seminary. The 22-year-old found the "rush and whirl" of the city thrilling and enjoyed immersing himself in "the perfect *flood* of humanity" on Broadway. But competing with the "grand gala-day" side of New York was something else: "an immense vat of misery and crime and filth."[3]

Brace found particularly compelling a sensational report that New York's first police chief, George Matsell, published in 1849. Matsell sounded the alarm against a breakdown of law and order, especially in the form of the staggering number of ragged, filthy street children who haunted the "lowest dens of drunkenness and disease." The chief's descriptions read less like an official report than a contribution to the emerging genre of urban reportage that, with lurid titles such as *New York Naked*, inflamed bourgeois fears of the urban poor. Brace agreed with Matsell that upright citizens must battle the dangers of poverty and vice.[4]

After touring Europe in the early 1850s, Brace was even more committed to that fight. For one thing, he had visited countries that were still reeling from the revolutions of 1848. In Hungary, his interest in the upheavals against what he viewed as "crushing injustice and tyranny and oppression" even landed him momentarily in jail. Authorities arrested him for possessing revolutionary materials and praising the Hungarian nationalist Kossuth. Brace's short stay in prison strengthened his resolve to help oppressed peoples. He grounded that resolve partly in ideas that he picked up from the Inner Mission, a new Protestant social work movement that was sweeping Germany. Advocates of the Inner Mission believed that genuine social service agencies were essential to stir a religious awakening and head off revolution among poor people with real grievances.[5]

Back in New York, Brace plunged into mission work. "I want to raise up the outcast and homeless, to go down among those who have no friend or helper," he wrote. To that end, he turned his attention to what one newspaper described as New York's "blackest and foulest spot," the Five Points section, a dense immigrant slum in a city whose population almost tripled in the 1850s, surging from 300,000 to 810,000. But he spurned the common evangelical strategy of "preaching sermons to the prostitute" in favor of a more active strategy of rescuing children. "Think of *ten thousand children* growing up almost sure to be prostitutes and rogues," he had written in 1849, one month after police chief Matsell released his influential report.[6]

II

Determined to help "the immense number of boys and girls floating and drifting about our streets," Brace formed the New York Children's Aid Society in 1853. During the society's first year he devoted special attention to a Newsboys' Lodging House where "*houseless boys*," or "little street rovers," could find shelter and hear the gospel. Initially, he viewed this project as "*the* thing" in working with street children, and he reported happily the first-night response of one young boy: "I'm glad I ain't a bummer to-night." By the 1890s, the NYCAS was operating five lodging houses for boys and one for girls, as well as a series of other refuges, including reading rooms, a summer home on Long Island, and 22 industrial schools (which were essentially workrooms where the youths learned various skills). The more marginal girls' projects were under the direction of women volunteers, who concentrated on the arts of domesticity—sewing, cooking, housecleaning, and virtuous motherhood.[7]

Brace developed a genuine affection and respect for the children, whom he described as a "happy race of little heathens and barbarians." He appreciated their street-smart independence, their ability to look out for themselves, their intelligence, and their "rough, hearty" temperament. He found himself admiring even "the skill and cunning with which the little rascals, some not more than ten years old," engaged in petty theft. Typically, however, he condoned such enterprising spirit in boys far more than girls, for whom boldness could be a precursor of "sexual sins."[8]

During the NYCAS's second year, Brace concentrated the society's energies on an elaborate scheme to place city children in the countryside. In March 1854 the society loaded a large group of 66 boys and 72 girls on a train for rural Pennsylvania. A few months later it sent 46 children to Michigan. Within its first 25 years, the society relocated around 40,000 New York City youngsters into farm homes as far west as Kansas. "Placing out" quickly became a popular and controversial strategy for dealing with homeless and destitute children.[9]

The idea was not new, although Brace publicized his work so well that people often assumed the "orphan trains" started with him. British colonization had included the transporting of poor people, including children, to distant places in North America and Australia. And for years the indenture system provided an early version of placing out orphan or destitute children. Brace's tour of Germany had introduced him to the "Friends in Need" program, in which wealthy individuals relocated homeless city children in rural settings. Brace was well aware, moreover, that in 1850 the Boston-based Children's Mission to the Children of the Destitute had started taking homeless children by train from Boston to foster homes on New England farms. The inspiration for the mission's program had reportedly been an innocent question a year earlier from a Unitarian minister's 12-year-old daughter when she saw poor children playing in the gutter. "Can't we do something for these poor little things?" she asked. Her father, the Reverend George Merrill, had promptly responded by soliciting funds from his congregation and Unitarian Sunday School children to save the "guttersnipes." Starting in 1850, the Children's Mission periodically took 30 to 50 waifs by train to farm families, with whom they were typically indentured. Charles Loring Brace knew well the mission's president, John E. Williams, and had served himself as one of the mission's officers before starting the NYCAS. After Brace started the NYCAS, Williams moved to New York to work with him.[10]

Although the NYCAS had numerous precedents, it represented a major legal departure from apprenticeships and indenture in that it did not require a formal contract. Like traditional apprenticeship arrangements, placing out involved an exchange of labor for room, board, and education. But families with whom the NYCAS placed children did not sign legal agreements, nor did the society relinquish custody of its young charges. In effect, the NYCAS instituted a free foster care system—free in the sense that families caring for children received no monetary reimbursement for their services. Any reimbursement would supposedly sully placement by turning it into a purely mercenary arrangement (known usually as "boarding out"). Granted, farm families would secure labor from the children. But Brace doubted that exploitation would be the result. For one thing, he was confident that "a child's place at the table of the farmer is always open; his food and cost to the family is of little account." Indeed, in Brace's mind, "a widespread spirit of benevolence" betokened a willingness to open "thousands of homes to the children of the unfortunate." This "spirit of humanity and kindness" was particularly strong within country families, according to Brace. If by chance an abusive situation developed, it would not last: "The chances . . . of ill treatment in a new country where children are petted and favored, and every man's affairs are known to all his neighbors, are far less than in an old." Brace was also convinced that the lack of a formal contract worked to the children's advantage, allowing them to leave unsatisfactory or exploitative situations.[11]

III

The nineteenth-century decline of apprenticeship was very much intertwined with the history of the NYCAS's placing-out program. Industrialization and surging population numbers devastated the apprentice system, which had long provided a way of caring for dependent children as well as a source of training in skilled labor. By the mid-1800s, factories and mass production were burying the older economy of artisans and small tradesmen. At the same time, waves of immigration threw impoverished adults into the labor force. For many employers, the apprenticeship arrangements, with their expectations of room and board, offered few advantages, especially as unskilled factory jobs proliferated. The demands for child laborers remained high in the late 1800s, particularly in industries such as textiles, mining, canning, and street peddling, where children who were no older than six or seven worked long and dangerous shifts. Employers were increasingly reluctant to accept responsibility for the youngsters' welfare. In this context, Brace believed that sending "street urchins" to western farms would relieve the overcrowded urban market and place "future laborers where they are in demand." He assumed that the children would receive better treatment in rural homes.[12]

Another contribution toward the weakening of the indenture system was the changing ideology of the family, with a new emphasis on maternal child-rearing and a protective, nurturing environment. By the 1830s courts were using the "best interests of the child" doctrine to redefine indenture, giving it a caretaker rather than a training role. Decisions in several courts thus made the parental apprenticing of children more difficult, limited the master's right to transfer an apprentice to someone else, and cast apprentices less as employees than as family members. In 1860 the Arkansas Supreme Court ruled that apprentices should live only with "persons proper to take the places of parents," and in settings that most accurately replicated "the parent-child bond." These words articulated the very rationale that made the old apprentice system less appealing to employers who increasingly tended to see the young employees as wage earners, not as children for whose care businesses were responsible. Involuntary apprenticeship did not disappear, however. Relief officials, more concerned about tax rates than about the welfare of children, still saw indenture as an economical way of dealing with homeless or impoverished children. In important respects, of course, Brace's placing-out program was a modified form of involuntary apprenticeship.[13]

The growing emphasis on family bonds nevertheless undermined the traditional apprenticeship system as surely as it implicitly challenged the spread of antebellum institutions for children. Just as Brace rejected the traditional indenture contract, so he criticized children's asylums. A basic NYCAS principle elevated "the superiority of the Christian family," and implicitly the Protestant family, over "any and all other institutions for the education and improvement of the poor child."[14]

IV

The midcentury emergence of modern adoption laws provided further evidence of a cultural tilt toward the middle-class family and tacitly encouraged placing-out strategies such as the NYCAS's emigration plan. In the history of children's rights, the formalization of the adoption process was crucial. There was nothing new, of course, about caring for someone else's children. But English common law, steeped in concerns over marriage, legitimacy, and inheritance, did not allow for transfers of parenthood; children outside the family's bloodline could not share legal status with natural born offspring. In the English colonies, informal understandings occasionally provided the equivalent of adoption. Sometimes, too, colonial (and, later, state) governments acceded to individual requests to recognize changes in children's names. When responding to such requests (which came typically via a last will and testament, or a private appeal to the legislature), the governments implicitly recognized the children's altered domestic status. In the 70 years before 1851, the Massachusetts legislature granted 101 private requests. Even then, however, the rights of the child under such arrangements were typically vague.[15]

With halting steps in the early 1800s, judges and legislatures moved toward a more general recognition of adoption. In the courts, the "best interests of the child" doctrine not only provided judges with greater discretionary powers but also required further clarification about the nature of childhood and the family. By midcentury, judges were increasingly willing to consider the place of affection, choice, and nurture in the family structure. In 1851 important custody cases in Pennsylvania and Massachusetts terminated the natural ties between parent and child. In one case, when a father attempted to regain possession of a girl he had placed with another relative for six years, the Pennsylvania court honored the child's request to stay with her new family. According to the decision, the child had been "estranged from the customs and government of her father's house" and had formed new "habits and views." Meanwhile, Massachusetts Chief Justice Lemuel Shaw argued that a father, by leaving his daughter with her grandparents for 13 years, had "surrendered his rights over the child, by a tacit understanding, if not an express agreement." It would be impossible, Shaw concluded, to return the daughter "without risking the happiness and interest of [the] child." More and more, judges moved the parent-child relationship from patriarchal kinship lines to a contractual relationship that reflected sentimental ties and emphasized child nurture.[16]

Not surprisingly, in 1851 the Massachusetts legislature codified this judicial trend by enacting a landmark "Act to Provide for the Adoption of Children." Here was a legal mechanism to substitute artificial ties for those of birth. The statute spelled out the procedures for adoption, placed decisions with probate courts, terminated the rights and obligations of the natural parents (after obtaining their consent or, if they were dead or missing, by using a court-appointed "discreet and suitable person" to represent the child), and emphasized the rights of the adopted child who stood in relationship to the adoptive parents as if he or she had been born to them "in lawful wedlock." The Massachusetts statute quickly became a national model. Its child-centered approach moved beyond a series of other midcentury general adoption laws in Mississippi, Vermont, and several other states, where the legislatures simply wanted to free themselves from handling individual adoption cases. The 1853 Pennsylvania statute attested both to the influence of the Massachusetts law and to the growing emphasis on protecting the child. In Pennsylvania the courts could permit adoption only when they were confident that it promoted the "welfare of the child." By the end of the century, adoption laws resembling those of Massachusetts and Pennsylvania existed in almost every state; and adoption, unusual before the Civil War, became routine, although disputes continued over matters of inheritance, custody, and the adopted child's care.[17]

V

The placing-out schemes of Charles Loring Brace and other child welfare reformers corresponded with the passage of adoption laws. In each case, the objective was to place children in caring, stable, moral family environments—a goal that reflected the triumph of the ideology of domesticity, with its emphasis on affection, romantic marriage, and innocent children. Contemporaries noted that the difficulties benevolent societies faced when seeking homes for foundlings had helped to inspire the 1851 Massachusetts statute. The popularity of adoption laws and the placing-out movement thus peaked during the same years. Agencies such as Boston's New England Home for Little Wanderers strongly encouraged adoption. Brace made less of adoption, because many of the NYCAS's charges were in fact children from destitute families rather than orphans. Instead, he favored an approach that resembled the later foster care system, although his scheme lacked formal agreements and rested on the hope that a placement family would accept the child as one of its own. Brace elevated the ties of what he described as "Christian duty and of affection" over legal bonds. He delighted in the news that one recently placed child "sits at the same table with the farmer's family, and goes to school with his children."[18]

In effect, as legal scholar Mary Ann Mason has observed, Brace found a middle ground "between the purely economic arrangement of involuntary apprenticeships and the child-nurturing focus of adoption." And he was unquestionably elated to receive letters such as one from a family with whom the NYCAS had placed a youth: "We surely love him as our own; and we have had visitors here for a number of days without once thinking that he was not our own child."[19]

Once Brace launched the NYCAS's program of transporting youngsters to the country, he became increasingly critical of institutions. Initially, he indicated simply that asylums could not cope with the growing number of dependent children. But within a few years he chastised even the best institutions as inadequate to youngsters' needs and, indeed, as agencies that would replace individual conscience with "drill-virtues" and "treadmill goodness." He was convinced that children's institutions, like charity as a whole, undermined self-reliance and initiative, thereby encouraging the habits of pauperism. Unlike institutions, he argued, emigration would build character and relieve the pressures of the overcrowded urban market. Emigration was thus a humanitarian response to the problem of street urchins; an economic answer to the problems of urban unemployment; and a social solution for the building dangers of a lower class whose poverty and violence endangered society.[20]

Recruiting children for placement was, however, a random and haphazard process. Some of them were in New York City's almshouses, House of Refuge, orphanages, and Newsboys' Lodging House. Some were in jail for vagrancy and homelessness. Some, including a little newsboy who wanted to " 'get West,' " reportedly came themselves to the NYCAS office in search of assistance. Some met Brace or his agents on the streets or docks by pure chance. Only hours before a small band of boys left on an orphan train for Michigan, NYCAS agents found two more youths, including a 12-year-old who simply claimed that he was homeless. In 1854 the Children's Aid Society placed over 200 boys and girls in rural homes. Thereafter, NYCAS agents accompanied "little companies" of from 5 to 30 children, numbering some three thousand in a typical year, westward to states such as Michigan and Illinois. Before the children left the train station, there was usually time enough only to bathe them, cut their hair, and provide a change of clothes.[21]

VI

Brace's genius lay partly in his ability to portray the NYCAS as a rescuer of friendless orphans even though most actually had homes. Among the "crowd of wandering little ones" who came under the NYCAS umbrella were, he wrote, "ragged young girls who had nowhere to lay their heads," "orphans who slept where they could find a box or a stairway," and "newsboys, whose incessant answer to our question, 'Where do you live?' rung in our ears, *'Don't live nowhere!'* "[22]

Such a poignant response—"Don't live nowhere!"—framed the NYCAS's ideology and provided a powerful rationale for rescuing victimized children. The image of a homeless child struck a popular chord, especially given the tendency of moral reformers and genteel urban residents to associate street children with disorder and future crime. "Send your child West for $10," the organization pleaded in its 1871 search for sponsors. The appeal won over people such as Mrs. John Jacob Astor, who between 1875 and 1884 subsidized the emigration of more than a thousand children to the Midwest. Some wealthy New York City families, such as the Vanderbilts, were strong NYCAS backers. City, county, and state funds also helped to underwrite the organization's expenses, even by as much as half in 1870.[23]

Such support drew certainly upon building fears of an urban crisis. During the 1850s in New York City, huge numbers of impoverished residents lived in miserable shacks, and the mortality rate of children under five surged to 52 percent. The economic Panic of 1857 threw 20,000 out of 30,000 in the city's garment trade alone out of work. In the pages of the frightening Tenant House Report of 1857, poor people emerged as "gaunt, shivering forms" with "wild ghastly faces," living in "fever-nests." According to the Association for the Improvement of the Condition of the Poor, "the dark, filthy hovels where many of them dwell" mocked the word "home."[24]

This was the context in which Brace and NYCAS agents responded to the city's street children. And that context very much colored what they saw and how they interpreted it. One agent thus wrote sympathetically about two poor children who lived with their widowed mother, a woman who struggled against horrendous odds to care for them. He watched her rub her offspring's hands, trying to warm them in an unheated, unfurnished tenement room during a cold winter day. But his final assessment of the woman was anything but charitable. Despite her struggles, which he had initially interpreted with some compassion, he had no confidence in her as a mother. Indeed, he said, "some cursed vice" of which she was probably guilty meant that she would destroy her children if they remained with her. Ultimately, the agent thus ignored the pitiful circumstances under which the mother struggled, and portrayed her as yet another depraved member of the feared "tenement classes."[25]

Similarly, Brace himself could describe with considerable poignancy the ordeal of a child's natural family and then turn harsh. In one household, for example, the father had lost his job because of illness and the mother, who had just given birth, was also sick. *They did not know what to do,"* Brace wrote plaintively. "Rent to pay, themselves to feed, fuel and all—and *no work!"* Yet Brace ultimately shifted attention from the parents' travails. He even observed callously in one instance that "the only hope for the children is that the mother will die."[26]

Brace's humane instincts faded quickly when he discussed poor immigrants. The "stupid foreign criminal class," in his opinion, represented the "scum and refuse of ill-formed civilizations." Brace contrasted this class with "true Americans," who valued "cleanliness, independence, good order, and decency." In that vein, the NYCAS's 1864 annual report distinguished between "the better portions" of U.S. society and the "*dregs*" of America's "foreign population"—the "foreign sediment" that settled in the slum districts and produced "pauper children." The NYCAS generally classified the urban poor as "social rats" bent on satisfying their "animal passions" and scurrying after dark into their "filthy lair." With such words, the NYCAS laced its relief efforts with condemnation. And by pointing an accusatory finger at indigent parents, it shaped an ideological legacy that long outlived Brace.[27]

At the same time, the NYCAS politicized the concept of childhood, using it as a lever for social change. Brace wanted to disassemble slum families, and the NYCAS's rendering of the street urchin provided a reason for action. Ironically, such a rationale unquestionably reflected sympathy for children but typically displayed little regard for the misery and misfortune of their parents. The pictures and rhetoric that permeated the NYCAS literature thus etched in the public mind a memorable image of the dependent child—the waif—who lived "nowhere," as the newsboys had said.[28]

Despite such images, most of the children with whom the NYCAS worked, at least during its formative years, were not rootless urchins from the streets. Brace rejoiced in taking "the children to the West . . . where the child finds his or her *first home*," but in fact the NYCAS's initial group of around four hundred children usually had at least one parent. Just as significantly, the children's families themselves often took the initiative and came to the NYCAS for temporary help during economic or emotional crises. Acting out of desperation, not cold-heartedness, and with hope that their families could soon be together again, such parents did not "abandon" their children but instead searched for ways to deal with misfortune and bad times. The children, moreover, tended to be older than the tiny foundlings who appeared in the NYCAS's drawings. Of the several hundred children whom the agency placed initially, the boys averaged 13 years of age, and the girls 12; only 14.5 percent were under age 11, and 16 percent were over 16. Almost two-thirds of them were living "at home" when their families surrendered them to the NYCAS. In only a few cases (around 16 percent) did the society's agents allege that the children were victims of abuse or neglect. Love and caring motivated many families to turn their children over to the NYCAS.[29]

One case involved the daughter of a widow who sewed and washed in a desperate effort to care for six small children. With the NYCAS's assistance, the daughter lived for 16 months with another family before returning to her mother. Another case concerned a 14-year-old boy whose mother, unable to work, asked the NYCAS to place him temporarily with a farmer. Twenty months later, the youngster thanked Brace's organization for its help and returned home. In other instances, parents reluctantly and sadly asked the NYCAS to find their children homes with better opportunities and conditions. A destitute Irish seamstress, for example, feared that her 13-year-old son would get into trouble if he did not find better surroundings. Similarly, an impoverished family in which the father could find no work asked Brace to place his 12-year-old son elsewhere. But the mother insisted that not just any household would suffice: The child needed to be in a "God fearing home as he has been religiously brought up." Significantly, within one 18-month period, around 70 percent of the NYCAS children who lived with at least one parent, and whom the society placed outside New York City, returned home. Among them was the 11-year-old son of a woman whose husband had deserted her and who had lost 9 of 12 children. After 10 months with another family, the boy rejoined his grateful mother.[30]

Older children sometimes used the Children's Aid Society as a kind of employment agency. In mid-1854, for example, 16-year-old William Betts happened to see the society's sign and stopped to see about job possibilities. Orphaned when he was an infant, he had lived in a poorhouse until age 10, when he was indentured to a farmer. After five years, he fled to New York City, where he lived briefly in the streets and then in a lodging house for two months before he showed up at the NYCAS looking for work. The society placed him with a Vermont farmer, with whom he lived for five years before going to sea.[31]

Such cases suggested that the Children's Aid Society initially provided youngsters and poor families with ways to cope, at least temporarily, with difficult times. But the cases hardly confirmed the NYCAS's public picture either of itself or of its clientele. The gap between the agency's image and reality was strikingly apparent in the case of 10-year-old John Quinte, one of the first children whom Brace personally rescued. According to the NYCAS, Quinte was a "homeless orphan child" whom Brace found under a cart in mid-1854, gnawing "like a dog" on a bone. The society chose not to publicize the important facts that Quinte had a mother who worked for different families, that the boy had run away from the Staten Island farmer with whom the agency placed him, that the runaway youth had returned to his mother, and that his mother brought him back to the NYCAS.[32]

These realities did not square with the society's portrait of itself as salvaging tiny, abandoned waifs from the "dangerous classes" who haunted the slums. Rather than focusing on the social and economic calamities that many struggling families faced, Brace and his cohorts chose to "manufacture" orphans. They also downplayed the NYCAS's early social service role in favor of a placement saga in which the agency saved children by moving them to farm families. "Get these children of unhappy fortune utterly out of their surroundings," the NYCAS urged in the mid-1850s, and relocate them "to kind Christian *homes in the country*." The agency assumed that such a home would serve as a kind of foster family and "a Reformatory Institution" for "the wild, neglected little outcast of the streets."[33]

Poor families understandably had a different perspective, one that made them apprehensive about Brace's emigration plan. Brace himself noted their resistance to long-term separation from their children: "The poor, living in their own homes, seldom wish to send out their children in that way." Betraying his preference for white, Protestant, middle-class parents, he angrily described poor immigrant parents as "narrow and pigheaded"—so ignorant and selfish that they "can't be talked or driven into saving their own children" by giving them up. In that regard, the orphan trains offered a strategic advantage to the NYCAS. The act of transporting the children long distances could discourage them from keeping contact with, or returning to, their roots. The NYCAS may even have deceived some parents who tried to regain custody of their children. It sympathized, for example, with employers who worried that a boy's parents might attempt to meddle "with our plans for his future training" if the parents knew his location.[34]

VII

During its first seven years the NYCAS placed almost four thousand children. Brace hailed it "as the most practical, economical, and successful remedy yet applied, for the evils among the juvenile poor of large cities." On the organization's 10th anniversary, he claimed that requests "for receiving our unfortunate little *proteges*" exceeded the number of children that the NYCAS could deliver.[35]

Such a claim erred insofar as it suggested that the placing-out movement was meeting the growing demands of child dependency. By 1865 the Civil War had sharply increased the number of dependent children, tripling in New York City alone the number of children in almshouses. Celebrated publisher and author William Cullen Bryant urged New Yorkers to help subsidize the relocation of "the homeless children of the city to comfortable farmhouses in the West, where they will be trained to industry and virtuous conduct, and grow up good citizens."[36]

By then Brace's emigration scheme had inspired a variety of imitators. Among the most prominent was the New England Home for Little Wanderers, which Boston Methodists founded in 1865 to shelter the children of Civil War veterans. Within five years, the organization cared for some 2,500 children, many of whom it sent on orphan trains to the Midwest. Unlike the NYCAS, however, the New England group downplayed the children-as-workers theme and emphasized the goal of formal adoption.[37]

Despite differing emphases, the various placing-out societies generally followed similar procedures. They sent advance agents to check with local officials and clergy about community interest in receiving several dozen children for home placement. In some cases, the local arrangements included identifying which families would accept which children. Bathed and with new clothes, the children boarded trains in eastern cities and headed westward with tags that matched those of their awaiting families.[38]

In other instances, the efforts to find families for children did not commence until the youngsters, accompanied by representatives of the placement agency, arrived at the local train station. "Asylum Children!" read a broadside in 1888 from the New York Juvenile Asylum heralding the arrival of an orphan train in Rockford, Illinois. "Homes are wanted for these children with farmers, where they will receive kind treatment and enjoy fair advantages." The asylum, unlike the NYCAS, sought to indenture the children, ages 7 to 15: "Those who desire to take children on trial are requested to meet them at the hotel at the time above specified."[39]

The train trip itself was often an ordeal. The adult chaperones typically faced major challenges. One recalled endless delays and difficulties when taking 27 children on the week's journey from New York to Peoria. In turn, one child viewed the adult agent as a witch. And another described bitterly the long trip to Nebraska, during which the children ate "red-jelly sandwiches three meals a day." Years later, he could not stand the thought of jelly.[40]

Predictably, the children's entry into the farm communities brought joy and tragedy. One woman had childhood memories of standing on a platform in South Dakota "while people came from all around the countryside to pick out those of us they wished to take home. I was four years old, and my sister was only two. . . ." Tired, anxious, excited, and probably frightened as well, the children came face to face with adult strangers who looked them over. Sometimes, when the children sensed they had found a good place to live, the results were indeed satisfying. Other times, children balked at living with particular families. "I didn't like her," recalled one orphan train passenger of the woman who had chosen her. "So I bit her."[41]

To a Minnesota charity worker the "distribution" of 40 children was "a pathetic sight." The children, "weary, travel-stained, confused," stood one at a time in front of a large crowd. As an adult described each of them, potential families looked them over. "It's quite a shock," recalled one individual. "You feel like you're on display." Some of the families who selected children had not previously filled out an application. When a man chose one little boy's big brother, the younger youth climbed on the knee of the man's aging father and begged, "I want to go home with you, and be your boy; I want to see my brother." Tearfully, the old man accepted the additional responsibility. A boy who arrived with an orphan train in Arkansas remembered that "folks were asked to take an orphan home for dinner." When the selection process subsequently began, he felt "sorry for the others because some of them were not chosen. I know now how much it must have hurt them to feel that nobody wanted them." Children whom no one picked boarded the train for the next stop. The children sometimes performed acts. "One boy told jokes and did acrobatic tricks," a participant recalled. Farmers occasionally inspected boys' muscles, a practice that at least one youth found offensive: "That was just like making a slave out of you." Spectators dabbed at tears when the children sang hymns.[42]

The number of children per train varied from a few to several hundred. Some of the larger troops came from the Catholic-sponsored New York Foundling Hospital, which the Sisters of Charity of St. Vincent de Paul founded in 1869 to care for children who had been abandoned before they were two years old. The number of deserted infants was a huge and growing problem. By the end of the 1800s, New York City's Bellevue Hospital alone was dealing with an average of four abandoned babies per day. The Foundling Hospital housed many such children in its own institution but also sponsored orphan trains, some that carried as many as three hundred small children to states such as Texas, Louisiana, and Oklahoma. As one youngster recalled, "[I was] with 200 other children and none of us knew where we were going or what was going to become of us."[43]

Sometimes, orphanage personnel encouraged youths to go westward on the orphan trains. Such was the case with Brooklyn's Harry Colwell, who had lived in several orphanages since age three with his older brother Frank. In 1894 after the NYCAS placed Frank on a western farm, the brothers quickly lost contact with each other. For five more years Harry remained in the privately operated Riverside Drive Orphanage in New York City. Although he found the institution's care quite good, he was intrigued when the superintendent told him about a Kansas farm family that was interested in sheltering an older orphan boy. "I was not long in deciding," Colwell remembered. "To me the 'West' meant cowboys, and Indians, a chance to ride horses and to participate in all sorts of exciting adventures." In April 1899 the 15-year-old left with around 50 other youths on an NYCAS-sponsored railroad coach. As the train moved toward Chicago, young Colwell became more anxious about his future. From Chicago on to his rural Kansas destination, he traveled alone, switching trains a number of times. At one isolated stop, a desolate railroad building called Garrison Crossing, he felt so lonely and depressed that he broke into tears. The next day, the apprehensive youth finally met the family with whom he would live. In retrospect, he believed that he received "the best possible kind of bringing up."[44]

Colwell's placing-out experience proved more fortunate than that which Eugene Smith had initially encountered in the same town several years earlier. Smith arrived with a group of youngsters from New York who had no designated families awaiting them. Unlike Colwell, they traveled with an Aid Society agent from place to place in search of a home. "Any farmer who took a fancy to a given boy could take him, with little or no ceremony," Colwell wrote later of Smith's journey. Smith ended up with an abusive man until Colwell's family rescued him.[45]

Not all of the orphan train children were as lucky as Colwell and eventually Smith, however. A young girl in Missouri did nothing more than cook and clean. "My foster mother was so cruel—oh, she was a crackerjack," the girl said later. One boy found his new family so uncaring that he decided he would be better off living in a garbage barrel. Another youngster endured thrashings and "three years of hell" before the NYCAS placed him elsewhere. In Minnesota, a farmer worked a youth all summer until harvest was over, then threw him out. A Kansas farmer gave another youth "the godawfullest beating" that the boy ever received.[46]

For children, the placement program too often resembled a kind of family grab bag. The NYCAS, especially in its early years, usually knew far too little about the prospective parents, and it also lacked the personnel and the resources to check on what happened to the children once they were placed. Thus, for example, 11 of 18 children whom the NYCAS took as a group to Kansas in 1867 simply disappeared. In Minnesota over a three-year period in the early 1880s, at least 40 of 340 youngsters dropped out of sight. Such bungling helped fuel a growing resistance to the orphan trains.[47]

VIII

Opposition to Brace mounted on several fronts, ranging from families to religious, regional, and institutional groups. By his own admission, impoverished tenement families typically regarded the Aid Society with suspicion. Most destitute parents seeking at least temporary refuge for their children understandably preferred a local institution to the NYCAS. A nearby asylum, whatever its deficiencies, would be far more accessible and accountable than some distant Midwestern farm. Still, because the NYCAS placed so many youngsters who were not true orphans, Brace invariably had to deal with attempts to reclaim them. To him, poor families who wanted their children back were selfish and inconsiderate. Some angry parents in turn accused the Aid Society of child stealing. Among them was an irate father who learned that the Aid Society, without his permission, had taken his daughter from a Brooklyn institution and relocated her on a Kansas farm. At the Boys and Girls Aid Society in San Francisco, which Brace's followers had founded in 1874, one superintendent said that it was "a truism in the most densely populated parts of San Francisco . . . that the 'Aid' exists for the purpose of kidnaping [sic]." Because of the organization's reputation, "fathers and mothers confess that they are afraid to ask our assistance lest their children would be taken away" permanently.[48]

Some people opposed Brace for religious reasons. Non-Protestants increasingly feared that the Aid Society was interested mainly in "rescuing" children from the Catholic and Jewish faiths. Although Brace maintained that his work was nonsectarian, his background, training, and disposition tilted him in a decidedly Protestant direction. He had no doubt, for example, that "the power of the priests . . . rests on ignorance," and he clearly had Protestantism in mind when he discussed moral training. At least once the NYCAS cooperated with a strongly Protestant organization, the American Female Guardian Society, to keep a Catholic father from recovering his son. "We dread Catholic influence more than the bite of the rattlesnake," the Guardian Society said when urging the foster family to hide the boy. An NYCAS official supported the Guardian Society's position. And at the Boys and Girls Aid Society in San Francisco, Edmond Dooley, the superintendent whom Brace had "warmly recommended" for the job, discussed the ongoing "warfare" with the Catholic church: "Nearly every child we receive comes as the result of a contest—a contest with the most degraded, malignant, and unscrupulous" opponent one could imagine.[49]

A number of non-Protestant groups countered the Aid Society by building their own children's institutions. Even before the formation of the NYCAS, Catholics had opened several orphanages to keep children within the Church. In 1846, for example, the Society of St. Vincent de Paul committed itself to stopping the "wholesale loss of our children" to Protestant agencies. And in 1863 the New York Catholic Protectory launched a major campaign to rescue destitute Catholic children from the reach of the NYCAS and other Protestant child-placing agencies. During its first seven years, the Protectory housed more than 3,500 children; in 1885 alone it sheltered almost 2,200. Meanwhile, several large Jewish orphanages also opened in the 1860s.[50]

In 1874 resistance to the Aid Society suddenly appeared from yet another quarter: Midwesterners accused it of dumping young criminals on their states. According to a Wisconsin delegate at the National Prison Reform Conference, the orphan trains carried "car loads of criminal juveniles, . . . vagabonds, and gutter snipes" westward, scattering them "among the peaceful homes and in the quiet neighborhoods of the state." Over the next decade this line of attack broadened and intensified. In 1879 the National Conference of Charities and Correction (NCCC) and the American Social Science Association heatedly debated the extent to which the Aid Society was unloading "young barbarians," "born constitutional thieves," and "tramps and burglars" on states such as Indiana. One prominent child welfare advocate from Michigan went so far as to say derisively that New Yorkers should honor Brace with a monument because he had gotten "so many incipient criminals" out of their city.[51]

By the early 1880s, Brace and the placing-out movement were constantly under fire. Participants at NCCC meetings criticized the Aid Society for its loose administration, poor screening processes, sloppy supervision, and exposure of children to slavelike conditions. Lyman P. Alden of the Michigan State Public School struck at the heart of Brace's program, attacking it for naively assuming that good families existed "by the wholesale" and that institutions were invariably bad for all children.[52]

IX

On August 11, 1890, Charles Loring Brace died. By then his son was in charge of the NYCAS, which continued sending orphan trains to states such as Kansas for around 40 more years. Brace was dead, but his influence clearly was not.

More than anyone, he had challenged institutional care for dependent children. Children's asylums grew in size and number throughout the late nineteenth century, but they no longer monopolized policy debates and they were increasingly on the defensive. Although Brace's own placing-out strategies likewise elicited disapproval, they spawned a host of imitators, most notably the New England Home for Little Wanderers in 1865, the Illinois Children's Home Society in 1883, and the Boston Children's Aid Society (BCAS).

The BCAS was one of a number of children's aid societies that formed after 1860, independent of the NYCAS but inspired by it. The Boston organization managed to avoid some of the problems faced by children of the NYCAS. Incorporated in 1864, the BCAS initially provided dependent boys with a period of adjustment and training on a nearby farm before relocating them, one at a time, with rural families. In 1866 it established a similar system for girls. However, the Boston group recognized early on that some children disliked agricultural life and would be better off in more urban settings. In 1885 the Boston society took a major step by hiring 25-year-old Charles Birtwell, a recent Harvard graduate who over the next several decades profoundly influenced the field of child and social welfare and became an expert on the subject of dependent children. Like Brace, Birtwell criticized long-term institutional care for children. Unlike Brace, he gave top priority to preserving families and viewed the placing out of youngsters as a last resort. Birtwell insisted that the BCAS assist destitute families by trying to "remove the very causes of their degradation" and helping them stay together. Under the inventive Birtwell, the BCAS developed a variety of strategies for placing dependent children: paying other families to board them, finding homes where single mothers could both work and keep their offspring, and carefully selecting and monitoring foster homes.[53]

Brace's goal was to find family homes for children who were homeless or in jeopardy. That goal connected agencies such as the NYCAS and the BCAS despite their variations. And it certainly encouraged the formalization of foster care and the passage of adoption laws. By seeking family environments in which relocated children were treated more like natural sons and daughters, placement agencies made adoption statutes more essential.[54]

The New York Children's Aid Society was surely flawed. Its assumptions were often naive and prejudiced, its procedures lackadaisical, and its omissions telling. It so overwhelmingly favored white children of American or Western European parentage that perhaps 95 percent of its placements from 1860 to 1890 came from those groups. Still, realities of the time suggested that the placement of African American or Eastern European children would have been difficult in rural, Midwestern communities. And Brace had to contend early on with Catholic and Jewish groups that were determined to protect "their own." Child placement was a tricky business, subject to local expectations and prejudices. The Catholic Sisters of Charity, for example, stirred up local furies by placing 40 Anglo children with Mexican families in the Arizona Territory. Irate Anglos raided the Mexican homes and removed 19 of the children. After the territorial court vindicated the mob action by saying that Mexican families could not raise white children, the other 21 youngsters were also resettled. Brace and the NYCAS, of course, sometimes intervened in the lives of poor and unfortunate New York families just as callously, and perhaps even as ruthlessly, as the Anglos in Arizona acted to remove the children from the Mexicans.[55]

Yet Brace and the NYCAS did more than legitimize intrusions into the lives of struggling families. Poignant descriptions and images of victimized waifs also heightened public awareness of the truly awful situations in which some children lived—a world of "blows and curses," in the words of the NYCAS. "'Twas always . . . a blow with mammy," one battered boy told Brace. In the mid-1870s, child welfare organizations launched a major movement to end cruelty to children. On that issue, as with so many others, Charles Loring Brace and the New York Children's Aid Society had pointed the way.[56]

4

Discovering Cruelty and Building More Asylums in the Late Nineteenth Century

Mary Ellen Connolly's life intersected with the major trends in late-nineteenth-century child welfare and also marked a turning point in the history of child protection. She entered an orphanage at a time when orphan asylums were growing at an unprecedented rate, from 170 before the Civil War to around 600 by the 1890s. But her story also fit with the era's push for home placement. After staying briefly in the orphanage, she lived on a farm in upstate New York with relatives of a charity worker who had taken an interest in her. When she ultimately started her own family, it included a foster child.[1]

It was in 1874, however, when Mary Ellen was only 10 years old and had not yet moved to the orphanage, that she became the focal point in the "discovery" of cruelty to children in the United States. Like tens of thousands of children in the early 1870s, she suffered horrible abuse and neglect. Unlike most of them, she attracted a huge outpouring of sympathy and publicity. Her shocking story filled newspaper columns, inspired songs, and triggered the formation of a major movement to halt cruelty to children. By at last making the physical mistreatment of children a public issue, the anticruelty movement facilitated outside intervention in behalf of helpless and brutalized youngsters. Yet because the discovery of cruelty was so laden with class biases, it tended to confuse the effects of poverty with purposeful neglect and abuse, and thus to subject poor families to special scrutiny and blame. That widespread tendency not only characterized the anticruelty movement but continued to haunt the history of children's asylums and home placement as well.

I

Until the highly publicized case of Mary Ellen, courts had generally refrained from acting in matters of child abuse. Out of respect for family privacy and parental rights, authorities had left matters of punishment and discipline to the discretion of parents, especially to fathers, with few exceptions. According to legend, Mary Ellen was able to break from this tradition because the American Society for the Prevention of Cruelty to Animals brought her to court as a member of the animal kingdom. When the founder of the Society had learned of the girl's pitiful situation, he had supposedly cried out in anguish, "The child is an animal. If there is no justice for it as a human being, it shall at least have the right of the cur in the street. . . . It shall not be abused."[2] In fact, the story was far more complex: Mary Ellen was indeed a victim of terrible mistreatment, but her rescue was less clear-cut than legend allowed.

In 1874 Etta Angell Wheeler heard about a small girl whose caretakers were beating her so badly that the neighbor could hear the youngster's wails through the walls. Wheeler, a charity worker for the St. Luke's Methodist Mission, investigated Mary and Francis Connolly. After one failed effort, Wheeler finally got a brief look at the miserable child, whose arms and legs were covered with whip marks. Wheeler located several asylums that were willing to care for Mary Ellen, but only after the girl had been removed legally from her foster parents. That objective proved virtually impossible. Charity organizations and legal officials advised Wheeler not to interfere in family matters. At the least, she personally would have to bring the girl to court and bear the burden of proving abuse. Frustrated, Wheeler picked up on her niece's suggestion to contact Henry Bergh, the founder of the American Society for the Prevention of Cruelty to Animals (ASPCA). Mary Ellen was a "little animal surely," according to the niece. But Bergh was reluctant to take action. For one thing, the wealthy New Yorker did not much like children, whom he viewed as too noisy. For another thing, he did not want to take up any cause that might undermine his crusade to protect animals—a commitment so unswerving that several publications had already rebuked him for ignoring endangered children. Such criticism may have prompted Bergh to instruct the animal society's attorney, Elbridge T. Gerry, to investigate Mary Ellen's situation. Even then, however, Bergh made clear that he was acting outside his official capacity as the ASPCA's president.[3]

Gerry brought his own agenda to the case. A descendant of famous patriot stock, the extremely wealthy lawyer had long worried about the baneful effects that poor immigrants had on American society. In an essay in 1852, he had used the concept of "the rights of children" to argue for protecting youngsters from the parental "tyranny" of such people. By the 1870s, escalating labor unrest and urban disorder only heightened the anxieties of well-placed conservatives such as Gerry. From their perspective, the issue of cruelty to children reflected larger social problems.[4]

When Gerry brought Mary Ellen to court, her appearance and testimony electrified the public. Weeping, wrapped in a carriage blanket, she indicated that she did not wish to return to the tenement because Mary Connolly "beats me so." She recounted almost daily beatings with a rawhide whip or cane. Only a few weeks earlier, Connolly had also assaulted her with scissors, inflicting an ugly cut that extended from her forehead to her cheek, narrowly missing her left eye. Years later, Mary Ellen's own children could still see her scars from the beatings. Mary Ellen also told them that Mary Connolly, in a fit of anger, once burned her on the arm with a hot iron. When Connolly herself testified before the court in 1874, she admitted that, for the past eight years, she had virtually ignored instructions from the Commissioners on Charities and Correction to report on the child's condition. The judge ultimately remanded Mary Ellen to the Sheltering Arms institution for dependent children.[5]

Mary Ellen's story became a social and cultural lightning rod. There were any number of other cruelty cases that might have similarly galvanized public opinion but did not. The pitiful fate of 13-year-old John Fox, for example, had that potential. Only a few months before Mary Ellen's case sparked a public uproar, Fox's father in New York City beat him to death for not going to the store to buy beer (which the boy had no money to purchase). But Fox's story had merited only brief and passing mention in the *New York Times*.[6]

In contrast, Mary Ellen's case catapulted into the public eye partly because it received substantial press coverage. At a time when the press's role in the United States was increasingly significant, Mary Ellen's cause benefited from the fact that Etta Wheeler, the child's advocate, was married to a journalist. And newspapers and magazines, by publicizing the Connolly case with great detail and poignancy, helped to elevate into a cause célèbre one of the myriad examples of brutality to a child.

During 1876, the nation's centennial year, at least two songs focused on Mary Ellen and her rescuers. "Little Mary Ellen," which the writer dedicated to Henry Bergh, described a weeping "infant, pale and feeble,/ Victim of her keeper's rage, / Tender flower crushed and broken, / Blighted in her budding age." The second song, "Mother Sent an Angel to Me," was dedicated to Elbridge Gerry and portrayed a healthy Mary Ellen on the cover of the sheet music. "Tell me, maiden," the song asked, "who has changed thee / From what once thou used to be? / Who has healed thy broken spirit / Saved thee from captivity?" At the Philadelphia Centennial Exhibition, the exhibit of Bergh's Society for the Prevention of Cruelty to Animals included, with pictures of abused animals, a photograph of the battered Mary Ellen.[7]

A sympathetic audience was ready to respond by then. For some time public sensitivity to the plight of children had been on the rise. Over several decades, the growth of children's institutions, the child-placing campaigns of

Charles Loring Brace, the debates over child placing, the drama surrounding the orphan trains, the legal turn of courts toward "the best interest of the child," and the popularity of sentimental literature about innocent young victims had in various ways produced a highly charged setting.[8]

A growing women's rights movement that was greatly concerned about family violence also played an important role in popularizing the Mary Ellen case. Drawing upon the ideals of female purity and the wife's special role in the domestic sphere, temperance reformers, many of them women, had for some time assailed a dominant male bastion, the tavern. The brutish, drunken male who beat his spouse and children became one of the era's chief villains. "In discussing the question of temperance," observed Elizabeth Cady Stanton in the 1850s, "all lecturers, from the beginning, have made mention of drunkards' wives and children, of widows' groans and orphans' tears." From this perspective, liquor victimized women and children, thus undermining home, family, and domesticity. If society protected children from violence, safeguards might emerge as well for battered and abused women. Here was an important rationale for closer outside scrutiny of the fate of children and women within the family.[9]

That rationale also drew upon sharpening sensibilities about cruelty and suffering. The antebellum era's antislavery movement had influenced those sensibilities by challenging the traditional tolerance for cruelty meted out as "discipline." By using gruesome accounts of slaves' agony, abolitionists had sought to stir public rage. Increased concern about pain and suffering was also apparent when, in 1849, medical doctors at Massachusetts General Hospital first used anesthesia, an indication that pain now seemed treatable. By then, many churches were downplaying a theology of suffering and instead portraying God as benevolent rather than punitive. Evangelicals, emphasizing religion of the heart, stirred their listeners to action by evoking moral sympathy. At the same time, the increasingly popular genre of women's sentimental fiction enlisted sympathy for the weak and afflicted. More and more, antebellum reformers expanded the earlier eighteenth-century attacks on excessive state power to include criticism of abusive private relationships, including those of spouses or parents and children.[10]

Additionally, as historian Linda Gordon has pointed out, the evolutionary theories of Charles Darwin "decreased the felt distance between humans and animals," and at the same time encouraged "standards of refinement and 'respectability'" that separated humans from beasts. In England, reformers founded societies to prevent cruelty to animals and, in 1857, a Society for the Protection of Women and Children. In the United States, the changing opinions of Jacob Abbott, minister and well-known childrearing expert, reflected the new shift in thinking. In 1841 he had defended mild whippings as a way to discipline children; by 1871, however, he rejected corporal punishment altogether as a danger to the child's nervous system and brain. Among at least some thinkers, the idea took hold that children, no less than horses and dogs, should be free from cruelty. Some two years before Mary Ellen's case reached the courts, one woman had publicly urged Henry Bergh to protect children as well as animals. Children, she told him, had "a far greater capacity for suffering." Moreover, she argued, animals were "dumb creatures" whom Bergh would not encounter in heaven; but, "if you rescue but one human being, angels will envy your reward."[11]

After Bergh finally acted to protect children in the Mary Ellen case, Etta Wheeler thanked him outside the courthouse and wondered if it was time for an anticruelty society to protect children as well as animals. She recalled that Bergh took her hand and said, "There shall be one." In December 1874 Elbridge Gerry took the initiative in founding the New York Society for the Prevention of Cruelty to Children (NYSPCC).[12]

Using his impressive social credentials and connections, Gerry put together a board of directors that included some of the most affluent and influential men in the United States, including manufacturer and railroad magnate Peter Cooper, banker August Belmont, and Cornelius Vanderbilt, the multimillionaire owner of ships and railroads. The elevated status and conservative nature of the anticruelty movement's founders helped to legitimize intrusions on family privacy in ways that had earlier been difficult. Still, the NYSPCC's all-male leadership moved cautiously, emphasizing that it did not object to corporal punishment. According to Henry Bergh, "a good wholesome flogging," if moderate and for good reason, was justifiable for "disobedient children." Because the NYSPCC enjoyed such prominent and respectable backing, it received wide recognition and exposure.[13]

II

Within a short time, a multitude of anticruelty organizations sprang up in major cities and small towns. Some resembled the NYSPCC by concentrating on children. Some were "humane societies" that initially protected both children and animals but, by 1906, included 61 of 240 chapters that focused entirely on children. A parallel group, the American Humane Association, which emerged in 1876 to rescue only animals, bowed to public pressure in the mid-1880s and started some child protective work. By 1914, 494 anticruelty societies existed in the United States.[14]

Some states empowered the societies to arrest abusers or to determine which children needed institutional care. At the least, local authorities were supposed to assist the societies' work. Some societies hired former police officers or firefighters as agents. In other cases, volunteers patrolled the streets, looking for examples of cruelty or investigating reports. They also dealt with children who had been abandoned or orphaned. But their objective was not to provide social services for needy families, or even to intervene if the cruelty occurred in homes they deemed temperate and industrious.[15]

Very much a product of their members' upper-class origins, the children's anticruelty societies (SPCCs) displayed a mix of social fears and altruism. Dread of Brace's "dangerous classes" intensified as the nation became more industrial and as threats of social chaos and labor upheaval increased. In Boston, for example, Protestants of British descent watched anxiously as first- and second-generation immigrants, largely Irish at first, then Italians and Russian Jews, moved from 46 percent to 74 percent of the population between 1850 and 1910. Tenement areas in the major cities grew more congested and dilapidated. Workers' discontent erupted in periodic strikes, which, in 1877, crippled parts of the nation. In this turbulent context, control of poor, immigrant, working-class families seemed more essential than ever.[16]

Yet although anticruelty reformers worried about the gathering social storm, they also exhibited genuine humanitarian feelings. John Wright, the NYSPCC's wealthy first president, had devoted himself to altruistic deeds since retiring at age 59. He spent time at the Home for Friendless Children in New York City, distributing candy and telling stories. And he deemed it his "religious duty to found a society for the prevention of cruelty to the little ones." Similarly, in 1882, Elbridge Gerry spoke movingly about society's obligation "to stretch out its hand and rescue from starvation, misery, cruelty, and perhaps death, the helpless little child who ought to have a protector. . . ." Gerry's view that "children have *some* rights, which even parents are bound to respect," was loaded with significance. Indeed, such a statement helped to provide leverage for a momentous shift: The anticruelty movement, as historian Joseph Hawes has observed, "was the first to articulate the idea of enforcing children's rights against their parents."[17]

The crucial questions, of course, involved which parents and which rights. At this point the SPCCs revealed a strong class bias, one laden with moralistic judgments about the urban poor. Sometimes the societies seemed less concerned with youthful victims than with ignorant, "depraved" parents—members of the working classes who were perceived to lack respectability and self-control, and whose violence plagued the larger society as well as their own offspring. When the volunteers of the anticruelty movement plunged into the streets looking for youthful victims, they were thus highly selective, policing families primarily in the tenements and working-class neighborhoods and generally ignoring middle-class families. And, in the process, they broadened their definition of cruelty to include neglect—a category that, according to the Massachusetts Society for the Prevention of Cruelty to Children in 1885, included not only inadequate food and clothing but also "exposure to examples of intemperance, dishonesty, falsehood, and vice."[18]

Although poverty typically resulted in insufficient food and clothing, the anticruelty people tended to place the blame elsewhere, on the questionable values and moral unfitness of workers and immigrants. Even moderate drinking supposedly attested to vice-ridden lives. Sometimes the complaint was vague: "Mother will never bring up her children according to American standards," one caseworker reported.[19]

In 30 percent of the cases that the Pennsylvania Society for the Prevention of Cruelty to Children (PSPCC) handled in the late 1800s, the agency removed the youngsters from their homes and placed them, sometimes temporarily, in institutions or with other families. The vast majority of these children were neglected (which meant typically that they received insufficient food and clothing, or were exposed to vices such as liquor) rather than abused. Indeed, no more than 13 percent of the PSPCC's cases during any of its first 10 years dealt with abuse. Often, in fact, the anticruelty societies seemed less interested in rescuing physically abused children than in pursuing drunken and neglectful parents.[20]

By intervening in the affairs of at least a few families, the SPCCs hoped to send a warning to all parents in the neighborhood. Usually the agencies acted with the approval of the courts, but sometimes they cut legal corners to gather evidence, entering tenement homes through windows or searching without warrants. As the Massachusetts society acknowledged in 1881, "If we rescue from a tenement house a child who has been neglected or abused, every family in that house and neighborhood are warned. . . ." For good reason, then, residents of working-class neighborhoods referred to the SPCC as "the Cruelty." When word got out that an SPCC agent was on the way, people shouted up and down the street, "Investigation! Investigation!"[21]

Critics then and later accused "the Cruelty" of insidiously and coercively spreading its octopus-like tentacles into the homes of poor families in an effort to control them. At the least, critics charged, the SPCCs were agents of harassment, bent more on moral policing than on protecting children. To gain public support and raise money, they publicized the most extreme examples of abuse, filling their literature with photographs of children "before and after" their rescue, and of discovered "instruments of torture," such as whips and straps. Viewing the world through the glasses of a privileged class, they refused to see that much of the neglect they encountered was a result of poverty itself. They failed to consider how a larger network of social services, or reforms that dealt with structural problems in the society as a whole, might more effectively protect children. Labor leaders in the late 1800s thus easily labeled the anticruelty movement as a sham. According to laborites, if the SPCCs really wanted to end child cruelty and neglect, they would oppose such evils as inadequate factory wages and unconscionably long workdays that forced parents to leave children unsupervised.[22]

In a number of ways, as their critics argued, the SPCCs were indeed smug, hypocritical, and arrogant. "The reformer will ever be considered as an intruding enemy by those whose vicious plans he seeks to circumvent," one

SPCC report said in 1892. The anticruelty societies certainly had sufficient authority to raise neighborhood fears of agents dragging children from homes. In 1881, for example, the New York state legislature granted agents the power of arrest and made obstructing the NYSPCC's work illegal. By 1890 the New York agency alone controlled the fate of some 15,000 children. The SPCCs were such a force that feuding families and neighbors threatened each other: "Don't cross me or I'll report you to the Cruelty." Tenement children played a game, "the Gerry Society," in which they portrayed the NYSPCC as a kind of bogeyman that was out to get them.[23]

Yet despite this well-warranted criticism, the identification of physical cruelty as an issue represented in itself a huge step in children's welfare. As one scholar has written, "Until the nineteenth century, when the term 'child abuse' entered the national discourse, most Americans saw the suffering of children pragmatically, as part of the human condition." The SPCCs were instrumental in reshaping that discourse for decades to come.[24]

Moreover, "the Cruelty" did not move through impoverished neighborhoods like an unwelcome juggernaut, imposing its will on resisting, previously autonomous families. That previous autonomy was in itself a myth. Historically, families have always been subject to myriad forms of social regulation, sometimes through the pressure of gossip or private intervention, sometimes through authorities who enforced conformity against dissent. Although the SPCCs indeed represented "outside" intervention, they often acted on the invitation of victims who wanted help—children and wives who traditionally lacked power within families and who desperately needed protection. In that sense, even the threat of reporting an abuser to "the Cruelty" might help to stop family violence. SPCC interventions that from one angle represented intrusions upon family privacy could, from another angle, enhance the rights of an abused child or battered woman.[25]

Relationships between the SPCCs and the poor neighborhoods were part of an enormously complex bargaining process. People in working-class neighborhoods sometimes appealed to the anticruelty reformers for support, and the reformers in turn found allies among the poor. Many working-class families celebrated the ideals of responsibility and character, and they did not have to look to the middle class for standards to emulate. For their own reasons and on their own terms, such families could appreciate efforts to keep a home together in the face of economic misfortune, just as they could abhor violence and neglect. One did not have to venture outside the tenement districts to find people who worked hard and loved their children. Their willingness to inform "the Cruelty" about abuse indicated that they wanted assistance in the battle against rough conduct and rowdiness. Neighborhoods were contested turf among the people who lived there, not just between the residents and outside intruders. In that sense, working-class people viewed the SPCC ambivalently, as a source of protection and as an agent of the police and the courts. The SPCC could in turn be both meddlesome and an ally of last resort.[26]

By the 1890s, however, the SPCCs seemed increasingly less interested in the child abuse issue than in a wider range of child welfare problems. As they depended on a more professional staff, trained in the new methods of social casework, and as they lobbied for a variety of causes ranging from juvenile courts to mothers' pensions, they sometimes gave the impression that abuse was no longer a pressing social problem. It would be another half century before child abuse was again "discovered." In the meantime, the anticruelty societies helped to boost the cause of orphan asylums.[27]

III

Between 1865 and 1890, the number of orphanages tripled. This was partly because the SPCCs and other agencies placed abused children in them. Another contributing factor was that family placement fell far short of meeting the rapidly escalating child welfare demands. Orphanages, moreover, proved very adaptable and many times provided destitute families with critical child care and support. Overall, orphan asylums offered at least minimal subsistence and shelter to tens of thousands of children in desperate need.[28]

Predictably, the Civil War created huge numbers of dependent children. By 1865 some 6,000 vagrant children wandered the streets of Boston; an estimated 30,000 were in New York City. Some widows who could not provide even for themselves implored institutions to care for their children. "How can we refuse them admittance?" asked one orphanage director.[29]

Some northern states contributed public money to private asylums to house children of Union troops, and, in 1865–66, eight states opened institutions for the dependents of dead soldiers. A decade after the war, Pennsylvania was subsidizing the care of more than eight thousand soldiers' orphans, most of whom were in orphanages. In New York City, the Union Home for Soldiers' and Sailors' Orphans was so full that it turned children away. For the three hundred children in the scandal-ridden Illinois Soldiers' Orphans' Home, there were only two bathrooms and no playgrounds or infirmary. For a while they also endured the cruel regime of "the cattle driver," a superintendent who worked them harshly. A three-year-old was scalded to death when several of the older children were placed in charge of baths.[30]

While the war increased the numbers of dependent children as well as governmental intervention in their behalf, the rapidly accelerating growth of cities also contributed to child dependency. On the eve of the war, almost 20 percent of the U.S. population was urban; within 60 years that figure exceeded 50 percent. Huge waves of immigration in the postbellum era were partly responsible for this trend, but so too was the growth of industry, which centered in cities and created wage laborers whose families were vulnerable to economic downturns. As impoverished urban neighborhoods became more congested, children wandered the streets in greater numbers, sometimes ending up in poorhouses and jails.

Even anti-institutional efforts sometimes added to the asylum population. Such was the unintended result of the important New York statute in 1875 that outlawed committing children between ages 3 and 16 to county poorhouses. Nineteen years earlier, a state legislative committee had chastised poorhouses as "the most disgraceful memorials of public charity," and certainly as "the worst possible nurseries." Proponents of the 1875 "Children's Law" wanted to move pauper children from the poorhouses and place them in families, but the mechanisms for doing so were so unclear that most of the youngsters ended up in private orphanages that were receiving state subsidies. This law that reflected the placement ideal thus ironically encouraged institutional care. During the 1880s, the number of private children's asylums in New York State jumped from 132 to 204; and the number of children in their care doubled from under 12,000 to almost 24,000.[31]

The asylums for dependent children that spread across the United States following the Civil War existed mainly in urban areas. They ranged in size from many that sheltered only several dozen to others that were massive, housing hundreds. Although by 1890 two-fifths of them were in the Northeast, they existed in every geographical region. By then, there were at least 564 orphan asylums, with a mean population of 85 children and housing altogether almost 50,000 youngsters. Only a few institutions were racially integrated, and 27 of them were limited to minority children, usually African Americans. The Thomas Asylum for Orphan and Destitute Indian Children, which the New York legislature converted into a public institution in 1875, cared for more than one hundred Native American boys and girls from within that state. In 1890, perhaps half of the nation's orphanages were Protestant, but the Catholic Church had 173 institutions and cared for some 23,000 youths. The nine Jewish asylums were among the largest orphanages in the nation. Around 6,500 children lived in 83 publicly managed asylums and 257 more in four institutions that fraternal organizations sponsored.[32]

A majority of orphanage residents were half-orphans (children with one parent), and around 20 percent had two living parents. These institutional demographics highlighted an important point: Many orphan asylums served as early welfare agencies by caring for the children of impoverished families. Destitute parents were understandably unwilling in most cases to surrender their children permanently. For a number of such families, orphan asylums provided temporary care that allowed parents to have at least some access to their children as well as the opportunity to reclaim them at any time. "Both [parents] living but could not keep the child on account of their difficult position," recorded one Cleveland orphanage, which for a while sheltered their eight-year-old girl.[33]

In this context, the era's notorious "baby farms" played a more problematic role than contemporary critics allowed. Ostensibly places that boarded

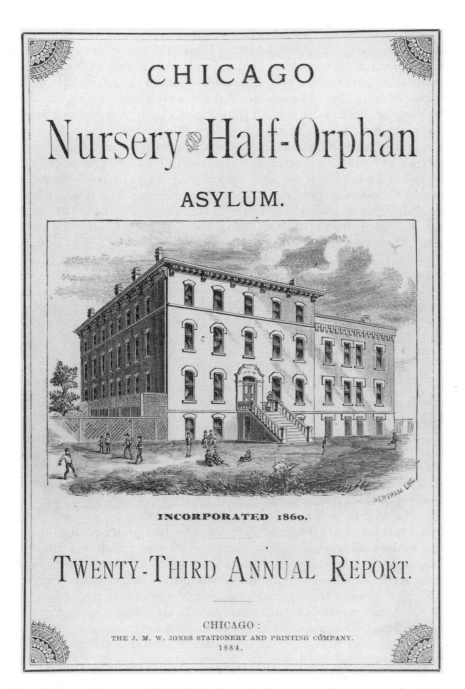

CHICAGO
Nursery ᴁ Half-Orphan
ASYLUM.

INCORPORATED 1860.

TWENTY-THIRD ANNUAL REPORT.

CHICAGO:
THE J. M. W. JONES STATIONERY AND PRINTING COMPANY.
1884.

The Chicago Nursery and Half-Orphan Asylum, one of numerous late-nineteenth-century institutions. By 1885 its population was around 160. Courtesy Chicago Historical Society.

infants for profit alone, they developed a reputation among SPCC reformers as slaughterhouses for abandoned babies. There was nothing new, certainly, about infanticide as a method for getting rid of unwanted babies. Abortion was expensive and, in the late 1800s, increasingly illegal. For individuals with illegitimate babies, or for whom additional children presented crushing economic liabilities, the choices were typically stark and agonizing. Without insurance or relief programs, a number of parents chose to abandon their infants. Each year in large cities, authorities found hundreds of tiny bodies in culverts, cesspools, trashbins, and rivers. In some instances, mothers left babies in public places so people could find them. Foundling asylums tried to save deserted infants, but typically the mortality rates were frightening, sometimes ranging over 90 percent. Baby farmers claimed to do better. "I take Infants from Berth [sic] up and keep them in my own home until I place them in a good home," said one of them. "My terms is fifty Dollars and If you can't pay the fifty cash you can Pay thirty-five Dollars and the Balance weekly." Supposedly, baby farmers cared for the infants until adoptive homes or alternative care was available. In reality, some of them simply disposed of unwanted babies, either because customers did not pay the boarding fees, or because destroying the children was their goal from the outset. By the late 1800s, sensational accounts about infanticide for profit, an underground "traffic in children," and child abuse attracted widespread attention.[34]

In important respects, however, baby farming was less about child neglect and abuse than about working-class efforts to devise alternative means of child care. Horrific baby farms unquestionably existed, and some specialized in disposing of unwanted children. But for working-class mothers, baby farming provided both a legitimate home-based occupation and a comparatively cheap place to board infants. Although such child-care provisions met genuine economic needs, popular stories about the "evils of baby farming" focused on murderers and tiny victims. To middle-class reformers, nervous about the laboring class and women in the workplace, baby farms were typically an affront to sentimentalized images of motherhood. To labor reformers, baby farming was yet another example of the terrible predicament that an exploitative market posed for workers. Some state and local authorities responded to dramatic exposés of particularly scandalous situations by establishing systems to license and inspect baby farms. A few groups and individuals founded homes where unwed mothers could remain with their infants.[35]

More than most nineteenth-century welfare reformers, the individuals who ran such homes, along with at least some asylum managers, empathized with poor, toiling families. Some orphanage superintendents, as a result of working closely with needy parents, came to see them as victims of bad luck rather than of moral depravity, and as individuals who loved their children deeply. Although the managers of a Brooklyn institution asserted in 1867 that intemperance and lack of character ruined some poor people, they insisted that unexpected tragedies such as unemployment, death, and illness were more typically the source of problems. Rather than blame destitute, struggling parents, a number of asylum directors agreed to shelter their children until the return of better times.[36]

In this respect, an orphanage could resemble a "poor man's boarding school," in the words of one student of orphan asylums. Working parents, or parents in the throes of economic or emotional crises, turned to nearby orphanages for at least temporary help. They often did so reluctantly, sadly, and out of desperation. They usually also kept close contact with the children. The common refrain in their letters to superintendents was: "I can take no peace or comfort until I get them back." One mother awaiting a small pension check begged the manager to treat her son well. A widow with six children in the Albany Orphan Asylum wrote, "Will you pleas rite back and let me no how the children is." An abandoned woman who had placed her three small children in the asylum worried that they looked ill when she visited them: "fore the love of god and heaven may some one help me to get them to gether" at home again, she pleaded. A widower whose job injuries, illnesses, and unemployment forced him to put his two young children in the asylum wrote, "this is humiliating." Some parents were terrified that somehow they might lose their children. "Do not let anyone take them," implored one parent. Such communications completely belied the prevailing view among reformers in the SPCCs, or the children's aid societies, that poor parents were indifferent or uncaring about their sons and daughters. Parents often expressed their love and pride in poignant letters to their children in the asylums. And they were anxious that their children learn to live in good, honest, and useful ways. "My Dear Son," a railroad worker whose wife had left him wrote his 12-year-old in the Albany orphanage: "I have bin to work hard all Day & to nite. . . . Pa hopes and prays that you will be a good Boy & try & learn so when you are a Man that you wont hafts do hard Laborious work. . . ."[37]

Although orphan asylums often assisted crisis-ridden families, some parents refused to entrust their children to such institutions. In 1879 a group of mothers in the Cook County poorhouse in Illinois objected to a plan to remove their children to private child-care institutions. In this instance, the institutions demanded that the mothers relinquish the rights to their children. Unable to stop the plan, the mothers searched frantically for alternative places to shelter their children. By the time the officials arrived to take the 75 youngsters, 58 of them were gone—eloquent testimony to the mothers' determination not to give up their offspring.[38]

IV

The quality of care varied greatly for children in private orphan asylums. Smaller institutions might approximate family-like settings rather well but be strapped financially. Larger asylums might be economically better off but unable to meet the almost universally shared goal of "homelike" care. The bigger institutions were increasingly dominant, housing a majority of institutionalized dependent children following the Civil War. In 1873 six asylums sheltered more than five hundred children each. Within three decades, 12 housed between five hundred and one thousand each; 9 cared for more than one thousand apiece. Even asylums that started small often grew quickly. When the Albany Orphan Asylum opened in 1832, it housed 150 children in a two-story building surrounded by pastures, gardens, and a low picket fence. By the 1880s the house included another story and several wings. The once-expansive grounds had given way to barracks-like buildings in which up to six hundred children lived. Only the small picket fence was a reminder of earlier days when the asylum looked far less like an institution.[39]

The large asylums typically required uniform dress, with numbered clothing items. Routines were usually strict and monotonous. Corporal punishment was common, in some cases for girls as well as boys. Often as many as one hundred children slept in dormitory rooms with rows of identical beds. In the New York Catholic Protectory in 1885, around nine hundred boys ate together in a huge dining room. Girls and boys were strictly segregated in these asylums, a fact that made many of them uncomfortable with the opposite sex later in life. Some institutions had barred windows and were surrounded by tall spiked iron fences—a setting that one resident recalled "helped to give us the feeling of being imprisoned, an 'inmate' psychology." Hunger was often a problem. Children in Cleveland's Jewish Orphan Asylum (JOA), for example, constantly searched for additional food, breaking into the kitchen to find raw potatoes or stealing from the asylum's garden and smaller residents. "They cheated, tricked, and frightened the younger kids out of their food," recalled one person. "We weren't properly protected from them. I was in constant fear." In another asylum some of these smaller children, as one resident recalled, "sneaked in the dining room after meal time and on their hands and knees crawled under the tables picking up the stray crumbs, even from the cracks in the floor."[40]

Because of the many rules and regulations in most asylums, critics attacked them as impersonal and dehumanizing. "The child is reared by the bell," one individual complained. "The bell rings in the morning to rise, the bell rings to dress, the bell rings for prayers." To most managers and staff who were responsible for feeding and clothing sometimes hundreds of children, and who had to deal constantly with health problems such as head lice, such strict rules and control were institutional imperatives. Some orphanages isolated their inmates as much as possible from outside contact.[41]

Some asylums undoubtedly set out initially with grandiose objectives of child reformation. "We can control what he thinks about, from the time when he gets up in the morning till he goes to bed at night," gushed one individual. "He never will run with the gang. He never will be out nights." German Jews who organized and ran the Jewish Orphan Asylum in Cleveland tried mightily to Americanize children of the new immigrant Jews from eastern Europe, whom they viewed with disdain and embarrassment as uncouth and inferior. Worried that Russian Jews would undermine the gains that German Jews had made for American Judaism, one longtime JOA superintendent tried assiduously to drive a wedge between the children and their surviving relatives by instructing the children to jettison their Orthodox culture and learn "American" customs and values. Elsewhere, a woman in Kansas who claimed in 1896 that she was building "the greatest home for girls that ever was seen" disparaged "the ordinary mother": "She does not understand the principles of child study, child culture, child nurture, and all those things." The woman's goal was to provide poor girls with the proper kind of upbringing, one that would allow thousands of them to become fine teachers and matrons—indeed, a "new race of women to become the mothers of the next generation." In reality, however, the day-to-day operations of institutions blurred such lofty dreams and turned the staffs' attention to more mundane matters of simple child care. Still, tensions unquestionably existed between middle-class managers who worked with children from working-class backgrounds, or between older and newer immigrants.[42]

The level of those tensions depended considerably on particular institutions and particular times. A change in superintendent or key staff members could produce dramatic shifts in tone and conditions. When some of the children at New York's Hebrew Orphan Asylum (HOA) objected to the terrible meals they received, superintendent Jacob Cohen showed little sympathy. He claimed, astoundingly, "that orphan children are more fastidious about their food than the children of rich people." His successor, Dr. Hermann Baar, who had himself been an orphan in Europe, was far more qualified and competent. But his emphasis on tighter discipline and military-style regimentation left an enduring imprint on the asylum and provoked its residents to say that they lived "behind the Baars." At the Cleveland Jewish Orphan Asylum, longtime superintendent Dr. Samuel Wolfenstein implemented a similar military model that emphasized, as historian Gary Polster has written, "the psychological use of power: the power of staff over children, the power of monitors over other youngsters, the power of big boys over small boys, and the power of wealthy, prestigious benefactors and trustees over the entire institution." Wolfenstein had no more faith in the working-class poor than did Charles Loring Brace or Elbridge Gerry. He, too, believed that city children were better off under his protection than they would be with their own impoverished parents.[43]

The children themselves responded to conditions in the late-nineteenth-century orphanages with emotions that reflected their varied backgrounds, personalities, and particular situations. An abandoned boy who lived for a while in the Albany Orphan Asylum wanted nothing to do with his mother if she showed up, "for she would surely make trouble." He noted bitterly "that a mother's duty does not end in the act of bringing into this world of turmoil children and then leaving them to take care of themselves. She abandoned us. . . ." A 17-year-old girl wondered what had happened to her family: "I do not remember there [sic] names." Some children were grateful for the care an institution provided. "I thank god that there is such a place," wrote one youngster. "What wood become of children if there was now place like that for them to go too." Another woman observed, however, that her brother "to this day . . . doesn't have anything good to say about the orphanage." Or there was Henry Bauer, the first full orphan admitted in 1860 to the newly opened Hebrew Orphan Asylum. He had much to complain about in the institution, ranging from the tedious diet and routine to the lack of playtime and the "black strap" that the superintendent occasionally used on him. But Bauer was not among the boys who ran away; he considered himself better off than he had been with a foster father who had beaten and starved him.[44]

Admission to larger institutions was particularly scary. Younger children encountered bullies who put them through rituals of initiation. One boy was

The Hebrew Orphan Asylum, ca. 1920s. One of the nation's largest orphanages, it housed more than 1,700 children in 1916. Courtesy American Jewish Historical Society, Waltham, Massachusetts.

awakened his first night when four older youths suspended him headfirst from a third-story window. In 1894, after their father died, seven-year-old Sarah Sander Wirpel and her sister Charlotte walked apprehensively up the steps of the Cleveland Jewish Orphan Asylum for the first time. They were bathed, given an institutional uniform, and suffered "great indignity" when a barber cut their long hair until they looked like boys. "I don't like to be here," Charlotte tearfully wrote her mother that first night: "I want to go home— you must take me home—you must take me home—you must take me home. . . . please take Sarah and me home." But after a year in the asylum, Sarah recalled, the sisters had gotten used to the regimen and accepted "each day in the spirit of the JOA world—obedience and duty." At the Hebrew Orphan Asylum, whose population soared in 1893 to 867 and in 1916 to 1,755, the first day was frequently terrifying. Frightened children sobbed, vomited, even defecated in their clothes.[45]

In the bigger orphanages, bells and lines marked the daily routine. There were lines into the washroom in the mornings. Children marched in columns into the dining room, where they sat at long tables. In the Hebrew Orphan Asylum, talking during mealtime was against the rules. So, too, was having more than one cupful of water, even though there was plenty of it. At night, the children undressed literally "by the numbers." At the command of three, for example, they took off their right shoes; at the count of four, their left shoes. During the daily inspections, the children stood with their shoes touching lines on the floor. In the Cleveland Jewish Orphan Asylum, the dormitory in the sprawling four-story building was so large that a resident in the 1890s recalled feeling "like an insignificant member of a herd."[46]

There was also the stigma of being an "orphanage kid," a stigma that prejudices regarding class, race, and religion sometimes exacerbated. When children of the HOA marched in a long column seven blocks to school, they suffered verbal abuse from Irish gangs, who taunted them as "sheenies," "Christ killers," and "kikes," and sometimes threw rocks or snowballs at them. In Cleveland, as one JOA resident remembered, "Every winter the Irish micks came from Kinsman Road and the slums of Superior Avenue to fight with the orphans."[47]

The living could be rough inside the asylums as well, where corporal punishment was common. When Hermann Baar was superintendent of the HOA, he moved with a rattan switch along the line of boys, smacking the palms of those with uncombed hair or dirty ears. For a while in the postbellum era, the HOA used male "wardens," who actually supervised the residents, including the girls. Some of these individuals were terribly abusive. One of them liked to watch the girls when they were bathing. He once punished a boy by locking him in a very small hall closet, and then forgetting him until the next day. When the boy was finally "dragged from the hole in the wall," according to one eyewitness, "he was unconscious, drenched, and soiled with the purgings of his bowels." In at least one asylum—but probably many more—bed wetters received whippings in the mornings.[48]

Still, in the late 1800s the huge number of needy children forced the enlargement of older orphanages and the formation of new ones. Within a year after its founding in 1884 outside New York City, St. Agatha's Home cared for 120 children. Altogether, the 29 institutions in New York City alone housed 14,245—and still the demand multiplied. By then, however, support for institutions was coming from a source that had been minimal before the Civil War: state governments.[49]

V

In the last half of the nineteenth century, many states assumed part of the burden of caring for dependent children by establishing public institutions, subsidizing private asylums, or boarding youngsters with families. Government's role was not new; public poorhouses had been around for decades. As late as 1900 only a dozen states had banned children from county almshouses; Illinois did not do so until 1919. In the mid-1890s reformer Julia Lathrop found between 50 and 75 children living in the Cook County poorhouse; many stayed with their mothers, a few were up for adoption, and "perhaps a third" were unadoptable because of their appearance or health. When they went to school across the street in their "hideous clothes," wrote Lathrop, "the outside children sometimes jeer at them." The superintendent of another county poorhouse claimed that as far as he knew during his 16-year administration, no one had taken a bath.[50]

Reformers hoped, of course, that an enlarged state role would produce better results and improve child-care conditions. In the late 1800s the states of New York, Michigan, Ohio, and Massachusetts established four main systems for dealing with dependent children. A few other states adopted their own versions of each.[51]

New York's approach was to help subsidize private institutions. In 1811 the state had set a precedent for this approach by awarding annual payments to the New York Orphan Asylum; by 1866 it was contributing to 57 additional institutions. Although a state constitutional amendment in 1874 ended lump sum payments to private agencies, a system developed whereby counties and towns paid per capita subsidies for most children within orphan asylums. California likewise made annual payments to private orphanages. These states thus provided public money for needy children without having to build and manage government-run institutions.[52]

Michigan, in contrast, gave no public money to private asylums but instead built a state institution for dependent children. The children became wards of the state and lived in relatively small groups of several dozen. Family placement was supposed to occur within a year.

In 1874 the Michigan State Public School for Dependent and Neglected Children opened at Coldwater. Of the 172 children who lived there the first year, 19 were orphans and 91 were half-orphans. A total of 98 came from poorhouses, according to the institutional record. Because parents forfeited all rights to children in the asylum, it did not provide temporary child care for families in crisis. To noted reformer Homer Folks this arrangement was nevertheless beneficial: It "discourage[d] parents from parting from their children unless such a course is really necessary." At Coldwater, the children wore uniforms, marched in lines, ate in a common dining room, and lived in "homelike" cottages designed to hold from 25 to 30 residents each. They received instruction in morality and "habits of industry" through at least three hours of work per day (gardening, scrubbing, sewing, helping in the laundry, for example) and regular drills to instill "obedience, order, precision, self-government, and promptness." Theoretically, the inmates were supposed to stay only a few months at Coldwater, before the state placed them in family homes, either through indenture or adoption. But, by 1887, 77 children had been there for more than two years. Finding placements for the children proved more difficult than the legislature had expected. Children with physical disabilities, or who were black or Native American, were virtually impossible to place. And, because of inadequate state supervision, placement in itself did not ensure good treatment. Although leading child-care reformers liked many aspects of the Michigan system, it was adopted in only a few states, such as Minnesota, which in 1885 opened its State Public School at Owatonna.[53]

The Ohio system grew out of an 1866 law that allowed each county to impose taxes to support its own asylum for needy children under age 16. Fourteen years later, however, only 9 of 88 counties in the state had built homes. Over the last two decades of the century, 30 more did so. By then, 9 others had chosen to pay private asylums per capita subsidies. Family placement was the goal in Ohio, but the system hardly encouraged it. Critics complained that county institutions were so anxious to get public money that they agreed to let "unworthy" parents institutionalize children temporarily, and at the same time refused to search energetically for placement homes. With variations, Indiana in 1881 and Connecticut in 1883 nevertheless adopted Ohio's county system.[54]

Massachusetts employed yet another model: subsidized boarding homes in which families received money to care for children. Initially, the state had followed the more traditional path of institutions and indenture. In 1866, for example, the legislature converted the public almshouse at Monson into an asylum for poor children whom officials were to place as quickly as possible into families, via either indenture or adoption. The task of overseeing the placements quickly engulfed the state agent, who in three months alone in 1866 tried to visit 160 children in families and find places for 30 more.

According to the institution's report, he encountered "many abuses," one involving a 12-year-old indentured girl who had been horsewhipped until bloody. Two years later the agent was so busy that he failed to visit 164 of the almost 1,000 children whom the state had placed. "In two instances," he lamented, "small boys came distances of eighteen and twenty miles on foot to lay their grievances before me." By 1869 the Board of State Charities admitted that placements were not working: Not enough families took children from state institutions, and those who did wanted mainly to use the youngsters' labor. The board recommended paying "a small sum per week" to keep dependent children in selected homes. In 1880, the legislature tried out the recommendation as a way of dealing with the staggering death rate of foundlings in the state almshouses—a rate so high that it amounted to what one critic described as an "extermination plan." When the foundlings' mortality rates dropped from almost 100 percent to 30 percent within two years, the state decided to board out children at Monson who were under age 10.[55]

Massachusetts's boarding system, which some opponents compared to baby farming, challenged existing fostering practices. Indenture, and often free foster care as well, rested on a child's ability to work. "Paid fostering" offered a novel alternative, especially for young children who otherwise had no value economically. A fee for parenting meant that even the unproductive child could still be a good bargain. Just maybe, too, as welfare reformer C. H. Pemberton hoped, the child in its new home might "awaken a sentiment" that would encourage the family to keep it after the payments ended. Charles Loring Brace scoffed at such expectations as utter nonsense. In his opinion, paid parenting vulgarized the home placement movement, turning a humanitarian ideal into a crass business arrangement.[56] The boarding system nevertheless reflected Brace's anti-institutional ideology. In 1895 Massachusetts closed Monson and stopped maintaining public asylums for dependent children. By the early 1900s only about 15 percent of children receiving public support resided in the state's institutions.[57]

Because many children still resided in institutions at private expense, however, that statistic was misleading. By 1904, for example, almost four thousand youngsters lived in 52 private institutions in Massachusetts. Indeed, under state law, local authorities continued to commit children in their towns not only to private institutions but also to the state's almshouses. In 1923 Massachusetts poorhouses still contained almost four hundred children under age 15.[58]

Although the deinstitutionalizing aspect of the Massachusetts system was exaggerated, boarding out helped lay the foundation for twentieth-century foster care. The Massachusetts approach was slow to catch on, perhaps mainly because it was expensive. In the nineteenth century only one other state, New Jersey (in 1899), adopted a similar plan. By 1923 only 10.2 percent of the nation's dependent and neglected children lived in boarding homes.[59]

Although the New York, Michigan, Ohio, and Massachusetts systems provided well-publicized models for dealing with dependent children, some states went their own way. Too often, this tendency meant doing little at all. In the South and West, private orphan asylums in the late 1800s rarely received public aid, even though such institutions remained the main support system for needy and neglected children.[60]

VI

Overall, however, the trend was toward a growing state presence in the lives of dependent and neglected children—a trend that appeared in a variety of places, ranging from a new paternalistic language to court decisions and new charity boards. An important shift in public discourse was under way, implementing an inventive vocabulary that justified state activism in behalf of children. In a society still wary of government intervention, the choice of words proved crucial. Child welfare advocates such as Elbridge Gerry thus spoke of the rights of children, but not in terms of personal liberty and independence. Instead, they referred to the right of innocent youths to be safe from risk and corruption.[61]

The idea that children constituted a special category of citizens had been around for some time, but in the late 1800s it exerted an increasingly powerful influence on welfare policies. To protect children from social and economic turmoil, reformers urged segregating them into a separate class. The founders of antebellum asylums and the children's aid societies had helped mark the way; and so, in the 1860s, had state legislatures, by subsidizing private children's institutions, establishing state-sponsored orphanages, and authorizing the construction of county children's homes. Meanwhile, Darwinian theory provided strong intellectual underpinnings for thinking about the developmental stages of life, particularly childhood. Popular literature had sentimentalized childhood for some time, providing a tradition upon which authors such as Horatio Alger built. In this context, a popular writer rendered with great emotion the plight of homeless children: "It is these forlorn creatures whose naked feet smear the gutter ice with blood, whose hands eagerly search the garbage barrels for morsels of food which the homeless dogs will not touch, but which they devour. . . ."[62]

Against this backdrop, the legal doctrine of "the best interests of the child" became even more elastic. On one level, the doctrine facilitated age-segregated laws restricting child labor and prohibiting children from purchasing alcohol or tobacco. On another level, it shaped adoption and custody laws.

Even in the South, judges seized on the distinctive needs of children as a means of chipping away at traditional parental power. "The increasingly child-centered legal process could be turned against parents," according to historian Peter Bardaglio, "since it rested on an assessment of the child's needs and the public good rather than the parent's interests." Before the Civil War, only once in a child custody contest did a southern appellate court (the Tennessee Supreme Court in 1858) deny custody to a natural parent. After the war, however, southern courts much more willingly granted custody to third parties. Most third parties were relatives of the children. Still, between 1866 and 1900, unrelated individuals and institutions won 39 percent of cases in which they were contestants. In 1894, for instance, when parents sought the return of a two-year-old girl whom they had given up voluntarily, the Texas Supreme Court awarded custody to her adoptive parents who, the judges said, could best protect her interests. Judges were also increasingly considerate of children's wishes and emotional ties.[63]

Like their northern counterparts, southern judges hastened state involvement in family life by more vigorously defending abused and neglected children. According to an Arkansas judge in an 1882 case in which a father and his second wife had badly mistreated their six-year-old son, there was a "natural presumption that . . . children will be properly taken care of . . . and that they will be treated with kindness and affection." Such reasoning continued to reflect class and racial biases, however. Courts had for years been willing to remove (and typically bind out) neglected children from poor families. That tradition not only persisted but impinged upon former slaves with particular cruelty. At the moment when newly freed African Americans rejoiced at finally receiving family autonomy, white authorities used new apprenticeship laws to bind out black children without parental approval for virtually any reason. In Maryland, according to historian Barbara Fields, ex-slaveholders quickly rounded up the children of former slaves, "whisking them off to the county seats, sometimes by the wagonloads, to be bound as apprentices by the county orphan's court."[64]

The legal turn toward protecting children's best interests thus sometimes masked injustices, just as it often ignored the volatile subject of sexual abuse. In the postbellum South, several legislatures took a tougher stand on incest; but judges in notable instances proved more lenient. Incredibly, in 1891, omission of the word "feloniously" from an indictment was sufficient reason for the Mississippi Supreme Court to reverse an incest conviction. Five years later, Texas's high court ruled against a female who accused her father of having forced himself sexually upon her since she was age six. The judges concluded unsympathetically that she had probably consented to having sex anyhow; and if she had not, they found no evidence that she had resisted. But even evidence of resistance refused to satisfy some judges. The Georgia Supreme Court ruled in 1900 against a girl who said that she had continually tried to stop her stepfather from having intercourse with her. The judges reasoned that she was too young to have made any mature decision regarding sex. Moreover, they concluded, "she in fact consented to it, so doing however with that reluctance and disinclination which would naturally be felt by any young girl in sustaining such relations with her mother's husband."[65]

Despite such examples of judicial insensitivity and inaction, courts in the late nineteenth century generally moved with the larger trend toward state mediation of familial matters. Growing state paternalism included the protection of children. Parental authority was, according to legal scholar Ernst Freund in 1904, "a power in trust. . . . The authority to control the child is not the natural right of the parents; it emanates from the State. . . ."[66]

As states assumed greater responsibility for the care and protection of dependent and neglected children, they relied on a new administrative arm: boards of charities. Massachusetts established the first state board of charity in 1863 to monitor public institutions and state programs. By 1894, 18 states had similar agencies. Over the next 16 years, that number doubled, setting the foundations for what later became state departments of public welfare.[67]

By the century's end, a growing child welfare crisis intensified debates about the best solutions. The terrible depression of the 1890s devastated many families. Poverty worsened, violence escalated, and street waifs begged on urban corners or, if they were "lucky," found institutional shelter. Perhaps 1 in 30 of New York City's children ended up for a while in crowded asylums.[68]

Infants on steps of a New York City almshouse, ca. 1900. Courtesy the Photography Collection of the Carpenter Center for the Visual Arts, Harvard University.

This startling statistic could only encourage institutional opponents who were championing family-like environments for poor, dependent, and neglected children. Advocates of such environments could point to the example of Mary Ellen, the child whom the NYSPCC had rescued in 1874. After having had a new start in a foster home, she adopted a daughter. Defenders of children's asylums could reasonably note, however, that Mary Ellen's case was in fact a cautionary tale about family placement and foster care. After all, the girl had been brutalized as a foster child.

On the eve of the twentieth century, child welfare reformers heatedly discussed the virtues of placement, the continuing role of institutions, and—of increasing importance—the role of the state in family intervention. Their debates helped to usher in one of the most creative and energetic eras in American child protection. According to one prominent welfare reformer, nothing less than "the century of the child" lay ahead.[69]

5

Innovation, Tradition, and Progressive-Era "Child Saving"

It was the first meeting of its kind—a gathering in early 1909 of almost two hundred leading child welfare advocates at a White House Conference on the Care of Dependent Children. "The problem of the dependent child," several of these reformers had advised President Theodore Roosevelt several months earlier, "is acute; it is large; it is national." At the landmark gathering, the conferees overwhelmingly endorsed the family ideal. "Home life is the highest and finest product of civilization," they resolved. From the 1890s to the 1920s—the Progressive reform era—that ideal prompted an expanded placing-out movement, a push to make the still-growing congregate children's asylums more homelike, and the formation of "anti-institutional institutions" with family-style cottages and self-governing formats. Most notably, however, it elicited from the participants at the 1909 meeting a declaration to keep children with their natural families whenever possible. That objective set the foundation for one of the era's most important innovations regarding child dependency and neglect: mothers' pensions to enable needy and morally "fit" widows to care for their children at home.[1]

Several tendencies were apparent in the progressives' discussions about child welfare. Reformers typically conflated problems of dependency, neglect, and delinquency. From this perspective, some children who had families were in fact considered "homeless," and real orphans who had broken no laws might be so degraded as to seem a danger to society; all of them needed "rescuing." The progressives thus expanded the definitions of dependency to include such conduct as visiting poolrooms habitually, using liquor or drugs, and wandering the streets at night. Additionally, because the reformers generally viewed problems within the larger social setting, they were inclined to subsume abuse—or purposeful acts of cruelty—under the category of neglect, which was often a consequence of unfortunate circumstances. But this tendency to consider the unfortunate conditions in which people lived was often insufficient to overcome a crucial part of the progressives' intellectual baggage: a class-based propensity to find parents, typically working-class mothers, culpable for bad lifestyles and poor methods of childrearing. Old assumptions proved hard to shake. As a result, the progressives responded to child dependency, neglect, and abuse in ways that were both innovative and traditional: They introduced the modern welfare state but at the same time encountered resistance and retained long-familiar judgments about poverty, the working class, and race.[2]

I

The 1909 White House conference was a potent manifestation of what the famed juvenile court judge Ben Lindsey described as "the gospel of child saving," a key aspect of progressivism. Reformers had for some time looked to children as crucial agencies of social reconstruction, but by the turn of the century the stakes seemed higher than ever. According to the noted journalist Jacob Riis, child rescue work constituted society's "chief bulwark against bankruptcy and wreck." "If we do not pull him up," boy's club organizer J. F. Atkinson warned of the street waif, "he will pull us down." A familiar cartoon showed a protective fence at the top of a hill and an ambulance at the bottom. The message was clear: Society could take action to save the endangered child, or wait passively until events were out of control.[3]

Reform journalists such as Riis and Lewis Hine helped to publicize the plight of needy children and gave a sense of urgency to their rescue. Photographs of urban waifs sleeping in stairwells or on street grates, or of filthy youngsters coming off long shifts in factories and coal mines, were powerful dramatizations of dependency and neglect. Likewise, sociologist Robert Hunter's landmark 1901 report, *Tenement Conditions in Chicago*, contained grim pictures of forlorn slum children, victims of poverty and unsafe living conditions.

A blend of impulses and strategies suffused Progressive-Era child saving. An essential element was a gender-based politics in which women, many of them constituting the first generation of college-educated females in the United States, blended women's rights activism with a larger social justice agenda. Sensitive to the subordination of females, they empathized with groups on the margins of power—the poor, the working class, the dependents. With special fervor, they pushed to the forefront issues involving family violence, poverty, and the plight of children. Their commentaries about innocent, vulnerable waifs implicitly spoke to the victimization of women as well. And in their struggles against inequities, reformers such as Jane Addams,

Florence Kelley, Julia Lathrop, and Grace and Edith Abbott helped to carve out new powers of the state.[4]

Strong religious convictions also informed progressive child saving. By the end of the nineteenth century, a number of ministers preached a Social Gospel, one that drew upon the model of Christ ministering to the poor and downtrodden. "I love organs and stained glass windows," said one minister, "but I love orphans and stranded saints more." The push for "applied Christianity," for a religion in which modern Good Samaritans assisted the unfortunate, inspired the formation of a host of organizations and institutions to help dependent and neglected children: "Nobody's Darlings," as one poem called them. By rescuing such children, society could save itself. Child saving thus had its own moral tableau, pitting innocent children against selfish interests.[5]

Another source of the era's child-saving campaigns was the ongoing organizational revolution. Order, expertise, efficiency—these elements of the emerging corporate economy influenced the interventionist bent of many reformers. As Jane Addams observed, "The trust is the educator of us all." Reformers thus sought to battle modern economic organizations with competing organizations: associations, institutions, and government agencies that spoke for the public against the monied interests. For many progressives the emerging social sciences were essential weapons in such a struggle. Child welfare reformers drew upon psychologist G. Stanley Hall's child study movement, which provided a scientific rationale for identifying childhood as a separate stage of life. In this context, Grace Abbott and other social workers discussed topics such as "Efficiency in the Care of Dependent Children" and regarded child saving as a kind of science involving trained experts.[6]

Child saving fit also with the progressive concept of dedication to service. Blending altruism and efficiency, reformers emphasized themes of civic responsibility, of decent citizens standing up to corrupt special interests. From this perspective, the cause of needy children seemed especially compelling.

II

A major progressive innovation in that regard was the juvenile court. In 1899 Illinois's Cook County created the first of these courts as part of "An Act to Regulate the Treatment and Control of Dependent, Neglected and Delinquent Children." By 1920 juvenile courts existed in all but three states. Their chief objectives were to treat needy and troubled youths separately and differently from adults, and to provide a central agency that was responsible for supervising the placement of children in foster homes or institutions. At the turn of the century in Milwaukee, for example, some reformers discovered to their horror that homeless children as young as eight still lived in adult jails.

Progressives who worked with the juvenile courts blurred the lines between dependent, neglected, and delinquent children; stressed the role of environmental factors in creating individual problems; and emphasized the positive aspects of government intervention. A common assumption was that dependency and neglect spawned delinquency. According to Timothy Hurley, a leading advocate of the courts, "A child who today is simply neglected may be dependent tomorrow, truant the next day and delinquent the day after that." Stories and photographs of dependent children appeared prominently in the monthly *Juvenile Court Record*. Beneath the picture of a ragged tenement child, the editors asked who was to blame for the small boy's condition: the dead father or the mother who was struggling economically? Neither, answered the journal. "It was your fault! Not you personally, but all of us" for abiding intolerable situations. The juvenile court was supposed to provide a remedy by acting in the child's defense as a friend rather than as a heavy-handed intruder. "The fundamental idea of the Juvenile Court is so simple," argued Hurley. "It is . . . a return to paternalism, it is the acknowledgement by the State of its relationship as the parent to every child within its borders."[7]

Kindly judges—like Denver's Ben Lindsey—and probation agents were supposed to intervene in behalf of children, and at the same time to consider the situations of individual families. From the reformers' perspective, these court officials were typically understanding and fair. "Father has just held a private session of our family juvenile court," read the caption under a photograph of a sobbing youth in the *Juvenile Court Record*. "As usual, I lost my case." In contrast to this scene, judges and probation agents were supposed to bring wisdom and sensitivity to their cases. They would be supporters, not adversaries, of struggling families; and they would help create a more just and equitable world.[8]

Yet intervention to "do good," to save children and their families, could all too easily become a weapon against poor, defenseless individuals. In that regard, the emerging concept of "moral neglect" easily reflected class prejudices and encouraged freewheeling court action against parents. Judge Harvey Baker of the Boston Juvenile Court, for example, had impressive legal credentials, but his judgments invariably reflected the biases of an upper-class, genteel bachelor. He suspected that lower-class immigrant families did not much think about matters of shame or respectability. In his courtroom, he sat on a platform to accentuate his authority, and he had difficulty relating to working-class children who stood before him, especially girls. By his own admission, the court did not focus on "just the particular offense which brought the child to its notice." Baker looked for bad tendencies, signs, and "habits" such as loafing. He also considered the children's race and ethnicity. "I feel such a mixture of Indian and Negro blood as I understand exists in her case makes a very difficult character to deal with," he said in one instance. Lower-class families had to approach him gingerly lest they lose their children to institutionalization or foster care. One of Baker's colleagues quipped: "Young children, when you prove unfit, / Are whisked away by sovereign writ."[9]

The potential arbitrariness of the juvenile court system rested also on the assumption that children did not need legal representation or other rights of due process when they came before a benevolent judge. But even the gentle Ben Lindsey sometimes handled cases in a heavy-handed way. He once sent a boy to reform school to become more manly, not because the youth had broken the law. "Frequently," Lindsey said, "we handle a boy whose only trouble is unchastity." As authorities lengthened the list of age-segregated crimes to include, for example, shooting dice or being out late, the distinctions between child protection and moral policing faded. The rights of parents to due process could also suffer. One juvenile court judge asserted that "the probation officer can go into the home [without a search warrant] and demand to know the cause of the dependency or the delinquency of a child." Such action was seen as a response to needs rather than as an infringement upon rights. In the judge's opinion, the officer "becomes practically a member of the family and teaches them lessons of cleanliness and decency, of truth and integrity."[10]

Although such thinking encouraged abuses of power, juvenile courts were not simply instruments by which reformers could pry into the lives of poor people. Like "the Cruelty" (the SPCC), the courts answered the summons of impoverished individuals. Time and again juvenile courts rescued children who were indisputably at risk. The courts sometimes acted reprehensibly, but they also conveyed a sense of civic responsibility for society's most defenseless members. Predictably, some juvenile courts were better than others. Judges like Harvey Baker had more open-minded counterparts, in particular the redoubtable Ben Lindsey. Some judges, moreover, benefited from working with the era's most tolerant reformers—people such as Jane Addams of Chicago's Hull House and Homer Lane of the Ford Republic, an institution outside Detroit for dependent and delinquent boys. During his weekly visits to Detroit's juvenile court, Lane liked to offer a home at the Republic to youngsters who seemed unwelcome elsewhere. "If that boy isn't first-rate material your Honour, I'll eat my shirt," he would announce loudly from the back of the room, trying from the outset to build the youth's sense of self-worth. The source of a huge majority of the Ford Republic's residents, a number of whom were homeless or impoverished, was the juvenile court.[11]

Across the country, juvenile courts bore considerable responsibility for the placement of dependent and neglected children. Although many children continued to arrive at orphanages via the larger court system, charity associations, and economically strapped parents, the juvenile courts handled large numbers of their cases. In 1915, for example, the Cook County Juvenile Court disposed of 1,886 cases of dependency—almost 40 percent of its workload. Many dependent and neglected youngsters who ended up in orphan asylums came through the juvenile courts. In 65 percent of child neglect cases between 1906 and 1916, the Boston court found an institutional solution.

Indeed, juvenile courts were greatly responsible for the huge growth in the population of all children's institutions, from almost 61,000 in 1890 to around 205,000 in 1923.[12]

For many children this trend was a mixed blessing. They may have been better off in institutions, but the improvement was too often minimal. Large numbers of dependent and neglected children ended up in reform and industrial schools because the juvenile courts were sometimes unsure about where else to place them. Some of the children, according to a court worker in Chicago, "have been so criminally neglected [that] even if they have themselves committed no offense, [they] are often contaminated by their surroundings." Judges reportedly placed them in reform schools simply "to protect the other dependent children whose experiences have not been demoralizing." A young victim of sexual abuse thus went to Illinois's state reform school at Geneva. Her stepfather, with the complicity of her mother, had forced her to have sex with him until, one morning, the girl resisted. As she explained from the reformatory, "They beat me so severely that I had bruises on my face. . . . I was sent here for my protection." In some instances, dependent and neglected children ended up in state-funded reform schools simply because penny-pinching local officials were trying to save money.[13]

III

That same desire to care for needy children without raising taxes kept much of the burden for child welfare on private institutions. Most of those institutions still relied heavily on a long tradition of private charity with religious support and inspiration. One minister in 1910 doubted that there was a better way to improve society than to plunge into the "dark continent of unexplored child suffering." In that spirit the National Benevolent Association of the Christian Church (NBA) opened eight orphanages at the turn of the century. By 1914 the association had "fathered and mothered" more than seven thousand dependent children in its institutions.[14]

Although dedicated to rescuing the "precious little ones," most church-supported orphanages also wanted to protect the faith. The NBA, a Protestant organization, thus hoped to save orphans from Catholicism and monitored the number of Protestant baptisms in its orphanages. One matron noted with pleasure that a six-year-old "Jewish lad, a fact of which he is not very proud," indicated "he'd rather be 'a 'Merican' than a Jew!"[15]

It was precisely such thinking, of course, that spurred Catholic and Jewish organizations to step up their own orphanage work. These non-Protestant efforts also responded to the huge influx of new immigrants from southern and eastern Europe. An average of one hundred thousand Jewish immigrants entered the United States each year from 1900 to 1910. In 1903 the spiraling number of abandoned, neglected, and homeless Jewish children pushed the Hebrew Orphan Asylum's (HOA) population over one thousand for the first time, still way short of the growing demand.[16]

Strained child welfare resources also forced African Americans in northern cities to search for institutional answers. Blacks had relied traditionally on neighbors and extended families to house orphans and needy children, but this informal child-care system could not keep pace with the accelerating black migration northward. Few institutions accepted African American children. By the twentieth century in Chicago the situation became critical. Even the Chicago Orphan Asylum, which had been integrated since opening in response to the 1848–49 cholera epidemic, eventually stopped accepting blacks. In 1899, 60-year-old Amanda Smith, the daughter of slave parents and a missionary for the African Methodist Episcopal Church, used her $10,000 in life savings to start an orphanage for African American children in Chicago. She hoped initially to house the children only temporarily, while searching for permanent placements. By 1911 Smith was in her seventies and caring for an average of 36 children at a time. Four years earlier, Elizabeth McDonald, an African American volunteer for the juvenile court, opened the Louise Home for dependent black children in her own house. In 1911, when her orphanage sheltered as many as 27 boys and girls per day, she covered 60 percent of the expenses with her own money. The two orphanages reorganized in 1913 into the Amanda Smith Home for Colored Girls and the Louise Manual Training School for Colored Boys. Most of the children came from parents in desperate economic straits. Both homes were severely underfinanced; the Smith Home lacked adequate heat and bathing facilities, and its young residents shared towels. The willingness of white officials to approve the two homes—the city's only certified orphanages for dependent African American children—showed the extent to which racial lines were hardening in Chicago.[17]

As the Smith and Louise orphanages struggled financially, institutions with greater resources underwent substantial trials of their own. Their expanding size tested mightily the quality of care they could deliver. The challenge of overseeing dozens, and in some cases hundreds, of children often overwhelmed the staff. "Did you ever spend a day indoors with a hundred children learning a yell?" one matron wondered on a rainy day. "I have not one minute to call my own," wrote another matron, "from five in the morning till eight at night when each of the weary 60 heads is quietly reposing on the pillow." One woman in charge of 70 children had so much trouble keeping track of just the special Sunday handkerchiefs that she "instituted a roll-call" to collect them by the day's end. Keeping track of the children was not easy either. Of the 65 youngsters from one orphanage who went to the World's Fair in St. Louis, four were momentarily lost. Supplies of food, clothing, and support staff in the asylums were usually inadequate. One matron referred to the difficult task of simply trying "to find something to cover the heads of 102 little ones." Raising money was a relentless task. "Stick Sixteen Cents on This Slip and Add a Foot to a Mile of Pennies for the Cleveland Christian Orphanage," read one appeal.[18]

Few crises, however, matched the terror of epidemics. Year in and year out the usual childhood diseases of measles, mumps, and chicken pox swept through asylums. In one orphanage 47 of approximately 100 children were sick at the same time. Several of them died. "It has never been my experience to cope with a situation so trying," reported a matron who had worked at the asylum for more than three years. In 1915, at an upstate New York orphanage, 58 percent of the infants under age two died.[19]

Although orphanage conditions and experiences were anything but uniform, some former residents found institutional life so painful that they later refused to discuss it. Others reflected upon their childhoods with only bitterness. Hy Newmark remembered little that was good about his nine-year stay in Cleveland's Jewish Orphan Asylum (JOA), which cared for around five hundred children. He entered the orphanage in 1913 with three siblings. He hated the spiked iron fence, the "abominable" food, the deteriorating buildings that were "infested with mammoth rats and bedbugs in our beds that ate you alive. We bathed only once a week. . . . Most of us had lice in our hair." He resented the military ambiance in which, for example, the inmates marched in columns of two when they went to eat. He also recalled the beating across the legs he received from the superintendent's nephew who wielded a long stick, one-inch thick: "I wept for hours afterward." Harris Gelder, who lived at the JOA from 1904 to 1914, never forgot the nagging hunger: "The last year I was in the home it was my job to take the stale bread to the horse. He very seldom got any." To see friends and relatives, to find privacy, or simply to get away, some children climbed the fence and ran to the river or parks. Edward Dahlberg, a JOA resident from 1912 to 1917, was among the many who chafed under the asylum's rules and tedium. He recalled how the superintendent, Samuel Wolfenstein, occasionally "clouted a kid." Wolfenstein himself described the children "as little savages" who needed instruction in "cleanliness, orderliness, and decency. . . . they are lazy, cruel, selfish, unreliable, and untruthful."[20]

Wolfenstein believed that his harsh tactics produced the desired results. His goal was to separate the immigrant children from what he saw as the rude ways of their Eastern European parents. In many respects, he succeeded. For the most part the orphans jettisoned Yiddish ways and Orthodox traditions and did not return to their old neighborhoods. From the children's viewpoint, however, the physical, emotional, and cultural price of such changes was high. Some of the residents, perhaps many, found little reason for gratitude.[21]

A former occupant of a large Protestant institution at the turn of the century had equally unhappy memories, starting from the moment he entered the "dismal brick building" at age nine and saw a long line of boys "all standing erect without a smile." Over the next few years the youngster felt "the smarting raps of [the superintendent's] hose" on his back. Chores and school occupied most of the day. There, as in other asylums, the chores were gender-related: Girls helped with the kitchen and laundry; boys did the janitorial and outside work. Typically, the boys and girls were segregated as much as possible, and even verbal contact between them brought punishment.[22]

A former resident of another orphanage resented how poorly the institution prepared him for life. When he talked of going to high school, the matron laughed at him and asked "who had ever heard of an orphan boy having a high school education." He received constant reminders that he was a pauper dependent on charity. Elsewhere, at the Rochester Orphan Asylum, small children watched enviously the youngsters who played in the "world beyond the fence," as a neighbor described it. When someone walked along that fence, the orphans peered through the wooden pickets and talked excitedly. "Those little ones looking out from an enclosure, fenced in," recalled the neighbor, "were allowed to go out only on special occasions, and then in uniform, marching two by two." The neighbor imagined how painful it was for the orphanage residents to look, "as they did, into yards where there were happy children with . . . freedom!"[23]

In reality, of course, even that outside world was no paradise for poor children. Diets, living conditions, and discipline in the asylums were in many respects no worse, and in some respects perhaps even better, than children expected in the tenements. When one girl left an orphanage to rejoin her father, she hardly found her new dwelling—a crowded room above a chicken coop—an improvement. A boy who was reunited with his mother recoiled from the setting outside the asylum: "Can it be that I am to call this neighborhood my home? . . . This is terrible." Hunger, malnutrition, and crowded quarters were not new to impoverished youngsters who, in some cases, welcomed institutional life. A small girl in a Baltimore orphanage, for example, was elated to have her own bed and a glass of milk each day. But even if institutionalized children were sometimes materially better off than before, they seldom received much personal attention and affection in the asylums. "Love is the thing I think they missed the most," said one former orphanage resident as she reflected on her experiences. "Some of those kids couldn't cope with not having somebody to hug them and kiss them, and those are the ones who thought it [the orphanage] was a terrible place."[24]

Such memories of emotionally cold institutions helped to confirm the increasingly negative public perception of asylums. The best-selling 1908 novel, *Anne of Green Gables*, although set in Canada, reinforced that perception. The heroine initially suffers in a dismal orphanage. By a fluke at age 13 she finds a kindly foster home, but she always fears that she will again end up in a dreaded institution.[25]

IV

During the Progressive Era, criticism that had long fallen on congregate institutions built into an avalanche. In 1907–09, a series of articles in the *Delineator* magazine exemplified the dislike of traditional asylums. Previously devoted to women's fashion and patterns, the magazine started, under new editor Theodore Dreiser, to examine social issues, particularly the plight of dependent children.

With a ringing essay in 1907, "The Child without a Home," the *Delineator* launched a "Child Rescue Campaign" in opposition to the "machine charity" of orphan asylums. A year later, Mabel Potter Daggett's "Where 100,000 Children Wait" provided a searing look at orphanage life. The essay's accompanying photographs showed lines of sorrowful children, with clipped hair and in drab uniforms, marching in lines to a spartan dining hall or to church. "Here come the orphans," read the caption of one picture that showed dozens of youngsters filing down a street. Daggett castigated the grimly "oppressive routine and discipline" that smothered the individuality of the youthful residents. Behind orphanage fences, she wrote, was "dangerous dynamite." Initially, the orphan felt only sadness "when nobody cares for him. . . . Later, when he cares for nobody, he is unsafe." Whether the children ended up in prisons or in almshouses, they remained dependents. As the *Delineator* attacked orphanages, it conducted a well-publicized campaign to bring homeless children and childless homes together. For several years each issue included photographs of dependent boys and girls who needed families. The magazine hoped not only to find families for its featured children but also to gain public support for the home-placing movement.[26]

As disapproval of institutions mounted, the home-placing movement grew more popular, despite its own blemished record. Orphan trains continued to transport youngsters westward from eastern cities. "Homeless Children Coming Friday," announced a North Dakota newspaper in April 1914. The youngsters ranged in age from 1 to 12. A few weeks earlier, some five hundred people had shown up at a town auditorium in South Dakota to look over nine "somewhat frightened 'kiddies'" from New York. Some critical observers likened the stage to an auction block. As the children soon discovered, home placing was still far from a science, or even a humane exercise. At one point three brothers stood on the stage. "The older, a freckle-face, red-haired urchin of 11 years," according to a newspaper account, "seemed to be unaware that his younger brothers would soon be separated from him." Three other siblings, ages six, four, and two, ended up with families in different towns. The placements sometimes failed. Two girls moved through a series of families. Five years after their placement, three of nine youngsters in South Dakota had disappeared. Several from the North Dakota groups had also dropped from sight, a fact that one local person brushed aside: The children, he said, had been "undesirables, whom the society wished to be rid of and thought they could give to the people out West who would not know any better." Orphan trains remained a familiar sight nevertheless. The children on board tended to be younger than their predecessors several decades earlier; few of them were now older than 12 or 13.[27]

Home placing gathered momentum in large part because of the rapid rise of state-oriented Children's Home Societies. In the mid-1880s, the Reverend Martin Van Buren Van Arsdale founded the first of the societies. After meeting a small girl in a county poorhouse where he had conducted a Sunday School service, he dedicated himself to "deliver[ing] children from such places." Initially, he brought the waifs to his own house where his wife cared for them while he searched for more. "When I heard a carriage drive up at night I knew there were children coming," she recalled. Between 1885 and his death in 1893, Van Arsdale chartered the Illinois Children's Home Society, inspired chapters in Iowa and Minnesota, and founded the National Children's Home Society. By 1908 chapters existed in 29 states. Working within state borders, each chapter tried to place dependent children immediately in private homes. "There's a child outside our door," the Home Society literature asserted, urging a family somewhere to welcome the "little wandering waif."[28]

If that child happened to be illegitimate, however, the Home Societies wrestled with an old dilemma that antivice reformers in the late 1800s had raised anew: Did rescuing such children encourage illicit behavior? When mothers wished to give up misbegotten babies, Edward P. Savage, superintendent of the Minnesota organization, did not want to facilitate vice or help immoral people "hide the consequences of their sin." And he was well aware of the strong opposition to sending "diseased bastard babies" into respectable families. Still, he wondered how fair it was to penalize a baby for its parents' wrongdoing. If no one would take an illegitimate child whom the mother wished to give up, what would happen to it? Savage suspected, moreover, that 90 percent of unwed mothers were unfit for parenthood anyhow. Ultimately, he sought a middle position whereby he placed illegitimate children only when their mothers were too poor to care for them. Between 1896 and 1916 at the Washington Children's Home Society (WCHS), perhaps one-third of the children whom mothers relinquished were born out of wedlock. For the mothers, most of whom were under 21, the choices were typically harsh: relinquish the baby or struggle with the stigma of immorality and the problems of child care, often with inadequate resources. The WCHS routinely accepted illegitimate children who came from rescue homes such as the Salvation Army's in Spokane or the White Shield in Tacoma. "Desertion" was apparently a convenient way of accounting for the children's relinquishment.[29]

Although the Home Societies fought for legislation to protect homeless, neglected, and abused children, their primary mission was home placement. Their efforts initially resembled scaled-down versions of the Children's Aid Societies' orphan trains. The more local focus was, however, supposed to ensure that a homeless child would find a deserving family.

Edward P. Savage, superintendent of the Minnesota Children's Home Society, complained that Charles Loring Brace had simply "brought the little street urchins out in car loads and distributed them to the farmers who took them largely for help." The Home Societies hoped to do better by matching dependent children with loving families. But the search for free foster or adoptive homes was demanding, exacting, and frustrating. Even the energetic Savage grew discouraged, noting wearily that "there is a limit to human endurance." Throughout the 1890s and into the twentieth century, he and an assistant moved by wagon and train across Minnesota's 84,000 square miles, finding and placing children. One assistant earned the nickname "the Stork." Lacking time and resources, Savage and his helper could not personally examine each prospective family carefully. As a result, they often depended on the family's reputation among local officials and church members. That measure of worth sometimes proved insufficient or misleading. "He is not the boy we want," or "I do not wish to keep her" were responses from families who returned children to Savage. One couple rejected a child because he practiced "self abuse," or masturbation, although they agreed to take him back if someone cured him of "the disgusting habit." Increasingly, Savage had to worry about children whom he could not place quickly. For a while, he and his wife kept some of them in the Savage household for several weeks. By the early 1900s, however, the Minnesota organization was relying on a "receiving home" that typically held from 25 to 50 children. The danger, of course, was that the receiving home would come to resemble a hated asylum.[30]

A prominent child-care worker nevertheless exulted in 1906 that "the home-finding idea has won. . . . [It] is the new, modern scientific and true solution of the child problem." Shortly thereafter, the prestigious 1909 White House Conference on Dependent Children solidly endorsed home placement as "the best substitute for a natural home." According to the 1910 census, an estimated 61,000 children were in foster care.[31]

The same census showed, however, that 111,514 children (90 percent of whom were orphaned, abandoned, or indigent) lived in 1,151 institutions— at least 836 of which were specifically orphanages. Still, these large numbers were not completely bad news for opponents of asylums. Among the children's asylums were a number of "anti-institutional institutions" that progressive child savers popularized.[32]

V

One type of anti-institutional institution featured a cottage-home, or family-style, format. Rather than living in congregate settings, children resided with small groups in cottages, each with a matron or supervisor. Ideally, according to the influential R. R. Reeder, the children would have different ages and share household chores, just as they would in "a well-ordered family." Reeder applied these ideas to the New York Orphan Asylum after he became superintendent in 1898. He believed the cottage-style system offered a refreshing counterpoint to institutionalization, where coercion, silence, "rote, routine and dead-levelism" smothered individual needs and personalities. His objective was to capture, as closely as possible, the features of a true home, a place "associated with children; with their freedom and spontaneity." At the turn of the century a number of new residences for needy and dependent children adopted the cottage format.[33]

Among them was Good Will Farm, which George W. Hinckley founded in Maine, on rolling hills along the Kennebec River. Anything but well-to-do himself, he built the farm through rigorous fund-raising efforts and by gaining sponsors for individual children. By 1914 almost two hundred dependent boys and girls lived in 13 cottages on five hundred acres. Hinckley would not permit drills, uniforms, or even similar-looking cottages. He was determined that, at Good Will, people would never encounter a situation such as the one he had read about as a young man. According to the story, when a visitor to an orphanage kissed a child, the youngster responded by saying, "That isn't in the rules, ma'am." Former residents of Good Will remembered Hinckley as "very fatherly," someone who developed close bonds with the children. "We just idolized him," recalled a 1909 graduate. By rotating tasks, youngsters earned money and supplies. Some even "rented" small garden plots, and then sold what they grew. Hinckley emphasized education and developed a superior academic setting that offered college preparatory work as well as vocational training. "Among all boys and girls who have spent a part of their life at Good Will," he said proudly, "there is not one that has been institutionalized." Evidence abounded that Hinckley's claim was not pure rhetoric. Over several decades, hundreds of youngsters flourished at Good Will Farm. Celia Jackson, for example, whose father died in 1909 when she was age nine, and whose mother could not care for four children, found emotional as well as physical support at Good Will. For Progressive-Era child savers, the challenge was always to find enough George Hinckleys.[34]

Among the individuals with Hinkley's kind of commitment, tenacity, and genuine concern for what he called "left-over" children were several founders of the junior republics—additional examples of the era's anti-institutional institutions. In the mid-1890s, William R. "Daddy" George had started the first and most famous of the republics, Freeville, in upstate New York. It was a scaled-down replica of the U.S. government and reflected the ideal of progressive education in which children learned by doing. At Freeville, they discovered the virtues of democracy and good citizenship by electing their own legislature and establishing a tiny society. Convinced that "the 'Republic Microbe'" was contagious, George established the National Junior Republic Association in 1908, which included little commonwealths in Maryland, Connecticut, and California.[35]

By then, other republics existed, including Edward "Cap" Bradley's at Allendale Farm in northern Illinois and Homer Lane's Ford Republic outside Detroit. The republics varied slightly. Some had rudimentary economies based upon their own scrip. Some had fledgling court systems. Some included both boys and girls. But all of them shared an aversion to congregate children's institutions where routine stifled individuality. "Laughter is the supreme affront to the institutional," said "Cap" Bradley. At Allendale, he thus looked "for some hopeful, lifeful signs of naughtiness" and himself joined the youths in footraces and snowball fights.[36]

Twenty years after its founding in 1895, Allendale Farm housed around one hundred dependent boys in eight cottages and included a school, gymnasium, church, and manual training shop. Bradley was convinced that in a rural setting with the features of family and self-governing community he could "recreate" the children, lifting them from lives of destitution and homelessness. He also introduced a self-governing system with elected officials (such as a mayor, game warden, and town messenger), a court, police department, and money system. One 13-year-old preferred having his privacy so much that he built his own hut from driftwood and scrap materials and put it under lock and key. "And it came to pass that I built my hut on land near the swamp and it was made fine," the boy said proudly. None other than Ben Lindsey lauded Allendale: "It comes nearer being ideal as a home for children than any elaborate institution could be."[37]

VI

Congregate asylums took notice of the new child-saving experiments. Facing mounting criticism and often showing the influence of new, younger leadership, they made a number of adjustments, sometimes adapting cottage formats and even trying self-governing schemes. In 1912, for instance, the Hebrew Sheltering Guardian Society moved its 480 children into cottages of 25 to 30 children each. It also established Boys' and Girls' Republics. The administrators of the 75-year-old Albany Orphan Asylum were so enamored of the cottage-style format that they sold the old building and in 1908 moved to new cottages. This transformation involved considerable expense and required a huge reduction in the number of residents. By the end of the Progressive Era, the Cleveland Jewish Orphan Asylum (CJOA) was using 65 volunteers to help institute a form of self-government, modeled after the junior republics.[38]

Asylums that had traditionally isolated the children from the outside world began to integrate institutional life into that of the community. Children obtained permission more easily than before to leave the orphanages for a few hours or even weeks to be with families and friends. Opportunities for

play and recreation expanded. Residents competed more and more in base-
ball, basketball, and tennis, sometimes joining teams outside the asylums.
Group day trips, once rare, became common, as the children had more
opportunities to attend concerts, dramas, circuses, or civic events. Institutional controls relaxed somewhat. To the residents' joy, several of the large
Jewish orphanages abolished the long-required uniforms. "There was a
Catholic Home not far from the HOA, and they were really regimented," an
HOA alumna remembered. When she and her friends saw the Catholic white
blouses and blue skirts, they felt liberated: "We'd say, 'Look at them; they're
all dressed up like penguins. They all look alike, but we're individuals' . . . I
think those kids kind of envied us."[39]

A number of asylum superintendents and board members themselves criticized institutional life. In some instances, they came from new immigrant
backgrounds and had even grown up in orphanages. Michael Sharlitt and
Jack Girick were prominent examples. After his experiences in an orphanage,
Sharlitt was determined to make changes, which he proceeded to do as superintendent of the Baltimore Hebrew Orphan Asylum, and then of the Cleveland Jewish Orphan Asylum. "Numbers to me were a symbol of something I
wanted to forget—the conventional anonymity of the orphanage," he wrote.
He thus made a point of calling children by their first names and celebrating
their birthdays. Girick, who entered the CJOA in 1902 at age six, later
became Sharlitt's assistant and fired a staff member on the spot for having
slapped a young boy hard. "It was a new era in the history of the home,"
recalled a former resident.[40]

Despite more flexibility and improved conditions within a number of
institutions, changes were perhaps more often rhetorical than substantive. In
1910 only 15 percent of orphanages used the cottage format. Financial constraints often prohibited restructuring congregate settings. A lack of money
kept the managers of HOA and the CJOA from moving to the cottage system,
even though they wanted to do so.[41]

Looking back, a former asylum resident scoffed at talk about revamped
orphanages: "Even in 1913 all the homelike things and kindnesses of such an
institution were but a show and a sham to allay the suspicions and idle curios-
ity of visitors and social workers (that radical and hated class)." Corporal
punishment hardly disappeared. Herbert Kirschner, who entered the HOA in
1916, recalled that the superintendent "had a heavy hand, beating the kids
until they would grovel on the ground and plead and beg, 'Please don't hit
me.' . . . He governed by fear, terrible fear." Kirschner also remembered his
first night in the asylum, when he bit the ear of the doctor who examined
him. "I was screaming my lungs out. . . . they took me and threw me in the
broom closet and locked the door for I don't know how long. . . . This was
my inauguration, my welcome to the orphanage." Looking back, he believed
that "most of us came out of there physically and emotionally warped. I know
I did."[42]

For many crisis-torn families, however, an orphanage continued to provide what they desperately needed: temporary child care. Significantly, a majority of the children in orphan asylums in 1910 were there at their parents' request. As one Catholic charity worker commented that year, orphanages thus existed because they had to: "It was the *demand* for them which created the *supply*."[43]

VII

Partly to reduce that demand, progressives instituted one of their most influential reforms: mothers' (or widows') pensions—"the first modern public welfare in the United States," according to historian Linda Gordon. Their purpose was to provide financial assistance to poor widows or deserted wives so that they could care for their children. Unlike Charles Loring Brace's earlier emphasis on any good home environment, the progressives' pension plan focused on keeping children with their families of origin. Few progressive social reforms caught on so quickly. In 1911 Illinois enacted the first statewide law; eight years later 39 states had their own versions. Oregon's passed with only one negative vote. Drawing on a large reform constituency, particularly among women's groups such as the National Congress of Mothers, the pension movement swept to victory despite the protests of private charity groups that government aid would erode the spirit of voluntarism.[44]

Mothers' pensions, like other forms of progressive child saving, attested to the appeal of the idealized family. "Home is the nearest point from which one may step into heaven," asserted a speaker at a 1908 convention on child welfare. According to prominent social worker Mary Richmond, "The old cry of 'Save the Children!' must be superseded by the new cry 'Save the Family!' for we cannot save one without the other." In 1911 a member of Congress received thunderous applause by telling his colleagues that "the touching cadence and simple majesty of 'Home, Sweet Home'" was more compelling than famous symphonies. Three years later, Congress unanimously established Mother's Day, an annual event to honor the nation's mothers.[45]

Such glorifications of Motherhood and Home masked nagging worries that the American family was endangered. As one child rescue worker said, "The good old-fashioned home has absolutely broken down." The evidence seemed all too clear. Divorce rates were rising. Urbanization and immigration seemed to encourage moral permissiveness. Tenement poverty forced women and children into the streets or exploitative jobs. A sensational press, cheap magazines, and "lurid" motion pictures undermined traditional sources of family solidarity.[46]

Unlike earlier welfare reformers who attributed poverty and crime to individual weaknesses and immorality, progressives were more inclined to blame an unjust social order. In 1910 an editor thus rebuked his readers after he received a pathetic appeal from a deserted mother of three children. "It breaks my heart," the mother told him, "but . . . to save my innocent children from hunger and cold I have to give them away." The editor wondered what kind of society would place a mother in that predicament. He hoped that such injustice would "kindle a hellish fire of hatred in every human heart." As one scholar subsequently described this progressive worldview: "The moral fault lines were clear—hungry children, innocent parents, guilty social order."[47]

To protect such children and parents, and to make the social order fairer, progressives favored an activist government. Juvenile courts represented one form of state and local interventionism in behalf of the nation's young. So did the various state visitation boards that reformers established to inspect, monitor, and license children's asylums. But progressives also looked to the federal government for help. They, for example, pushed for national child labor laws, held the 1909 White House Conference on the Care of Dependent Children, and, in 1912, established the U.S. Children's Bureau. The bureau had little money and a small staff, but its investigations of problems such as infant mortality fueled reform causes. Bureau chief Julia Lathrop mirrored progressive optimism that government could use experts, facts, and science to solve problems and abolish traditional inequities. "Science," she said, "refuses to accept the old fatalistic cry 'The Lord gave, the Lord hath taken away, blessed be the name of the Lord.' "[48]

Mothers' pensions epitomized progressive activism in defense of the family. They represented a way "to save not only the child but the mother too," in the words of juvenile court judge Julian Mack. In that context, Ben Lindsey referred to "the Parenthood of the State," whose purpose was in part "to see that no child suffers because of poverty where the home is helpless."[49]

Although aid for poor widowed mothers to keep their children at home was hardly novel, mothers' pensions marked an important step toward legitimizing public assistance. Earlier forms of outdoor relief had provided goods and money from private organizations, or emergency supplies such as coal. Mothers' pensions, via state laws that authorized local governments to use public funds for aid, tilted away from the nineteenth-century emphasis on privately based social welfare. Moreover, insofar as mother's aid was "a subsidy for the rearing of children," as the Massachusetts Commission on Mothers' Pensions recommended, it had the potential of becoming an across-the-board entitlement, not selective charity. This entitlement would reward women for their domestic labor while improving the children's conditions. A few advocates of mothers' pensions had that very goal in mind.[50]

Ultimately, however, mothers' pensions delivered a blow to the concept of an entitlement, or across-the-board aid. The Massachusetts Commission, for example, emphasized that the childrearing subsidies should go only to "the fit and worthy poor," who needed to prove their eligibility. In Massachusetts and elsewhere, only a very small percentage of families in fact received assistance, and the amount of aid was woefully inadequate. The well-known social worker Edith Abbott concluded in 1917 that the pensions had rocketed to popularity precisely because they had not really threatened vested interests, whether in the form of the older charity organizations or taxpayers.[51]

For a brief moment, the future of family welfare, and of aid to dependent children, nevertheless hung in the balance. On the one hand, the progressives' stress on the environment engendered sympathy for poor people as victims of circumstances. From that perspective the conferees at the 1909 White House conference resolved, in the words of organizer and participant Hastings Hart, that "under no circumstances should a child be taken away from parents simply from poverty." Because such separations occurred all too often, champions of mothers' pensions searched for ways to build a reform constituency. To that end, they rallied around the image of the blameless widow. As a symbol of victimization and stoic virtue, the widowed mother provided a compelling reason to enlarge public responsibilities. Mothers' pensions thus emphasized public obligations in contrast to the older, punitive social policies that stigmatized pauperism and blamed its victims of idleness. For this reason, the pensions marked a significant point in the history of American social welfare.[52]

On the other hand, progressives could not break completely from the older charity distinctions between the "worthy" and "unworthy" poor. The 1909 White House conferees showed their divided thinking. Poverty, they agreed, was no reason to break up a home; yet "inefficiency or immorality" were justifications. Most states thus established "suitable home" provisions for receiving aid.[53]

Such criteria necessitated some form of investigation and surveillance and at the same time inevitably reflected the standards and preferences of the pensions' administrators. A Pennsylvania social worker, for example, worried that a Czech-born widow with three children "spoiled" her two-year-old "by petting him" and allowing him to sit on her lap. When illness forced the children into the hospital, the mother became frantic about losing them. The social worker warned her that "if she cried this way she was not fit to look after the children." Afraid that authorities might take her children, the woman became very compliant and followed the social worker's dictates. In other instances, eligible mothers sometimes had to receive instruction in subjects ranging from English to cooking and childrearing (keeping pacifiers from babies, for example). Intemperance, waste, or refusing to keep a clean and orderly home were reasons for losing support in Connecticut. "Unfitness" could also include using tobacco or not attending church.[54]

A large number of counties chose not to provide pensions at all; indeed probably only 40 percent of the counties who could legally grant them did so. Others awarded only a few pensions and had long waiting lists. At one point in Philadelphia only 24 percent of the applicants received pensions, and the wait could be as long as two years. Across the country, ethnicity and race provided grounds for exclusion or smaller allowances. In Los Angeles, Mexican immigrants were not eligible. Few African Americans received pensions anywhere; in Houston, where they constituted 21 percent of the population, none was eligible.[55]

A number of desperate women nevertheless viewed pensions as vital to keeping their children at home. "I am only a poor frail little mother, left with six children," wrote one widow. "I do not ask for charity. . . . I care nothing for the pension only as a last resort—that is to keep me from being *seperated* from my *precious babies*." Another widow pleaded for help to preserve her family. "I have been trying to keep them together and hate so much to part them, but will hafto do some thing with them pretty soon if I don't get help from some wheres pretty soon."[56]

Mothers who qualified for aid were usually caught in a double bind: The meager pensions often forced them to earn wages for extra income, but employment made them vulnerable to charges of neglecting their children. Working while at the same time providing adequate supervision for their children proved a monumental task for many poor single mothers. In 1919, for example, Chicago's Family Welfare Agency estimated that Mary Legaikas, a Lithuanian widow with five small children, needed a monthly budget of $89.50; yet her pension was only $55. For additional funds, she worked three days a week in a factory. She was lucky enough to find a neighbor to watch the children, but authorities monitored the situation carefully via home visits and checking with the schools.[57]

Pension recipients in some states were supposed to supplement their income with outside work. A 1923 Children's Bureau study of almost a thousand recipients in nine locations discovered that over half of them held jobs, and a majority of those jobs were outside the home. "By not paying single mothers enough to stay at home but preventing them from (openly) working full time," historian Molly Ladd-Taylor has argued, "the mothers' pension system perpetuated women's marginal position in the wage-labor market and reinforced their economic dependence. . . ."[58]

Ironically, a system that was supposed to preserve families could in fact jeopardize them. Without some kind of inexpensive and accessible child-care arrangements, working mothers sometimes could not find responsible individuals to watch their children. Or if they relied on their offspring to earn money peddling or collecting odds and ends on the streets, they could appear exploitative and unloving. Mothers' pension laws may therefore have redefined at least some dependent children as neglected. And because neglect was a reason for child removal, the laws perhaps inadvertently broke up, rather than preserved, at least some homes.[59]

Mothers' pensions thus pointed forward and backward. On the one hand, reformers took the radical step of saying that poverty was not grounds for child removal. "If the poverty of the mother forces her to neglect her child the poverty should be removed and not the child," Kansas City juvenile court judge E. E. Porterfield asserted eloquently. On the other hand, progressive policies were still indebted to the long-established tradition of moral-reform charity, a tradition that offered aid, in the words of the Massachusetts Commission on Mothers' Pensions, "hesitatingly, without assurance, and under abundant supervision."[60]

VIII

Overall, the Progressive Era was nevertheless one of the most beneficial periods in American history for dependent and neglected children. It improved institutional care and provided some creative "anti-institutional" alternatives to the traditional format. It gave special priority to keeping poor children with their birth families, a trend that was apparent in mothers' pensions as well as in the courts' greater willingness to grant custody to poor but "worthy" mothers—"a radical departure," according to legal scholar Mary Ann Mason. And it enlarged the principle of public responsibility for needy children by establishing new government agencies and programs. At the state and local level, juvenile courts collected information about dependent and neglected children and decided matters of placement. New state visitation agencies enforced more rigorous standards for private children's institutions and placement services and prepared the foundations for subsequent child welfare departments. Emerging groups of professionals, some attached to the juvenile courts, others to schools, social work, or the developing field of child psychology, focused their expertise on the special needs of children. In Chicago, the efforts of pioneering social workers Edith Abbott and Sophonisba Breckinridge documented the crises that confronted the city's African American families and dependent children.

Elsewhere, Kate Barnard, Oklahoma's first Commissioner of Charities and Corrections, unearthed a major scandal that exploited hundreds of the state's Native American orphans, and thousands of other Indian children. Under the Dawes General Allotment Act of 1887, which broke up tribal lands for individual distribution, every Indian minor was supposed to receive property. An example of the mass fraud by which non-Indians had plundered these Native American allotments was a system whereby, in Oklahoma, 40 county judges oversaw the property rights of some 60,000 Indian minors, 143 of whom were orphans in two state asylums. These judges connived with appointed "guardians" to seize control of property valued at $150 million. Some of these guardians were responsible for dozens, even hundreds, of Indian wards, whom they neglected while stealing from them. The problem was particularly shocking in the case of the 143 institutionalized orphans, whom the state housed as paupers in dismal conditions. Many other dependent Indian children lived in equally appalling places outside the state's asylums. When Kate Barnard discovered the scandal, she pushed for a law to make the guardians financially accountable for managing the children's estates, and she specifically sought authority to intervene in behalf of all orphans housed in Oklahoma's public institutions. Eventually, via hundreds of legal proceedings, she recovered more than $1 million in property that belonged to Indian orphans.[61]

On another reform front, a few progressives launched what one educational journal dubbed a "crusade" against corporal punishment in the public schools. In doing so, they moved beyond the bounds of the nineteenth-century anticruelty movement, which had concentrated on the working classes and immigrants. By 1908 at least seven major cities had banned corporal punishment in the schools. A survey showed that 55 of 83 superintendents opposed corporal punishment altogether, or accepted it in only the most exceptional circumstances. "It is not right; it is not wise; it is not pedagogical; public opinion will not sustain it," one of them argued. "It tends to brutalize both teacher and pupil," said another. "Even in the training of horses blows are not permissible." According to the head of a military department in a large secondary school, "No well-poised, just, self-controlled, warm-hearted man or woman needs to, wants to, or would, beat a child."[62]

Some reformers pointed to a different kind of abuse—one resulting from impoverished living conditions. "The power to maintain a decent family living standard is the primary essential of child welfare," observed Julia Lathrop, head of the Children's Bureau. Lathrop's simple statement provided further evidence that, wherever one looked during the Progressive Era, child welfare seemed a vital part of the nation's agenda.[63]

From another angle, however, much appeared the same. In Oklahoma, Kate Barnard's battle to secure legal protections for dependent Native American children dissipated in the face of quashed indictments and a lack of interest among other reform groups in her cause. The campaign against corporal punishment in the schools also lost momentum and virtually disappeared in the twenties.

Despite mothers' pension laws, which by 1923 allowed 120,000 dependent children to remain in their own homes, many offspring of poor women still ended up in orphanages or foster care. Into the 1920s, the number of children in institutions continued to grow. One deserted mother in Ohio was so terrified about losing her seven children to an orphanage that, in 1919, she killed them and afterward committed suicide. In 1921 only a relatively small number of around 46,000 families received pension aid. "The interest of the public in the humanitarian principle was," as one social worker noted, "overshadowed by a desire for economy." Despite the initial promise of the mothers' pension programs, the miserly stipends and their gathering aura of old-fashioned charity for the poor threatened to make such aid more symbolic than substantive.[64]

State inspections and monitoring of children's institutions and placements all too often seemed mere gestures as well. Illinois's Department of Visitation, for example, was badly underfunded and understaffed. The state had launched the department in 1905 to visit children whom the juvenile and county courts and state-funded agencies had placed in foster homes, and also to inspect institutions that received state money. But by its third year, two overworked visitors were trying to review almost five thousand placements in 95 counties. In 1917 the Department of Visitation merged into the new Department of Public Welfare. Two years later a chilling exposé of terrible conditions and sexual abuse in homes that boarded dependent children in Chicago resulted in a state law requiring the annual inspection and licensing of boarding homes. The department had more supervisory powers but faced ongoing problems of funding and staffing.[65]

Although institutions across the country probably improved overall in the early twentieth century, horror stories abounded. In 1919 two children died in Chicago when the deteriorating Amanda Smith Home for Colored Girls burned to the ground. Five years earlier, a state report had described conditions in the orphanage as "dreadful," but officials had done nothing. A year later, the Louise School closed, leaving virtually no institutional alternatives for Chicago's African American children. Elsewhere, a former resident of a Kansas orphanage found little that was "progressive" there. She compared her living conditions to "an auction yard." Visitors came to "look us over to see if we were what they wanted." After a family took her three-year-old brother, the girl could never forget the expression on his face as he looked helplessly back at her. When she fled in tears to the asylum bedroom, one of the matrons dragged her out by her hair. "They were so inhuman you can't imagine." Subsequently, in a foster home, she found only more hard times. "They needed a hired boy, but there weren't any, so I did the work."[66]

The progressives' "gospel of child saving" had achieved much, but many problems regarding dependency, neglect, and abuse obviously remained. By the 1920s, however, that gospel was a spent force with a diminishing audience. As the crusading elements of grassroots child saving steadily gave way to the "scientific" scrutiny of emerging professional groups, public concerns about dependent, neglected, and abused children faded. Indeed, over the next several decades such children virtually disappeared from the public eye.

6

The Issues Fade, 1920–1960

From the 1920s to the 1960s, issues of child dependency, neglect, and abuse received little sustained national attention. Child welfare policies and strategies shifted, but quietly and with little public awareness. After three-quarters of a century, orphan trains stopped running. Although the Great Depression momentarily pushed the population of orphanages to an all-time high, their overall trajectory was one of decline as they either closed their doors or concentrated on children whose problems were mainly emotional or physical. State mothers' pensions were transformed during the New Deal Era into the pathbreaking federal Aid to Dependent Children (ADC) program, which was hugely significant in its acceptance of national responsibility for needy children, but which was largely an afterthought and encouraged the illusion that matters of child dependency, neglect, and abuse were no longer notable issues.

The virtual disappearance of such issues from the national conscience during these decades resulted from several developments, starting with the waning of progressivism. An especially important factor was the decline of the women's rights movement, whose advocates were the chief shapers of progressivism's social welfare reforms. More generally, as reform zeal gave way to an exhausted sense of the limits of social change, many organizations concentrated on businesslike efficiency rather than on narrowing the chasm between social classes. Additionally, professionals defined the problems of children within a framework of therapeutic casework, thereby directing attention away from the larger social and economic threats to child welfare and toward individual aberrations. The crises of the depression, World War II, and the early cold war, moreover, were not such as to highlight the specific needs of children without homes or from impoverished families, or whose experiences resembled those of a resident of Washington, D.C.'s, alleys: "When I was a little girl about six or three / My father took a stick and beated me."[1]

I

A long era in the saga of dependent children ended in 1929 when the New
York Children's Aid Society (NYCAS) terminated its emigration department.
By then the NYCAS and other placement agencies had transported at least
two hundred thousand infants and youths to distant locations. The emigration program fell victim mainly to state laws prohibiting the shipment of children across boundaries, the growing commitment to keeping children with
their own families, and compulsory school attendance laws that discouraged
farmers from looking to orphan trains as a supply of young labor. Also, the
developing social work profession discarded some time-honored welfare
strategies, including that of indenture.[2]

Of all the systems for dealing with dependent children, indenture had
one of the longest and most sordid histories. Until the nineteenth century, it
had been the dominant form of social welfare, and even the new antebellum
institutions had typically been mere bridges to it. But the system's popularity
had declined notably during the late 1800s. During the Progressive Era, the
Children's Bureau had criticized it as "a relic of sixteenth-century England."
Still, in 1927, 12 states continued to permit and even use it. In Wisconsin, a
Children's Bureau study in 1923 found only two agents supervising some five
hundred youngsters whom the State Public School had indentured across the
state. The youths served essentially as unpaid laborers, often without schooling and subject to overwork and cruelty. Pennsylvania finally abolished
indenture in 1927, labeling it "intolerable." Although the New York Children's Aid Society had long distinguished its kind of placing out from indenture, the obvious similarities encouraged opposition to the NYCAS's emigration work.[3] "Don't forget," recalled an individual who rode one of the last
orphan trains, many families were basically "looking for labor." He remembered standing at train stations while people checked his muscles. One man
grabbed his jaw and inspected his mouth, "sort of like buying a horse or
something."[4]

At their conclusion, the orphan trains seemed not to have traveled far
from their origins three-quarters of a century earlier. Memories of the children who made the last trips in the 1920s sounded much like those of their
predecessors. Lorraine Williams was fortunate when a farm couple who
wanted a daughter chose her at one of the stations. "My parents took me for
love," she said. "I was their child. I was never an adoptive child, or an
orphan. I was their child." In contrast, the five Panzer brothers were bitter.
Sixty-seven years after their journey westward in 1922, one of them still had
to fight back tears when he reflected on the experience. "It's quite a shock,
you know," he said, when remembering how prospective foster parents had
inspected the children. "You feel like you're on display. That brings back
memories I have problems with." Similarly, a woman remembered little that
was good about the family with which she lived. She allowed that having "a

roof over your head . . . was better than nothing," but her so-called mother was "very vicious psychologically." George Meason had equally painful memories. At one train station, chaperones put his older brother Julius on a different train. "No, no, don't take him," screamed the younger boy. "I just grabbed him and held on to him and Julius was holding on to me." Adults finally forced the sobbing brothers apart and sent them in different directions. "Many a time I went to bed at night, crying," begging for Julius, Meason said. The foster family's response was anything but sympathetic. He received "a good hard whipping" and orders to get to sleep. When he later married, he and his wife vowed that their own children would never be without love.[5]

The orphan trains stopped running in 1929. What they had attempted was nothing short of monumental: the movement of literally tens of thousands of poor and in some cases homeless children to new starts in the West. "The concept," as one historian has written, "is both appealing and appalling." In retrospect, even those who rode the trains could not agree upon the choice of adjectives.[6]

II

Despite a combined population of more than 132,000 institutionalized children by 1923, many orphanages seemed as doomed as the orphan trains. Perennially underfunded, the asylums as a whole had trouble refurbishing their aging buildings, let alone constructing new ones. Boards of directors who wanted to modernize equipment, hire more staff, and adopt new methods constantly battled the constraints of limited budgets and the political mood of the twenties, which was largely unfriendly to social welfare programs. As a result, many institutions deteriorated.[7]

Aging almshouses and soldiers' orphans' homes were prime examples. As late as 1922, almshouses admitted almost five thousand children under age 16. In Pennsylvania, which housed 541 youngsters in county institutions, officials explained that it was difficult to place them. The evidence suggested, however, that placement efforts faltered because state subsidies for boarding children were so miserly that foster families were reluctant to assume additional child-care obligations. This same stinginess meant that almshouses were not serving the children very well either. In 1921 a visitor to a county poorhouse in Pennsylvania believed that it "seemed the last spot for children." Seventeen of the children, ranging in age from 19 months to 14 years, lived a short distance from the main almshouse in an overcrowded, decrepit house that was filthy and had a leaky roof. The kitchen was nothing less than a "hole," and the cook had only half a gallon of milk to dispense daily. There were no books, toys, or even individual washcloths. The boys and girls shared toilets and bathrooms. In 1929 a social worker in another state wanted to cry out, "Did you know that they kept babies at the County Home till they were two, with no chance to play normally or get the right food and training, shut up all day with a bunch of old women of all sorts, in a room reeking with disinfectant. . . ?" Conditions in the Illinois Soldiers' Orphans' Home, the state's only public institution for dependent and neglected children, were just as bad. The setting was so oppressive that, according to a committee report in 1920, the children "seem more like little scrubbing machines than human beings."[8]

Surveys of other children's institutions in the twenties found abominable conditions. In a Midwestern state in 1925, children in one asylum still ate their meals in silence and shared towels and combs; their toothbrushes were packed together into a single jar. In a city institution in a Middle Atlantic state, around 30 "shaven-headed children, four to six years of age," peered onto the street from an ancient brick building. Passersby looked up to see "barred windows, tiny hands clutching the bars, against which are pressed listless white faces." The pathetic scene had one benefit: It reportedly helped to raise money for the institution. "Those children you see clinging to the bars of the windows bring in thousands of dollars to us," one person explained. "Why should we move to a place where no one would see them?" If passersby could have seen the conditions inside the building, they might have reached even more willingly into their pockets. The several dozen children shared one washcloth, used the same basin of water, and ate a noon meal that consisted of "a heap of cold mashed potato, a huge soggy biscuit and a tin cup of skimmed milk, the daily contribution of a charitably inclined milk dealer." A girl who at age 11 entered what was reputedly one of the better institutions felt as if she were part of "a bunch of cattle." She resented the strict rules against leaving the grounds. "We had to sit behind high iron fences and there gaze longingly out at the people walking or riding by," she recalled. Most of all she regretted "the lack of affection. I felt so lonely and forlorn."[9]

Nor were these bleak situations unusual. A survey in 1926 of Pennsylvania's children's institutions produced dreadful statistics. Of the 240 institutions, 84 had no toothbrushes, 93 lacked adequate bathing facilities, 99 were without individual combs, and 91 were without individual towels. Only 55 kept medical and physical records, and 92 maintained individual records of any kind; 104 provided sufficient amounts of milk, and 144 served some kind of fruit daily. Fifty-four of the asylums had only cold water in the washrooms; 103 had no books.[10]

Even orphanages that offered better physical care tended to place their own financial needs above the interests of the children. The admission procedure of several respected Jewish orphanages in New York City and Brooklyn typified priorities. According to Hyman Bogen, a former resident and historian of the Hebrew Orphan Asylum (HOA), the orphanages played "a form of roulette" with children's lives. In the early 1920s, a blackboard in the Department of Welfare kept a daily tally of empty beds in each Jewish orphanage. Children went wherever available beds existed at particular times, regardless of their personal needs or situations that forced siblings apart. Because the orphanages could not survive a low vacancy rate, the Jewish institutions insisted on this system of "blackboard roulette" as a way of equitably dividing up the city's per capita child subsidies. Even worse, according to Bogen, when the orphanages' vacancies became too plentiful, the admissions procedure arbitrarily rotated children from foster homes back to the asylums. This procedure finally ended in 1922, but only with the insistence of the Department of Public Welfare. To its credit, the subsequent Jewish Children's Clearing Bureau, largely under the control of child welfare professionals, was more sympathetic to the children's needs. Beds in institutions remained empty unless the children's own distress justified their return to an orphanage. As a consequence, however, institutional populations declined, placing the future of the orphanages in doubt.[11]

During the twenties the future of all orphanages was increasingly uncertain because of the growing competition from foster care and mothers' pensions. In the decade after 1923, the number of children under age 16 in institutions fell by one-third. Asylums had to wrestle with a pressing question: "If children belonged in their own homes and their poverty was a public responsibility," in historian Marian Morton's words, "who belonged in a private institution?" Virtually no one, was one answer. In 1927, for example, Baltimore's Hebrew Orphan Asylum closed after 55 years. Only a few years earlier, it had housed 120 children. Now, suddenly, in what the last secretary described as heartrending scenes, sobbing children learned one at a time in the office that they were being dispersed to foster families. A number of other institutions decided by the end of the twenties that to survive they needed to concentrate on children with behavioral and psychological disorders.[12]

An emerging group of certified professionals facilitated this shift in focus with varying results. By relying on medical models and psychoanalytic theories, they broke from earlier moralistic judgments and suggested that people could improve themselves through self-understanding. The new psychological approach also broadened definitions of neglect and abuse to include emotional criteria. However, by turning attention to individual cases, the reliance on psychology very much narrowed the earlier reform vision of child welfare work: Matters of personality ultimately seemed more important than conditions of poverty. An emphasis on personality favored case studies, tests, measurements, therapy, and labels such as "deviancy" and "maladjustment." That emphasis unfortunately tilted child saving from a cause to a job in which the experts detached themselves from their "clients" and elevated "objectivity" over moral outrage and "involvement."[13]

For institutions, the influence of psychodynamic theory was profound. Casework focused increasingly on aberrant situations. By broadening neglect to include emotional factors, psychological analyses eased the transition of some orphanages to treatment centers for troubled youths. In Cleveland, for example, longtime orphanages not only revamped their facilities and mission but also changed their names. The Jewish Orphan Asylum became Bellefaire. Catholic institutions such as St. Mary's Female Asylum, St. Joseph's Orphan Asylum, and St. Vincent's Asylum, all of which existed before 1865, consolidated as Parmadale. The Protestant Orphan Asylum, whose origins went back to 1852 and which at the turn of the century had housed around one hundred children, became Beech Brook.[14]

III

The broadened concept of neglect also accounted in part for the growth of child placement throughout the twenties, a growth that sustained some very old problems. As had been the case for decades, placements in both foster and adoptive homes still lacked adequate supervision, usually separated siblings, shuffled children from one place to another, and sometimes placed children with abusive parents. According to Howard Hopkirk, one of the era's best-known child welfare workers, "probably half of the states did not have a single child-placing agency or institution that had attained the standards recommended by the Child Welfare League of America." A survey of one New England institution in 1928 was reminiscent of endless reports over the years from many placement agencies: "forty-six of the fifty-two placed-out children had never been visited since they were placed." In another state six field workers spent so much time raising money for the agency that they had only eight days per month to review the conditions of 443 children in 91 counties.[15]

All too often children went to families about which officials knew virtually nothing. In one instance, a married couple simply showed up at a county orphanage in Ohio looking for a boy. Because the man introduced himself as "Doctor," the superintendent assumed that the family was respectable. Around 20 youths assembled in the parlor so the couple could choose whom they wanted. The superintendent barked instructions at the boys as they stood for inspection: "Here, no, look up, and don't hang your head, Sam, just when the Doctor might pick you out and take you home to be his boy." While the youngsters waited with a mixture of hope, anxiety, and discomfort, the couple looked them over. Finally the man and woman settled on Bill and John but could not agree on which boy to take. For the next few minutes they debated the virtues and weaknesses of each. When they chose Bill, the youth beamed at winning the competition. By the time he left the orphanage a half hour later, however, he was less eager. After living in the institution for eight years, he was not sure he wanted to depart for unknown territory with strangers.[16]

Even formal adoptions sometimes occurred with little scrutiny. The travails of three-year-old Edward in Massachusetts in 1927 provided a pitiful example. When the boy was only a few weeks old, his natural mother deserted him. A judge, acting on a lawyer's recommendation, sent him to an adoptive family. But the father was an alcoholic and the adoptive mother disappeared eight months later. An investigation showed that the lawyer knew nothing about the adoptive parents and that they had paid him to secure the child. The adoptive couple had in fact only recently moved into town from communities where they had broken the law—the man for drunkenness and the woman for forgery, larceny, and breaking and entering. The adoptive family's checkered background was well documented. "But there was no way to tell the judge these facts," the Massachusetts Society for the Prevention of Cruelty reported. "Nobody appeared in court in Edward's behalf."[17]

The haste that marked Edward's adoption was not unusual. In several Pennsylvania counties during the early twenties, courts granted one-third of adoption petitions on the same day they were submitted; another third were granted within a week. One couple that petitioned to adopt three children, ages 7, 9, and 11, got them within 24 hours. Only later did officials determine that the adoptive couple ran a bootlegging operation out of a dilapidated farmhouse. The children had attended school for only four weeks during the year. After the arrests of their adoptive parents, they went to a children's home. More troubles awaited them, however, when their mother, on a suspended sentence, kidnapped them. When she ended up in jail, the children returned to the orphanage where they awaited a judge's decision on whether they would live with their father after he completed his bootlegging sentence. A state commission cited their predicament as an example of "the vast number of children who are adopted through our courts without adequate study of the home from which they come and of the home to which they are going."[18]

In some instances, the adoption process bypassed even the courts. During a two-year period in Pennsylvania, 27 children in 13 counties were simply deeded by their natural parents to adoptive parents. Such transactions required only a notary public's signature. As one writer said, "A person may thus deed away his child with as little ceremony as he disposes of a bit of real estate."[19]

IV

Despite these many problems and injustices, the 109 top professionals who in 1930 reported to President Herbert Hoover on dependent and neglected children were upbeat. They had worked for months to prepare their findings for the White House Conference on Child Health and Protection. "Today," they wrote proudly, "the principle of the preservation of the home is fully established as public policy," and institutions housed a smaller percentage of children in relation to the national population than had been the case 20 years earlier. Some of those institutions, moreover, had shifted to a cottage-style format, and some had programs that assisted children so they could remain with their families. Altogether, around 1,600 institutions and 400 child-placing agencies were helping approximately 280,000 dependent children who lived away from home; nearly 40 percent of the children resided with foster families. Although these numbers were encouraging, the White House conferees conceded that many more children, especially racial minorities, needed aid. To improve the situation, the conferees had no doubt that "child protection is a proper function of government." And they listed poverty at the top of the list of dangers to children.[20]

By late 1930, when the White House conference convened, the threat of poverty had become frightening indeed. The depression had worsened rapidly, throwing millions out of work and in search of relief. Homeless people wandered the country in unprecedented numbers. By 1933, probably at least 150,000 of them were children.[21]

As the nation struggled through the searing economic crisis, children were often the invisible victims. Unlike the documentary photographs familiar to the Progressive Era, those of the Great Depression focused particularly on adults in unemployment and relief lines, or on the road, or scratching out a living in parched rural areas. At the turn of the century, Jacob Riis and Lewis Hine had photographed urban waifs, street urchins, exploited breaker boys and textile girls. In contrast, the famous 1930s pictures typically ignored orphans and, rather, showed children with stoic sharecropper parents or, in the case of Dorthea Lange's classic picture, a migrant mother.

While headlines and policy discussions centered on the devastated economy, the problem of growing numbers of dependent and neglected children quietly overwhelmed agencies and institutions. In 1933 an estimated 120,000 children stretched the foster care system to its limits. Moreover, at the very time that the openings were scarce, the costs of foster care reached unprecedented amounts. The system had depended earlier on free homes in which foster families received no reimbursements. Indeed, at the end of the nineteenth century probably no more than 10 percent of foster children lived in subsidized boarding homes. That figure rose to 30 percent in 1923 and soared to 74 percent by 1931. For families that hoped to supplement their incomes in economically difficult times, paid foster care was an appealing option. "We were worth twenty-five dollars a month per child," recalled humorist Art Buchwald, who spent much of the thirties in foster homes. "The foster parents were more interested in the money they received," he was convinced, "than in the children." In his case, the families were at least not unkind, even though they were mainly concerned about the money. A major problem with the huge shift from free to paid foster care, however, was that, in the midst of the depression, placement agencies were running out of money. "Thousands of children are being refused care," complained C. C. Carstens of the Child Welfare League of America in 1933, "because neither public nor private agencies in their respective communities are in a position to provide such care." Dozens of agencies turned away hundreds of children.[22]

Suddenly, children's institutions were again in demand. By the midthirties, their population rebounded to an all-time high of 144,000. But that growth literally destroyed many orphanages. Few of them had ever enjoyed substantial resources to begin with. Private institutions typically relied on contributions from service groups, church congregations, and interested citizens. The superintendent of one private orphanage recalled waiting until each mail delivery before he went shopping for the day's food. "It would depend on whether a couple of one dollar bills or a five came in, whether I could buy a quarter's worth of sugar or a full sack of flour." As the depression dried up contributions, institutions resorted to slashing expenses, borrowing money, and dipping into capital funds. Even if they survived the ordeal, they would be in terrible shape, physically and financially. In the meantime, like the foster care system, they were running out of space for children. Ohio's 56 county orphanages housed more than eight thousand youngsters in 1933. In a large Kentucky orphanage, two children slept in each single bed and others ended up on the floor. At the State Home for Dependent and Neglected Children at Waco, Texas, the enrollment mushroomed from 42 in 1923 to 307 a decade later; in the baby cottage, as many as three infants shared the same crib.[23]

In 1932 the population of New York's Hebrew Orphan Asylum (HOA), including children it was boarding out, reached 1,800, the institution's largest enrollment to that point and up by almost 400 within two years. Sixty-three percent of the children had both parents, but the families were so economically crushed that they could not provide for their children. Across the country, other struggling parents turned desperately to asylums for help. Of 513 families that placed around 800 children in Cleveland's orphanages in 1933, over half had no jobs whatsoever and only 97 were receiving any form of relief.[24]

The swelling enrollment may have helped to account for superintendent Lionel Simmonds's increasingly quick temper and sometimes fierce corporal punishment at the HOA in the thirties. He once administered the "most brutal beating" that another HOA resident had ever seen. On another occasion he slapped with "hard roundhouse blows" four boys who had stolen some stamps. By 1936 the HOA was caring for 2,500 youths, a majority of whom it boarded out because of lack of room. Among them was Art Buchwald, whose mother had entered a state hospital and whose father was economically broken by the depression.[25]

When the six-year-old Buchwald and his three sisters first saw the HOA, he did not like it. "The architecture," he joked later, "was early Sing Sing." In retrospect, he compared the building to a "giant castle out of medieval times" and to a "warehouse." When he lived there, the woolen uniforms itched; the constant fighting, wrestling, and badgering frightened him; and he found no friends. "I felt locked up," he said later. "I couldn't relate to anyone there." At least his stay was brief. Because the orphanage was overcrowded, the HOA boarded him out within a few weeks. He was a foster child for 11 years, until he ran away to join the Marines in 1942. Looking back, he believed that humor had allowed him to survive a disheartening childhood. Even the HOA-sponsored summer camps were trials. "My nose used to bleed a lot because HOA kids did not like the foster home boys," he recalled.[26]

As Buchwald's experience suggested, orphanages hardly resembled the sentimentalized version that Hollywood presented in the popular 1938 movie *Boys' Town* starring Mickey Rooney and Spencer Tracy. At the HOA, youngsters got a hard dose of reality, not film fantasy. "The children of the Thirties were likely to view it as a benevolent prison," wrote Hyman Bogen, who lived there from 1931 to 1941. Weekly paddling sessions occurred on Thursday nights when the boys lined up for punishment, leaning over a bed and receiving licks with a paddle across their bottoms. The monitors devised rules and punishments as they wished. One girl who made a banana sandwich for lunch without permission ended up in a locked room for an entire afternoon. But the HOA youngsters in the thirties were more inclined than their predecessors to fight back. In 1939, 80 of them angrily surrounded a monitor who was slapping one boy hard. The "revolt" not only stopped that particular beating but finally ended corporal punishment at the HOA. By then, however, the institution was in its last days. "A ghost asylum," in Bogen's words, it officially closed in September 1941.[27]

"Ghost" institutions abounded by the early 1940s. As they again faced plummeting enrollments and pressure from the advocates of adoption and foster care, many institutions shut down, altered their missions, or sought new leadership. For example, when William Hammitt became the superintendent of The Baby Fold in 1939, he discovered what he described as "a 19th century Dickensian orphanage." Since its founding in 1902 this Methodist institution in central Illinois had cared for hundreds of infants and small children. But the depression had taken a terrible toll. The children's iron bedsteads lacked mattresses, and equipment, including a furnace and an ancient washing machine, kept breaking down. Rats were a major problem. Hammitt recalled one night when the screams of a small girl brought him running: "a full-grown rat had tried to jump from her bed to the windowsill, and had landed in a metal wastebasket with a mighty thud." Like managers of orphanages across the country, Hammitt faced the challenge of trying to save an institution. "We had to bring it into the twentieth century," he said. That task involved such basic changes as introducing systematic record keeping and implementing a standardized admissions form. During its first four decades, The Baby Fold had not kept permanent files. "The only information available was notes jotted down on the back of envelopes and found in a common box," Hammitt recalled. He struggled successfully over several decades to modernize the buildings, tap new sources of financial support, secure changes in legislation regarding adoptions and foster care, and, ultimately, shift the institution's main attention to children with "special needs."[28]

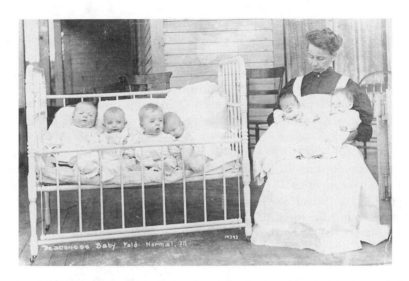

A few of the dependent infants in the care of The Baby Fold in Normal, Illinois, ca. 1908. Photo by C. U. Williams. Courtesy The Baby Fold.

Children ready for a walk outside The Baby Fold, ca. 1915. Photo by C. U. Williams. Courtesy The Baby Fold.

Similarly, Bellefaire, which until 1929 had been the Cleveland Jewish Orphan Asylum, abandoned altogether its care of dependent children and became a residential treatment center for emotionally disturbed children in 1943. Four years earlier, the Brooklyn Hebrew Orphan Asylum sent all its residents to foster homes and closed down. In the 1950s Good Will Farm, which George W. Hinckley had founded over half a century earlier to care for dependent, underprivileged youths, became a prep school; dormitories replaced the cottage system.[29]

States also phased out programs and institutions that had housed dependent children. Starting in 1936, the Indiana Soldiers' and Sailors' home, which had existed since 1865, began seeking alternative placements for as many children as possible. Within seven years, the asylum's enrollment fell from more than nine hundred to less than four hundred. In 1941 the Missouri legislature abolished the state home for dependent children at Carrollton and limited its enrollment to youngsters who were "feeble-minded" or had epilepsy. Four years later the Minnesota State Public School also stopped sheltering dependent, neglected children and accepted only trainable youths with learning problems.[30]

V

A major federal program, Aid to Dependent Children (ADC), hastened the decline of traditional orphanages and marked a watershed in child welfare. As Title IV of the 1935 Social Security Act, ADC represented the most important federal commitment to dependent children up to that point in U.S. history. Yet the complex planning and legislative process relegated it to a secondary position, sharply limited its application, and left it vulnerable to attack as a stigmatized form of public assistance.

ADC grew out of mothers' pensions, which all but two states had established by 1935. The wide state support for such pensions was misleading, however, because mothers' aid was minuscule (as low as $4.33 per month in Arkansas and under $25 in 26 other states), permissive (which meant that most local areas did not in fact participate), tied to vague "moral fitness" criteria, and at the mercy of local politics and prejudices. For example, in 1931, Florida and North Carolina each granted aid to only one African American family. In Marion County, Indiana, where African Americans comprised 11 percent of the population, none qualified for pensions. A study of the racial composition of mothers' pensions across the nation revealed that 96 percent of the mothers were white, 3 percent were black (with around half of them in Pennsylvania and Ohio), and 1 percent were "other." Moreover, the level of support was shrinking because the depression forced many counties to discontinue pensions altogether. In 1931 probably less than 1 percent of all children under age 14 benefited from mothers' aid. Still, despite their meager allotments, the pensions very much influenced ADC.[31]

By 1933, with the coming of President Franklin Roosevelt's New Deal, the economic crisis had raised more forcefully than ever the issue of government's responsibility to provide at least some collective security against the vicissitudes of the market, illness, injury, and retirement. The widening effects of social misery galvanized a variety of groups and movements that demanded not only immediate emergency relief but protection from subsequent social and economic disasters as well. Citizens expressed their discontent by joining unemployed councils, labor unions, Dr. Francis Townsend's old age pension movement, and Louisiana senator Huey Long's Share the Wealth campaign. Under increasing pressure from these grassroots protests and from his advisers, Roosevelt in mid-1934 created a Committee on Economic Security (CES) to draft a "social security" plan that went beyond the New Deal's emergency relief programs and established permanent governmental strategies to deal with recurrent problems such as unemployment. He specifically rejected controversial public works and medical insurance programs.[32]

Although the CES turned its energies primarily to devising an unemployment program, there was little doubt that dependent children would receive some kind of assistance. In the House of Representatives, for example, Arkansas Democrat Claude Fuller ringingly endorsed aid for "the helpless mother, the dependent, neglected, and crippled children." He envisioned a future in which "the dependent and neglected boy who never knew the love and guidance of father and mother" would grow up "extolling the grandeur of his country and the loyalty due the Stars and Stripes." Fuller also summoned up images of "the careworn and dejected widow" shouting with happiness after learning that she would receive financial aid for her children. Although no controversy existed about including ADC provisions in the envisioned Social Security Act, the nature of those provisions was neither clear nor of central concern to the CES. To draft an ADC program, the CES turned to the Children's Bureau.[33]

ADC's secondary status within the contemplated social security program was evident immediately in the CES decision not to include Bureau representatives in its top councils. And on Capitol Hill, Fuller's words attested more to the appeal of childhood and motherhood than to Congress's willingness to fund a major program. Edwin F. Witte, the economist whom Roosevelt chose to direct the CES, subsequently emphasized that Congress had "little interest" in the Social Security Act's sections pertaining to children.[34]

Even the women at the Children's Bureau, who hoped mainly to lay the foundation for a federal public health program, responded timidly to ADC and recycled the central assumptions of mothers' pensions. The Bureau remained a bastion of the "mothers' aid group," in the words of one New Dealer. Under the guidance of Progressive-Era social work pioneers such as

Katharine Lenroot, it continued to champion policies by which professionals used social services, including mothers' pensions, to educate and rescue individuals from the grip of poverty. These aging progressives did not attribute poverty to character flaws, but they believed that poverty encouraged bad habits that individuals could overcome through the tutorial guidance of trained caseworkers. And to erase the stigma of charity from programs that aided children and single mothers, the progressives had built mothers' pensions around "deserving" women. In that spirit Edith Abbott, a social work trailblazer, assured a congressional committee in 1935 that the 50 percent or so of needy single-mother families that would qualify for ADC would be "nice" and have "really nice children." Although the Bureau's staffers continued to see children's assistance as the cornerstone for a larger welfare system, they also clung to the belief that parenting was primarily the mothers' responsibility. Not surprisingly, the ADC provisions that Lenroot, Grace Abbott, and Bureau assistant chief Martha Eliot drafted for the CES reflected these assumptions.[35]

To a number of key New Dealers, however, the Children's Bureau overlooked the real issue: income maintenance. Roosevelt adviser Harry Hopkins thus dismissed the Bureau-type social workers as "pantry snoopers" who were more interested in meddling in the lives of individual families than in providing a necessary income. Within months after Roosevelt took office, Hopkins became the administrator of the Federal Emergency Relief Act (FERA), the first federal aid program, and immediately poured millions of dollars into emergency relief. Although the FERA did not concentrate on children's needs, its generous programs helped perhaps three times the number of children as did mothers' pensions. Hopkins favored an ambitious, comprehensive welfare program, free of the elitism and condescension toward the poor that he associated with the Children's Bureau. FERA representatives such as Josephine Brown thus pressed Witte's planning group to place aid to dependent children within the larger context of income maintenance, rather than limit ADC to a child-oriented service. Direct economic assistance, from this perspective, was more important than rehabilitating families. In this context, the FERA defined need broadly and, according to Brown, "would have provided aid within the limits of available funds to practically every family in need in which there was a child under sixteen."[36]

Indeed, the FERA was able to push its sweeping definition of child dependency into the Social Security bill that went to Congress: Dependent children included anyone under 16 for whom "no adult person, other than one needed to care for the children," could "work and provide a reasonable subsistence compatible with decency and health." This definition broadened the concept of dependent children to include those who live in two-parent families in which unemployment or underemployment prevailed, or in foster homes, or with relatives. Members of the Children's Bureau had lost this stage of the legislative battle. To them, such wording undercut hard-won standards of child care and represented a throwback to the inadequacies and stigma of poor relief.[37]

Congress, however, not only rejected the FERA definition of child dependency but also adopted a Social Security Act that made ADC an "also-ran" program, inferior in every respect to the law's adult-oriented sections. The act's final version demonstrated the strength of two main forces: policy-makers who favored social insurance and the grassroots champions of old age pensions. Planners such as Witte viewed social insurance as a way to provide security to wage earners by spreading the risks of the marketplace. More sweepingly, it would vitalize and rationalize the national economy by evening out the employment cycles with predictable, across-the-board entitlements, rather than arbitrary, stigmatized forms of public assistance. The social insurance thinkers gave little attention to children's (or mothers') issues because they assumed that unemployment insurance would automatically benefit dependent children. Because they were determined to distinguish the controversial Social Security programs of Old-Age Insurance and Unemployment Compensation from the dole, they separated them from public assistance programs such as ADC. On Capitol Hill, whereas social insurance had the support of wage earners and the elderly, children had no equivalent lobbying group. In the words of one scholar, "The dependent children, unfortunately, cannot vote," and poor, single mothers hardly constituted a powerful constituency.[38]

As a consequence of these factors, the Social Security Act established a two-track welfare system. One track was oriented toward social insurance, whereby government would make up for wages lost through injuries, unemployment, or retirement; the other focused on public assistance. Within this dual scheme, social insurance (in the form of unemployment benefits and old age pensions) flowed automatically from one's condition; public assistance (in the form of ADC) was discretionary and smacked of charity.[39]

ADC's final provisions dramatized the marginal position of programs relating to children. Congress rejected the FERA's broad definition of dependency in favor of one limited to children who were "deprived of parental support or care by reason of the death, continued absence from the home, or physical or mental capacity of a parent." The maximum funding that the federal government provided was $18 for the first child and $12 for any others—a sum that Edwin Witte described as "utterly inadequate and completely out of line with pensions of $30 per month to individual old people." Congress also made clear its priorities by limiting federal matching funds for children to one-third of that spent by state governments—as opposed to one-half for old age and disability pensions. ADC's designation as a public assistance program added to its second-class status; it was charity, in contrast to the social insurance programs, in which people contributed to a fund and supposedly got back what was theirs. At the end of the legislative process, even the Children's Bureau lost out. In the original bill, the Bureau was to administer

ADC; in the final version, ADC became the purview of a new Bureau of Public Assistance, housed within the Social Security Board. "It was only at the last minute that I knew the administration of mothers' pensions had been changed," a dumbfounded Katharine Lenroot wrote Grace Abbott, who worried that ADC would now resemble poor relief. The altered administrative responsibilities marked a shift in emphasis. Although the Children's Bureau, like Congress, favored a nonuniversal program such as ADC, the Bureau had historically been an advocate for children whom it viewed as the entering wedge for a more general system of social services. This "children-first strategy" collapsed with Social Security, as historian Linda Gordon has written. The result was "a system in which children are arguably the social group least well served by welfare policy, particularly in comparison with the elderly."[40]

Congress also chose to weaken ADC by enlarging state control over it. Virginia senator Harry Byrd successfully removed from the original bill a proviso that states had to guarantee "reasonable subsistence compatible to decency and health" to qualify for federal funds. By allowing states to determine the level of public support, Byrd's amendment aided local authorities who feared that wage earners might refuse to work for low pay if they did not have to worry about supporting dependents. ADC thus lacked consistency of coverage or standards. In addition, some states chose not even to join the program. Mississippi, for example, quickly implemented the old age pension part of the Social Security Act but did not start an ADC program until 1941. Louisiana started a program in 1936 but in 1943 stopped or refused assistance to anyone whose labor was needed in the cotton fields. Arkansas in 1939 paid families under ADC only $8.10 per month.[41]

Another major concession to state interests came in the form of a "suitable home" eligibility requirement. Although the Social Security Act did not require the eligibility condition for aid, it permitted states to do so. The various morals criteria, like those of mothers' pensions earlier, implicitly raised suspicions about single mothers' laziness and sexual permissiveness—suspicions that haunted ADC. From the beginning, the administrators of ADC had trouble setting priorities: whether to meet the economic needs of children or judge the morals and values of adults. As historian Roy Lubove has written, "vague moralistic imperatives competed with objective economic needs," undercutting any claims that dependent children had a right to public assistance. Moreover, the "suitable home" requirements tended to be sharply discriminatory, especially against African Americans in the South. One ADC field supervisor reported from a southern state that local boards saw "no reason why the employable Negro mother should not continue her usually sketchy seasonal labor or indefinite domestic service rather than receive a public assistance grant." The boards assumed "that 'they [African Americans] have always gotten along,' and that 'all they'll do is have more children.' "[42]

As halting and limited as ADC was, it nevertheless marked an important beginning. Whereas mothers' pensions had been state programs, ADC represented a federal commitment to aiding dependent children. Over the years, the program grew. After Congress increased the federal matching funds to one-half (as opposed to one-third) in 1940, states such as Illinois and Mississippi finally started ADC programs. Within a year after Illinois joined ADC in 1942, three times as many children were receiving aid as had been the case under the earlier mothers' pension law; in Cook County that figure was six times as many. Nationally, in 1931 only 94,000 families in the United States had received mothers' pensions; in 1940, however, 372,000 families benefited from ADC and received larger monthly payments ($32 as opposed to $22). Nevertheless, the number of destitute children across the United States who received little or no assistance remained huge. *Washington Post* columnist Ernest K. Lindley noted that some 13 million children under 15 lived in families with less than an $800 annual income. The Social Security Act, he believed, had short-changed them.[43]

But even a limited ADC program was politically vulnerable, largely because its beneficiaries had little power. That vulnerability increased in 1939 after a Social Security amendment moved deserving widows and their children into the Old Age Insurance program (which at that point became Old Age and Survivors Insurance). "The ADC example we always thought about," said the first executive director of the Social Security Board, Frank Bane, "was the poor lady in West Virginia whose husband had been killed in a mining accident, and the problem of how she could feed those kids." After 1939, ADC's constituency included mainly single mothers who had been deserted or were divorced or unmarried—people for whom the public had less sympathy. Moreover, the administrative unit within the Social Security Board had neither the experience nor the inclination to fight in behalf of single mothers and their children. By the forties, the political logic of the situation thus did not augur well for ADC. It was politically "an orphan," in the words of one scholar.[44]

VI

Child dependency at least gained a tenuous place within federal welfare policies, whereas issues of child neglect, abuse, and placement were generally ignored. Reductions in child welfare agencies and staff during the depression and war partially explained the downplaying of these issues. (As late as mid-1946, fewer than one in five counties in the United States hired at least one full-time child welfare person.)[45] Another reason reflected the general reluctance to judge too harshly families who were coping with depression and then war. As the nation struggled through some of the worst crises in its history, popular culture and professionals alike encouraged family unity. Where abuse was evident, authorities typically tried to resolve the problem, not prosecute the offender. True, the wartime employment of many women raised fears about "eight-hour orphans" and "latchkey" children. For example, in 1943 a Los Angeles social worker found 45 infants locked in cars in a parking lot of a war plant where their mothers worked. J. Edgar Hoover of the Federal Bureau of Investigation warned that latchkey children faced "a dismal future," one that could include delinquency, imprisonment, and, ultimately, even "maiming and plundering." Overall, however, the children of working mothers were not victims of neglect. Most of the mothers worked out arrangements whereby relatives, neighbors, or friends supervised the children during work hours. At the time, moreover, even those children who did suffer neglect and abuse hardly distracted the public from other wartime concerns. News about the battlefront and domestic efforts to win the war overwhelmed reports of "eight-hour orphans." The prevailing view seemed to echo the conclusion of the 1930 White House Conference on Child Health and Protection that "the grosser forms of physical cruelty are not so prevalent as they were a few decades ago."[46]

Psychoanalytic thinking helped to bolster such a conclusion among a new generation of child-care professionals, eager to shed what one of them, Dorothy Berkowitz, described as the "unconscious Jehovah complexes" that had characterized their predecessors. Whereas in 1916 a private family caseworker had instructed a client "to stop drinking," many social workers by the thirties were inclined to see such instructions as counterproductive and authoritarian. But as they became more appreciative of the complexities of the human condition, they also lost a sense of optimistic possibilities. "If we could not cure," wrote Berkowitz, "we could not help at all." In this context, child protective work came to represent "the drudgery, if not the downright dregs, of our case loads."[47]

By then, too, a dominant theme in psychoanalytic thinking discounted childhood sexual abuse as largely fantasy. The fate of Sigmund Freud's "seduction" theory was vital in this respect. In the late 1890s Freud had decided that his earlier attribution of various psychological problems to childhood sexual traumas was incorrect. He concluded that memories of childhood sexual abuse rested on unconscious wishes rather than actual experiences.

Psychiatrists subsequently tended to ignore his continuing belief that sexual abuse of children was nevertheless a reality. Freud, for example, was appalled when a patient told him that her father had raped and infected her with gonorrhea when she was two. In the face of such horror Freud drew upon a line from Goethe: "A new motto: What have they done to you, poor child." In spite of this, psychiatry's overall rejection of the seduction theory encouraged the view that sexual abuse was rare and that children often lied about it. In 1937 two prominent American psychiatrists not only denied that sexual assault traumatized most children but argued that "the child may have been the actual seducer rather than the one innocently seduced." A year earlier, an American Bar Association report had recommended psychiatric evaluations of women and children who brought charges of incest, rape, and molestation. According to the report, "the erotic imagination of an abnormal child of attractive appearance may send a man to the penitentiary for life." The report's main author, legal scholar John Henry Wigmore, claimed in his textbook on evidence that the "innocent man" was usually the real victim.[48]

Blaming the child or treating cruelty in a lighthearted fashion surfaced in popular culture as well. When the hero in the 1945 movie *Frontier Gal* spanks his daughter, she is grateful that he treats her "like other girls." Subsequently, the daughter tells another person, "If he beats you, it's because he loves you."[49]

In this popular and professional climate, youthful victims of abuse received little hearing, particularly if sex was involved. A sampling of children who lived in orphanages during World War II, for example, suggested that although sexual abuse in such institutions was substantial, it was dormant as an issue. Indeed, as late as the mid-1950s, a psychiatric supervisor was furious when a social worker told him about a 12-year-old client who divulged that her father had for two years engaged in incestuous relationships with her. The supervisor was angry, not about what had happened to the girl, but about the social worker's conversation with her. The girl, he argued, obviously felt guilty about wanting to sleep with her father.[50]

While concerns about abuse and neglect ebbed, child placement also faded as an issue. Demographics played a crucial role in this respect. In the midthirties, foster care started a downward trend that lasted for more than two decades. A record 59 of every 10,000 children in the United States were in foster care in 1933; by 1960 the number was 38 per 10,000. ADC contributed heavily to this trend by providing federal funds to keep children in their own homes. The once-compelling slogan of the Children's Home Society—"There is a child outside our door"—no longer seemed relevant.[51]

Typically, however, statistics obscured actual experiences. In 1943 a survey of 10 homes in Tennessee that boarded children found twin two-year-olds in the care of a 79-year-old blind woman who was losing her mind. Officials also discovered 16 children living in the attic of a home that failed to pass a fire inspection.[52]

The experience of Richard W. Carlson was bittersweet. In the early 1940s in Boston, his mother, a high school student, left her illegitimate baby at the Home for Little Wanderers. "Home Wanted for Foundling," the orphanage advertised in the city's newspapers. Carl and Florence Moberger, who already had three children, agreed to care for Richard while letting families look him over for possible adoption. The Mobergers wanted to adopt him themselves but the orphanage preferred to find a childless couple. For two years Richard lived happily with the Mobergers while prospective parents stopped by occasionally to see him. "I would have the chocolate wiped from my face, my hands washed and would be trotted out," he recalled. At the time, the youngster never understood why people were visiting him. Then, in the spring of 1943, three women came to the Moberger home. Florence Moberger sensed immediately that they were there to remove the child, but she decided not to tell him what was happening. She also chose not to summon her three children from school or her husband from work to say good-bye to Richard; in her opinion, the moment would simply have been too wrenching for them. Knowing that he liked to ride in cars, she told the child that the women wanted to take him for a drive. As Moberger informed him 40 years later, when she and Richard finally saw each other again, "You waved at the house from the back seat of the car as you all drove away. That was the last time we saw you. We never did get over it." Richard, in contrast, eventually forgot all about the Mobergers. Looking back, he considered himself lucky that the Mobergers and, subsequently, the Carlsons had taken good care of him. "It wasn't a perfect beginning, but it was better than many. Life is tough."[53]

VII

For many dependent, neglected, and abused children, life was indeed tough, but the public barely noticed, even without the distractions of the depression and World War II. During the immediate postwar era, institutions continued to decline or alter their missions; the growing ADC lists provided paltry support to relatively few families while evoking intense criticism; adoptions increased, but with all too little scrutiny, as the number of children in foster care dropped; and child abuse was a seldom-discussed subject.

In 1944 Howard Hopkirk, director of the Child Welfare League of America, offered a generally discouraging report on the falling status of children's institutions. Although he believed orphanages still met an urgent need, he found far too many "backward institutions" that were mismanaged and depressing. He bemoaned "the ignorance of the personnel, the insufficiency of clothing and diet, and the severity and discipline." Vocational training in most institutions was little more than "a maximum of drudgery" that included "prolonged hours of hoeing, weeding gardens, washing pots and pans, ironing, scrubbing or polishing floors." Probably half of the nation's institutions, in his opinion, showed no more concern for the children than had the earliest orphanages, and a "confusion of responsibilities" within states made a bad situation worse. Separate studies in Illinois in 1940 and 1943 confirmed Hopkirk's conclusions. Within the Illinois system, poor record keeping and a "bewildering maze" of agencies prevailed; outside the system, large groups of children received no services.[54]

ADC helped growing numbers of these children, albeit inadequately. In 1950, 651,000 families received ADC benefits, a jump of 75 percent from a decade earlier. Although such support allowed more children than before to stay with their mothers, its trifling amount kept families in poverty. Across the nation by 1960, the average monthly cash payment was only $30 per recipient.[55]

National developments, moreover, helped to build an unfriendly political climate for ADC. Although the depression was over, the end of World War II brought its own kind of economic and social discontent. Some communities that boomed during the war slumped afterward. Many people uprooted themselves in search of better opportunities in other areas or nearby suburbs. An increase in divorces as well as the growing size of the population of children under 18 (from 40 million in 1940 to 65 million in 1960) added to the number of families that needed aid. Although the divorce rate dropped after hitting a record high in 1946, broken marriages stirred considerable uneasiness. "The American Family in Trouble," warned *Life* magazine in mid-1948. Given the sense of dislocation and instability that bothered many Americans in the forties and fifties, ADC's vulnerability to political and racial attacks was not surprising.[56]

ADC became a popular target of postwar opposition to the New Deal's welfare legacy. Politicians attacked welfare fraud, typically tying it to the issue of race. After the 1939 Social Security amendments moved widows and orphans from ADC to social insurance, ADC's evolving clientele included more nonwhite and illegitimate children, a change that made the program more vulnerable to criticism. "Baby Racket?" asked *The Atlanta Constitution* in 1951, summoning up images of a host of ADC "chiselers." Although an investigation of California's Department of Social Welfare in 1958–59 turned up only about 1.5 percent of families that received aid fraudulently, ADC critics bandied about the figure of 15 percent and even referred to fraud as a "caseload characteristic." In 1959 Arkansas governor Orville Faubus declared that, "by taxing the good people to pay for these programs, we are putting a premium on illegitimacy never before known in the world." A city council member in Newburgh, New York, insisted first that "this is not a racial issue" but then referred to "a naturally lazy people." A panel in Atlantic City, New Jersey, objected that "immorality, promiscuity, and unwed motherhood seem to be rewarded and encouraged by the easy allowance made upon a simple application of need." By 1961 journalist Meg Greenfield found a "strong conviction that the poor are carrying out some sort of . . . conspiracy in a depressing world where vast numbers of chiselers and slug-a-beds buy not only whiskey but automobiles with their relief money."[57]

In the 1950s a number of states added to their vague and subjective "suitable home" eligibility requirements. Efforts to find a man in the house— "Rodger the Lodger" was one nickname for him—accelerated because children who lived with two able-bodied parents were not eligible for ADC. The assumption was that "men in the home" were in fact "substitute parents." Officials used various kinds of surveillance, from round-the-clock observation of homes to surprise visits. Investigators reportedly received instructions "to look in the bedroom, look in the closets, look behind the shower curtain, look in the drawers for articles of clothing." Without a warrant, a Chicago investigator barged past a nine-year-old girl who answered the door while her mother was taking a bath. Because the investigator found a man's suit in the closet and assumed that the woman was living full-time with a man, he discontinued ADC.[58]

Louisiana took the most drastic steps, however. In 1960 the legislature ordered that no ADC assistance should go to a child living with a mother who had given birth to an illegitimate baby after she started receiving benefits. The law was retroactive, according to the state's attorney general, which meant that it applied even to mothers whose children had been born out of wedlock many years before. Between June and September 1960, more than 6,000 Louisiana families with 23,459 children suddenly lost their benefits. Fewer than 1 percent of the mothers who lost assistance were guilty of neglect or abuse. The issue was overwhelmingly that of illegitimacy.[59]

By 1960 these campaigns in Louisiana and elsewhere against "unsuitable" ADC homes ensured that many destitute children received no aid. Seventy-nine of 1,000 children under age 18 in the United States lived in families whose annual incomes were under $1,500. Yet ADC grants went to only 33 out of 1,000.[60]

The issue of illegitimacy affected not only ADC but child removal as well. By the forties, social workers were rethinking their position on illegitimacy and adoption. A few years earlier the main objective had been to keep mother and child together, and to use adoption only as a final resort. But as one child welfare worker wrote in 1943, the newly dominant and "equally sincere conviction" held that an unwed mother would probably not be a good parent and her child would be "overpoweringly stigmatised."[61]

This revised opinion reflected the growth in illegitimate births among teenagers, especially during the war. But it also attested to the swelling demand for adoptions. That demand owed much to the continuing sentimentalization of childhood—the recognition that, although children were no longer "useful" economically, they were "priceless" objects of affection. Little girls were especially popular in this regard, according to one source, as dolls upon which doting parents "could tie pink sashes." Adoptive parents tended to come from the emerging middle class, as a Minnesota study in the twenties discovered; the fathers were usually professionals, managers, or at least white-collar workers.[62]

In the decade after 1934, legal adoptions tripled. Between 1944 and 1955, they increased by another 80 percent. Many white adoptive parents, anxious to join the postwar rush to build families, ignored the traditional wisdom that illegitimate children carried the taint of sin. The result was a "postwar white adoption mandate," according to historian Rickie Solinger. Although this emerging adoption mandate continued to stigmatize illegitimate black children, it made "market commodities" of "white, pregnant, unmarried women and their babies." As relatively well-to-do, childless families searched for adoptive babies, an illegal network flourished, especially in the quest for white infants. "The baby market is booming," reported one journal as early as 1937. "The clamor is for babies, more babies. . . . We behold a country-wide scramble on the part of childless couples to adopt a child." Magazines featured articles on baby "boot-legging," "Bargain-Counter Babies," and "Moppets on the Market." In 1940 a celebrated "baby farm" exposé in Chicago showed that, over a seven-year period, almost two thousand babies, some of whom were kidnapped, had been sold out of a home on Winnemac Avenue.[63]

By 1938, to discourage this underground marketing of small children, 37 states had enacted licensing systems for placement agencies, and an almost equal number had by the early forties revised antiquated adoption laws. The old laws, according to William Hammitt of The Baby Fold, were typically no more than simple legal transactions that gave the adoptive family "a clear title of ownership." Matters of "character, health, mentality, or moral fitness" were, he recalled, virtually irrelevant. Shortly after becoming superintendent of The Baby Fold in 1939, Hammitt cochaired a drive to modernize what one reporter described as "Illinois' archaic, 70-year-old adoption law." Under the law's no-questions-asked policy, the state's courts processed one-sixth of the adoptions in the United States. "We have become for adoptions what Reno has become for divorces!" Hammitt protested in 1944. Many state judges and politicians nevertheless liked the system. "They felt," Hammitt recalled, "that what they were doing with movie stars and political figures [who] were flying in and out of Cook County [to adopt a child] was wonderful, and that it was great for these children who could be put in such homes." In 1945, however, the reformers prevailed, securing a law that required an investigation of the backgrounds of the child and the adoptive parents, the birth mother's written consent, and a six-month probationary period before the adoption became final.[64]

Five years later a major scandal erupted in Tennessee, which had no such law. Since the 1930s a number of respected people in the state had profited from a black market baby-selling business. The legislature facilitated the operation by refusing to modify a 1937 law that permitted adoptive parents to come from out of state, get their new child, and leave the same day. The Tennessee Children's Home Society in Memphis, in league with key officials, used various kinds of duplicity to find and place the children, in some cases with movie stars. In September 1950 Governor Gordon Browning broke the news about the scandal at a midnight news conference. He described a shocking adoption-for-profit scheme that had involved some 1,500 babies over the previous 10 years. Fraud and deception had been rampant. In some instances, poor parents had not known they were relinquishing their children permanently. Adoptive families had received fictitious information about the backgrounds of children. Physicians and attorneys had coerced unwed mothers to give up their babies. Key individuals behind the scandal used other strategies, such as searching for a father of small children who had just lost his job. A judge would then promptly label the children as dependent and neglected, remove them from their family, and formalize an adoption agreement without the natural parents' consent.[65]

Even after the Tennessee scandal, stories continued to surface about questionable and illegal interstate adoptions elsewhere in the United States. In 1955 the reports prompted Tennessee senator Estes Kefauver to conduct hearings to publicize an interstate commercial racket that reportedly netted $15 million annually from the traffic in children. A year later the Senate approved legislation outlawing interstate adoptions of children for profit, but the bill died in the House of Representatives. The bill met a similar fate in 1963 and 1964.[66]

VIII

By the end of the 1950s, there was thus much to lament about the status of dependent, neglected, and abused children in the United States. Yet hints of change were also evident. Despite the backlash against ADC, by 1960 a record number of 803,000 children were receiving benefits, and Louisiana's decision to deny assistance to more than 23,000 of them spurred federal action to strengthen the program. Overall, as well, a sustained economic boom augured well for additional child welfare funds. The budding civil rights movement favored the rights of children generally, as well as other groups. And in 1961 a symposium of medical leaders focused on child abuse, setting the stage for a concept that jolted the public: the "battered child."[67]

7

Children's Issues as Battleground, 1960–1980

Few years have been more significant for dependent, neglected, and abused children than those from the early 1960s to the 1980s. In the sixties, a rights explosion and the medical "discovery" of the "battered child" propelled children's issues to unprecedented levels of public awareness and action. States responded to physicians' shocking reports about the physical abuse of children by creating a flood of reporting laws and by redefining neglect. Between the end of 1960 and February 1969, Aid to Dependent Children (ADC), by liberalizing its qualifications, added eight hundred thousand families to its rolls—an increase of 107 percent. Foster care and adoption also received unparalleled attention and generated major policy changes.[1]

Yet these changes hardly signified a general agreement on policy or even the nature of the problems. Indeed, policies moved in contradictory directions and invariably touched off heated opposition. Confusion, not consensus, prevailed. As a result, one of the most productive eras regarding child welfare was also among the most embattled.

I

In the 1960s the civil rights movement galvanized a dramatic rights upheaval that exerted a profound influence on the status and welfare of children. Significantly, the Supreme Court's 1954 *Brown v. Board of Education* decision, one of the landmarks in the civil rights movement, centered on children; by seizing the issue of racially separate but unequal public schools, civil rights advocates found their most effective weapon against segregation. Another of the movement's compelling moments occurred in May 1963, when thousands of African American children marched through the streets of Birmingham, Alabama, bearing witness against segregation. "What really sticks in my mind," recalled one individual, "is seeing a K-9 dog being sicced on a six-year old girl. . . . a big, burly two-hundred-and-eighty-five pound cop siccing a trained police dog on that little black girl. And then I got really involved in the Movement."[2]

The quest for civil rights spread like a chain reaction, producing what sociologist Herbert J. Gans labeled "the 'equality' revolution." By the end of the 1960s cries against discrimination and demands for rights echoed across the nation, from the slum neighborhoods of Newark and Detroit to the barrios of the Southwest and San Francisco's Chinatown district, from feminist protests to Gay Liberation parades, from shouts of "student power" on campuses and in high-school classrooms to the symbolic takeover of Alcatraz Island by a group of Native Americans. In that context, the cause of children's rights also gained support.[3]

Fifteen-year-old Gerald Gault was an unlikely protagonist in that struggle. Police arrested him in the midsixties for making obscene telephone calls, and an Arizona juvenile court judge sentenced him to reform school. But in 1967 the U.S. Supreme Court ruled that the juvenile court system had denied the boy's basic procedural rights. "Neither the Fourteenth Amendment nor the Bill of Rights is for adults alone," ruled the Court. According to the *Gault* decision, children were guaranteed basic constitutional rights to an attorney, to confront witnesses, and to refuse self-incrimination. The justices in the *Gault* decision, moreover, rejected the logic of the famous 1838 *Crouse* ruling that institutionalization was treatment, not punishment. Because the Court limited its decision to "delinquents" subject to incarceration, however, the *Gault* ruling allowed officials to devise new labels and "alternative" punishments for juvenile offenders. Juvenile courts thus continued to carry heavy administrative loads that often included newly designated "persons in need of supervision"—noncriminals whom some states continued to deny the procedural rights that *Gault* otherwise required. Still, despite its narrow focus, the *Gault* decision advanced considerably the idea of children's rights by saying that the Bill of Rights did not apply solely to adults. *Gault* and a number of subsequent rulings made the important point that the state must treat children justly.[4]

Such concern for the fair treatment of children featured a new twist. Traditional child protection campaigns had been steeped in paternalism, emphasizing not the autonomy of children but the responsibility of society to ensure their safety. But in the sixties, some activists promoted a liberationist view that paternalistic safeguards in fact placed children at risk by denying their basic rights.

By the midseventies the liberationist message appeared in several noteworthy publications, especially Richard Farson's *Birthrights* (1974) and John Holt's *Escape from Childhood* (1974). Describing children as "powerless, dominated, ignored, invisible," Farson urged society to recognize children's "right to full humanity," and to do so on their own terms, as children, "not just as potential adults." Holt regretted that childhood smacked of subserviency and dependency, "of being seen by older people as a mixture of expensive nuisance, slave, and super pet." Like Farson, Holt insisted that children should have the same rights as adults, or, in Holt's words, "the right to do, in general, what any adult may legally do."[5]

In 1977 the Carnegie Council on Children observed that recent legal trends had moved "decidedly in the direction of granting children greater legal rights and responsibilities." That year the American Civil Liberties Union (ACLU) helped to document this trend by publishing a handbook, *The Rights of Young People*. The ACLU's goal was not to articulate the liberationist message but simply to catalogue existing legal rights that children should know about in areas that included adoption, foster care, and neglect. A main point in the handbook was that "many laws which purport to protect young people have in practice rendered them subject to arbitrary and excessive authority exercised by parents, custodians and the state."[6]

These discussions of rights once again revealed the ambiguous nature of childhood. In response to the liberationists, some skeptics warned against having children rely on the courts and adversarial processes. The 1977 Carnegie report applauded the growing recognition of children's rights but fretted about an incoherent case-by-case approach. The popular children's writer Shel Silverstein twitted the liberationists: "Strike! Strike! For Children's Rights / Longer weekends / Shorter school hours / Higher allowances / Less baths and showers / No Brussels sprouts / More root beer / And seventeen summer vacations a year / If you're ready to strike—line up right here."[7]

Some critics believed that the liberationists themselves endangered children. In the midseventies, one law professor warned against "abandoning children to their 'rights.' " A decade later, in 1986, a Cincinnati juvenile court judge took that warning to heart when he ruled against 16-year-old John Grundy, who had just won a $1 million lottery and wanted the court to emancipate him from his divorced mother so that he could, among other things, buy a car. The judge concluded that Grundy was not yet ready for adult status that would, in fact, place the teenager at risk. "We have a sixteen year old boy who has dropped out of the seventh grade, who has no plans for accounting or investing," the judge said. "Granting him his adulthood would not be in his best interests." Wait until you are 18, the judge instructed Grundy.[8]

II

Although the liberationists raised significant questions about children's rights, the familiar paternalistic logic of child protection dominated child welfare policies throughout the sixties and beyond. That logic was essential in breaking down some of the "suitable home" limitations on Aid to Dependent Children. After Louisiana in mid-1960 summarily bumped more than 23,000 children from its ADC rolls, a public outcry pressured Arthur Flemming, President Dwight Eisenhower's secretary of Health, Education, and Welfare, to intervene. On January 17, 1961, just before leaving office, Flemming ruled that Louisiana had to reinstate the children. "A state plan for aid to dependent children," he said, "may not impose an eligibility condition that would deny assistance with respect to a needy child on the basis that the home conditions in which the child lives are unsuitable, while the child continues to reside in the home." States, in sum, still had a responsibility to look out for the children's welfare. In this regard, Flemming echoed well-established child protectionist arguments. He did not, however, challenge the states' moral eligibility standards. His point was simply that a state needed to continue assisting children while it was either improving their home conditions or arranging for foster home or institutional care. According to the "Flemming Rule," in other words, states could still use "suitable home" requirements to punish certain mothers by removing their children. But the expense of finding alternative care for the children in effect discouraged a strict application of such criteria.[9]

ADC soon underwent significant modifications. In the early sixties a combination of the "rediscovery" of poverty, optimism about the nation's future, and the new John F. Kennedy administration resulted in several amendments. Immediately after World War II, in the early phases of the cold war, most Americans had virtually willed themselves not to see poverty in the United States. The media and scholars alike contrasted the nation's prosperity, lack of social turbulence, and apparent classlessness with conditions in the communist world. When the subject of poverty surfaced in the early 1960s in a spate of articles and books, the development owed less to doubts about the future than to a burst of confidence in the United States. America, from this vantage point, was wealthy and inventive enough to combat poverty and could do so without depriving the middle classes. In this setting, poverty became an unacceptable moral blemish—indeed, something that was downright un-American and that had to be defeated. Kennedy and his chief advisers shared this judgment and looked for ways to sustain economic growth, which would in turn, they believed, diminish poverty.[10]

Before Kennedy took office, he consulted a number of experts on Social Security and health about possible legislation to combat poverty. Among them was Wilbur Cohen, who had served on Edwin Witte's Committee on Economic Security during the midthirties. By the time Kennedy entered the White House, Cohen's task force had a series of recommendations regarding welfare reform. Kennedy received additional advice from his secretary of Health, Education, and Welfare, Abraham Ribicoff. As governor of Connecticut, Ribicoff had been "appalled" at the costs and problems of welfare. He informed Kennedy that welfare reform was a "hot issue . . . conservatives are up in arms over the reports of welfare abuses—the ADC mother with a dozen illegitimate kids." The "new direction" that Ribicoff favored would "substitute (over time) services for cash," thereby rehabilitating people on relief and preventing the growth of poverty. Kennedy agreed. The needy, he said, should receive not just a relief check but "positive services and solutions." Many legislators liked the services approach, which they saw as a means to dry up the need for welfare. In 1961–62, with Wilbur Cohen doing the legwork on Capitol Hill, the administration successfully prevailed upon Congress to amend ADC.[11]

Two temporary amendments in 1961 set the stage. One of them endorsed the Flemming Rule by authorizing, for 14 months, ADC funds for foster care when officials removed children from "unsuitable homes." Another amendment, a one-year antirecession measure, provided matching federal funds to states to assist two-parent families in which the wage earner was unemployed and no longer entitled to unemployment benefits. Here was a legislative breakthrough. Under ADC-UP (for "Unemployed Parent"), federal grant-aided assistance was available for the first time to children with two able-bodied parents, if unemployment forced the family income below what the state deemed essential. Although some conservative legislators opposed the program, it appealed to a congressional majority as a way to keep unemployed fathers from deserting their families.[12]

With the 1962 Public Service Amendments to ADC, the federal government moved somewhat more boldly, although still very much within the framework of state permissiveness. Of great symbolic importance, it changed ADC to Aid to Families with Dependent Children (AFDC), a modification that emphasized the larger service objective of getting families off the welfare rolls by, for example, providing counseling. As an inducement to the states, Congress increased federal funding for rehabilitative services from 50 percent to 75 percent. Congress also prolonged indefinitely foster care payments under the Flemming Rule and extended the "unemployed parent" provision for five years. Although only a few states initially chose to participate in the AFDC-UP program, most sought the federal funds for rehabilitative and preventive social services.[13]

Some people believed the amendments did not go far enough. One critic said they offered "an ounce of prevention—and a pound of cure-all." According to a labor activist, the goal of rehabilitation was "almost obscene," given the fact that more than 4 million Americans were jobless. Moreover, although states pursued the 3–1 matching funds to help pay welfare costs, AFDC recipients complained that the resulting social services were insignificant, "little more than a relatively infrequent, pleasant chat," according to one survey. On the other side of the political spectrum, conservatives held up examples of welfare cheats and promiscuous, unmarried mothers.[14]

Despite the criticism from both sides, by the end of 1964 the AFDC rolls numbered 975,000 families. During the next four years, as one of the weapons in President Lyndon Johnson's War on Poverty, AFDC expanded even more dramatically, by 58 percent, enrolling more than 1.5 million families. Additional aid came through the new medical assistance and food stamp programs.[15]

Several factors contributed to AFDC's massive growth. For one thing, the baby boom had expanded considerably the population of children, a growing number of whom lived in single-parent families. For another thing, the advocates of the War on Poverty were genuinely determined to eradicate destitution within the United States. They believed in both the ideal of opportunity and the practical need to free the national economy from the anchor of poverty. The battle against poverty was thus portrayed as good for the soul and a sound investment in the country's economic future. Nor was poverty a mere fantasy. A 1967 survey of AFDC families discovered that 24 percent lacked running water and almost half had been unable to afford milk for their children within the last six months. Partly to bring pressure upon unsympathetic local officials and restrictions, partly to circumvent the federal bureaucracy's traditional interest groups, and partly to involve the relief recipients in their own program, antipoverty planners set up community action centers and neighborhood legal services—"competing institutions for the traditional services of government," as one Johnson adviser described them.[16]

Some welfare mothers seized the opportunity to speak out against the welfare bureaucracy. By the midsixties these mothers had activated a welfare rights movement, mobilizing poor people to act in their own behalf. Organizations such as the National Welfare Rights Organization (NWRO) lobbied for new laws, initiated court cases, and took to the streets. In the fall of 1966, for example, hundreds of New York City clients staged a huge campaign for winter clothing by disrupting four of the city's welfare centers. The next spring, welfare rights protesters in Boston staged a sit-in demonstration at the welfare office, remonstrating against callous and insensitive treatment at the hands of the bureaucracy. A brutal police reaction touched off three days of rioting.[17]

Opposition to AFDC intensified. Some critics opposed it for ideological reasons, as an example of creeping communism. In 1961 Joseph Mitchell, the city manager of Newburgh, New York, had attacked AFDC as the product of "all the mushy rabble of do-gooders and bleeding hearts in society and politics [who] have marched under the Freudian flag toward the omnipotent state of Karl Marx." But the program drew even more fire because of its rapidly changing clientele—mothers who were increasingly nonwhite and unwed. The percentage of unwed mothers who headed AFDC families increased from around 21 percent in 1961 to over 28 percent in 1967. By then the proportion of nonwhites receiving AFDC approached 50 percent. "The problem," as one Illinois child welfare worker had already observed, was becoming "too big and too black." Concerns mounted about a "welfare crisis." Louisiana senator Russell Long described AFDC mothers as "brood mares" who kept adding to the nation's dependent children. Newly elected California governor Ronald Reagan declared, "We are not going to perpetuate poverty by substituting a permanent dole for a paycheck."[18]

In 1967 Congress signaled its nervousness about both the rising social disorder and welfare costs by amending AFDC in favor of "workfare." The focus shifted from "social services" to "employment." To receive AFDC assistance, individuals with children over age six now had to register for work and training. Because such individuals were overwhelmingly women, the amendment marked a dramatic transition in congressional attitudes toward working mothers. Originally, at its incipience in 1935, ADC was supposed to assist poor mothers in caring for their children at home. By 1967 legislators assumed that motherhood was not full-time work and that a solution to poverty was to get jobs for poor women. Before 1967, earned income forced a dollar-for-dollar reduction in AFDC benefits; under the new Work Incentive (WIN) amendment, workers could calculate benefits by exempting from their earnings all work-related expenses, the first $30 in monthly earnings, and one-third of their remaining income.[19]

AFDC expenses still rocketed upward. "It can't go on, it can't go on, but it does," welfare administrators lamented. In part, the growing rolls attested to the success of the NWRO in publicizing welfare rights, distributing information, and encouraging applications. The NWRO received help from the Supreme Court, which in 1968 banned the man-in-the-house rule. "Destitute children who are legally fatherless," the Court ruled unanimously, "cannot be flatly denied federally funded assistance on the transparent fiction that they have a substitute father." A year later, the Court abolished state residency requirements.[20]

Competing trends were also under way, however. "A welfare backlash," according to a September 27, 1970, essay in the *New York Times Magazine*, "was alive in the land." Viewing AFDC as a malevolent creature from the sixties, President Richard Nixon looked for an alternative. When he first campaigned for the presidency in 1960, he had grudgingly indicated that he would have to give a speech on "all that welfare crap." Several advisers, including Arthur Flemming, preferred the term "meeting human needs," but Nixon had snapped back, "I don't care. It *is* crap." As president, according to his chief of staff, H. R. Haldeman, Nixon told his aides "that you have to face the fact that the *whole* problem is really the blacks," who belonged to "the only race" that historically had not been able to build "an adequate . . . nation."[21]

But Nixon surprised many people in 1969 by advocating a substantial welfare reform—a negative income tax, or what the former Harvard scholar Daniel Patrick Moynihan described as an "income strategy" as opposed to a "service strategy." Economist Milton Friedman had originally proposed the idea, which was straightforward: Eliminate the welfare bureaucracy via direct cash payments that would guarantee a subsistence annual income to all individuals who made less than the minimum liable for the federal income tax. The proposed Family Assistance Plan (FAP) included, in the words of an administration memorandum, "a federal floor of income, much work incentive, [and] provisions that if there is an opportunity to work the recipients must work." But the plan encountered opposition from many sides. Liberals worried that the guaranteed income would be inadequate, whereas conservatives feared it would diminish the work ethic. And Nixon himself privately helped to scuttle the FAP. "About Family Assistance," Haldeman wrote in July 1970, Nixon "wants to be sure it's killed by Democrats and that we make big play for it, but don't let it pass, can't afford it."[22]

By 1974 almost 11 percent of American families were on AFDC, up from around 6 percent in 1969 and 4.3 percent in 1965. Although cash payments provided only 38 percent of an AFDC's family's income in 1974 (according to a study of recipients in New York City), in-kind benefits such as food stamps and Medicaid buoyed families up to the poverty line. Over the previous decade, the United States had experienced nothing short of a revolution in social welfare. Most of the growth had occurred in non-means-tested categories such as Social Security, but AFDC had made substantial gains, enrolling 11 million recipients by 1972. "In truth a phenomenal reduction of absolute poverty" had occurred, historian James Patterson concluded. "According to the official, absolute definitions, the number of poor Americans decreased from 39 million (22 percent of the population) in 1959 . . . to 25 million (13 percent) in 1968, to 23 million (11 percent) in 1973."[23]

Yet this success story won little applause. Welfare was an increasingly contentious issue, and AFDC provided the main target for criticism. As the attacks grew, the cries of taxpayers drowned out those of dependent children. Strictly speaking, of course, AFDC centered less on the needs of children than on the economic status of their parents. Indeed, as two social welfare scholars observed in the early 1970s, no program existed yet in the United States "to provide for children because they are children or because they are in need." But even the truth of that statement could not obscure the fact that, because of AFDC benefits, more dependent children were better off than ever before in American history. And it was precisely the fate of those children that the building backlash against AFDC called into question.[24]

III

At first glance, the Supreme Court's 1971 decision in the *Wyman v. James* case seemed just another product of that backlash. When a caseworker visited the home of Barbara James to approve AFDC payments for two-year-old Maurice, the mother refused her entry on grounds that the visit violated Fourth Amendment protections against unreasonable search and seizure. With the backing of

NWRO and affidavits from 15 other AFDC recipients who objected to intrusive social work visits, the case ended up before a Supreme Court with an increasingly conservative reputation. The Court voted six to three against James. Writing for the majority, newly appointed Justice Harry Blackmun noted that James's home had not been subject to forcible entry or snooping. "The caseworker," he wrote, "is not a sleuth but rather, we trust, is a friend to one in need." Historically, of course, such reasoning had provided the rationale for the intrusions of "the Cruelty" and welfare authorities. The three dissenting justices, all holdovers from the Court's more liberal era, viewed the prescribed casework visits as an assault on the rights of poor people. "It is a strange law indeed," asserted William O. Douglas, "which safeguards the businessman [who receives government subsidies] at his place of work from warrantless searches, but will not do the same thing for a mother in her home." The NWRO interpreted the decision as additional evidence of the shifting weight against welfare clients.[25]

The dissents were telling, but Blackmun intimated that he was concerned primarily about the toddler, Maurice. From this perspective, the issue was not about poverty and welfare; it was about the rights of Maurice, the "one in need" who badly needed a friend. The boy had a dent in his head, apparently the result of a mysterious skull fracture. There was, in other words, strong evidence of abuse.[26]

In that context, Blackmun's opinion fit less with the backlash against AFDC than with the recent "rediscovery" of child abuse, largely through the technology of pediatric radiology. Since the mid-1940s, new X-ray techniques had allowed several radiologists to attribute various kinds of "infant trauma" directly to physical abuse—not, as doctors had traditionally done, to diseases such as rickets. Over several years these findings appeared in a dozen or so technical articles in highly specialized journals.

In the midfifties several important reports appeared on the subjects of child abuse and neglect, but they failed to capture much interest. One, in 1955, was the product of Vincent DeFrancis of the American Humane Association, who had conducted the first national survey on the subject a year earlier. DeFrancis wanted child protective workers to deal more actively with instances of suspected neglect, and he urged the federal government to help strengthen protective services. Shortly thereafter, in 1957, the Children's Bureau issued the first major statement from a federal agency that child abuse deserved national attention—a recommendation that state child welfare departments confront abuse and neglect more aggressively.[27]

In Denver, meanwhile, Dr. C. Henry Kempe worried increasingly about the number of children's injuries that, he was certain, parents had deliberately inflicted. Kempe, whose Jewish family had fled Nazi Germany when he was a teenager, had taken charge of the department of pediatrics of the University of Colorado's medical school at age 34. He was dynamic, demanding, and relentless. "When something has to be done," he advised, "forget about your principles and do what's right." In his case that advice meant facing up to the terrible truth that even respectable middle-class parents were brutalizing their children. He pressured several colleagues to gather evidence of suspected child abuse in the Denver hospital. To their surprise, they determined that probably 10 percent of the children whom they treated in the emergency room were victims of mistreatment.[28]

On October 3, 1961, at a dramatic morning session of the American Academy of Pediatrics's 30th annual meeting in Chicago, Kempe and his colleagues conducted a symposium for more than a thousand people. The symposium's title was deliberately provocative: "The Battered-Child Syndrome." A year later Kempe and his collaborators published a seminal paper under the same title in the prestigious *Journal of the American Medical Association*. The journal's accompanying editorial contained a shocking estimate: Abuse killed more children than did diseases such as leukemia or perhaps even auto accidents. "The battered-child syndrome," according to Kempe and his four coauthors, was "a clinical condition in young children who have received serious physical abuse, generally from a parent or a foster parent." Significantly, the abusers were often "people with good education and stable financial and social background." Moreover, there was some evidence "that the attacking parent was subjected to similar abuse in childhood." Kempe and his team urged their colleagues to report child battering to the authorities and recommended treatment for the abusers.[29]

With stunning quickness, the "battered-child syndrome" triggered a huge response. By focusing on the child as victim, the label evoked sympathy. And because the concept bore the stamp of the highly respected medical profession, it seemed authoritative and scientifically objective. Within four years some three hundred scholarly articles appeared on the subject. Although there was no evidence that child abuse was a greater problem than before, the enlistment of physicians in a campaign against it weakened the traditional ideal of family privacy. For the moment, the issue of the battered child overcame the public's instinctive dislike of government intervention. Between 1962 and 1966 all 50 states adopted laws requiring physicians who worked with children to report suspected incidents of child abuse. In Kentucky, the consensus was so strong that no one testified against such legislation. With subsequent laws, states expanded their reporting mandates to include teachers, social workers, and other individuals who worked with children.[30]

Sympathy for battered children also surfaced suddenly in popular culture. In October 1962 the *Saturday Evening Post* used Kempe's work as the point of departure for a lengthy treatment of "Parents Who Beat Children." Within a short time, *Life* featured an article, "Cry Rises from Beaten Babies," *Good Housekeeping* discussed "The Shocking Price of Parental Anger," and *Time* focused on "Saving Battered Children." Popular television shows, including "Ben Casey," "Dr. Kildare," "The Nurses," and "Dragnet" included stories about child abuse. In 1965, 90 percent of the public reportedly recognized child abuse as a problem. Three years later, for the first time, the Library of Congress made "Child Abuse" a keyword listing in its reference materials.[31]

In November 1970 the plight of a California girl, Genie Clark, received front-page treatment in the *Los Angeles Times* for a week. "Girl, 13, Prisoner Since Infancy," the headlines declared. Authorities discovered her condition by accident when her virtually blind mother, fleeing an abusive marriage, accidentally entered a welfare office. The media soon made public Genie's terrifying story. Her father had imprisoned her in "a small bedroom, harnassed to an infant's potty seat," according to one chilling account. "Unable to move anything except her fingers and hands, feet and toes, Genie was left to sit, tied-up, hour after hour . . . day after day, month after month, year after year." At night she slept in a homemade straitjacket. If she cried, her father beat her with a club. Often she went without food. When authorities took custody of her, the 13-year-old had still not learned to talk, was incontinent, could barely swallow, had vision problems, and was unnaturally stooped.[32]

As reports of abuse proliferated across the United States, a kind of panic ensued. In Florida, a mass media information campaign about child abuse and the installation of a toll-free hot line resulted in a staggering increase in reports, from 17 in 1970 to more than 19,000 a year later. In that context, Congress took action.[33]

In 1973 a new Senate subcommittee on children, with Minnesota Democrat Walter Mondale as chair, opened hearings on the subject of child abuse. The Nixon administration had blocked Mondale's recent efforts to secure comprehensive social services for children, so the senator looked for an issue that might advance social welfare legislation. "Not even Richard Nixon is in favor of child abuse," he joked, as he focused the subcommittee's attention on that problem. The hearings illuminated a gallery of domestic horror: "stories and photos of children, many of them infants," as the genuinely shaken Mondale recalled, "who had been whipped and beaten with razor straps, burned and mutilated by cigarette lighters; scalded by boiling water; bruised and battered . . . and starved and neglected and malnourished." Expert witnesses claimed that the United States was witnessing an outbreak of child battering. Dr. Kempe's testimony reflected the hearings' tilt toward medical, as opposed to social, explanations of child abuse. Kempe, whose National Center on Child Abuse and Neglect in Colorado was doing pioneering work in treating abusive parents, emphasized therapeutic strategies.[34]

In the wake of the hearings, Congress overwhelmingly passed the Child Abuse Prevention and Treatment Act (CAPTA). To protect children from abuse, the 1974 legislation endorsed professional intervention in crisis-torn families. It involved the federal government in the detection process by establishing a national clearinghouse for child abuse data, and by providing federal funds to streamline state reporting laws. States, to qualify for those dollars, had to meet federal guidelines regarding reporting, investigating, and having sufficient personnel and facilities to provide treatment. Without realizing it, the legislators had opened a Pandora's box. They had no idea that the subsequent avalanche in reporting would produce a huge expansion of child protective services—and an angry backlash against those services.[35]

Reports of child abuse cascaded across the nation. They swelled from around 9,500 in 1967 to almost 300,000 in 1975 and 669,000 in 1976—"the 'new math' of family violence in the United States," as one scholar called it. Reporters and experts cited wildly fluctuating statistics, all reflecting the illusion that it was possible to determine the incidence of child abuse. Testifying before the Mondale subcommittee in 1973, a member of Congress claimed that abuse and neglect constituted the "number one killer of children in America today." Two years later the United Press International (UPI) reported that an "epidemic" of child abuse was killing two hundred thousand children annually. That information came from an interview with Douglas Besharov, the initial director of the CAPTA-created National Center on Child Abuse and Neglect. Besharov indicated that the press had somehow misinterpreted his estimate that two thousand children died each year of abuse. Still, the figure of two hundred thousand continued to show up in discussions among officials and experts. In February 1977 CBS News announced the results of a survey that reportedly "shocked even the researchers": Parents had shot, shot at, or stabbed at least one million children between the ages of 3 and 17. Such figures showed the dangers of extrapolating from small numbers—in this case a survey of around 1,500 parents.[36]

A related problem concerned the shifting definitions of abuse and neglect. Immediately following Kempe's identification of "the battered-child syndrome," the public had focused on excessive physical violence against very young children. Gradually, however, child welfare professionals expanded the meaning of abuse. "What is 'CHILD ABUSE'?" asked one public service pamphlet in 1976. "It's REPEATED MISTREATMENT or NEGLECT of a child by parent(s) or other guardian resulting in INJURY or HARM." This maltreatment could be physical, emotional, verbal, or sexual. Verbal cruelty included "excessive yelling, belittling, teasing," and, according to at least one child protection expert, was "probably the most heinous form of child abuse."[37]

Definitions were critical in light of the report of the 1970 White House Conference on Children, which found "vast neglect" of America's children. But neglect could be an even slipperier term than abuse. In 1975 only eight states had, as legal scholar Sanford Katz and several colleagues discovered, "a statutory definition for the term 'neglect' and/or 'neglected child.'" A number of states simply used other terms "such as 'deprived,' 'dependent or neglected,' or 'dependent child.'" Intent was usually crucial in determining neglect. To what extent, for example, were parents responsible for the poverty, illness, or unemployment that denied their children basic care? At what point were circumstances within parental "control"? Even the professional groups, such as police and social workers, who dealt with maltreat-ment, typically brought different perspectives to the problem. Conflicting accounts, along with the limits of time and money, often hampered investiga-tions. And, as always, racial, ethnic, and class biases shaped individual judg-ments.[38]

Against this backdrop, the protective custody provisions of the 1974 law created what one leading social work professor described as "a monster." According to CAPTA, state child welfare agencies could remove endangered children from abusive or neglectful families for three days and, during that time, file for custody of the children. New horror stories surfaced, but now they were about parents who lost their children because of false accusations, child protective workers who ignored parents' basic constitutional rights, and children who were ripped from their homes for no good reason and placed unwisely in foster care. Douglas Besharov contended by the mid-1980s that 60 percent of abuse reports were unfounded. He complained that people call-ing emergency numbers such as 911 "cannot distinguish between life-threat-ening crimes and littering." As a result, even "marginally inadequate child care" resulted in the removal of children from decent families. Many of those children ended up in foster care, which was itself increasingly under attack.[39]

IV

Between the late 1950s and late 1970s, the fortunes of foster care rose and fell quickly. In 1958, for the first time, more children were in foster care than in institutions (although the ratio of 38 per 10,000 in foster care by 1960 was still far below the high of 59 per 10,000 in 1933). By 1969, 77 percent of dependent children were in foster homes, and in the midseventies the num-bers peaked at well over 400,000 (or 75 per 10,000 children). The new child abuse reporting laws accounted substantially for the increase, but there were other factors as well: the rise in births among young single mothers unable to raise children, the lowering of discriminatory barriers in child rescue work against racial minorities, the initiation in 1962 of AFDC payments to foster families, and the ongoing decline of children's institutions.[40]

"Orphanages Vanishing for Lack of Orphans," the *New York Times* announced in late 1974. In some respects, the headline was misleading. Although the number of full orphans in the United States had by then dwin-dled to less than 25,000 (80 percent of whom were adopted or lived with rel-atives), orphanages had traditionally housed many children who had one and sometimes both parents. As late as 1966, in fact, 60,000 dependent and neglected children still lived in institutions. Of that number approximately 45,000 exhibited no particular emotional or behavioral problems. Most were adolescent boys slightly over the age of 12 (only 1.8 percent were under age

2). They typically came from poor single-parent families, 25 percent of which received money from AFDC. A growing number of them were African American. Still, although orphanages continued to care for some dependent children, many observers were writing institutional epitaphs. By 1966 interest in orphanages "varied from minimal to zero," observed Alfred Kadushin, one of the foremost scholars of child welfare. "The professional literature is almost devoid of references to the experiences, activities, and problems of such institutions. It is as if they have been written off."[41]

Many orphanages were indeed either shutting down or finding a different clientele. Around 60 years earlier, The Baby Fold in Normal, Illinois, had opened one of the first nurseries for homeless young children in the state. But in 1971 the institution closed its nursery and began to provide group care and individualized programs for emotionally troubled preschoolers. In Chicago in 1974, the Angel Guardian served Christmas dinner to senior citizens for the first time. For over a century it had been an orphanage, caring over the years for around 30,000 children. Meanwhile, after 138 years, St. Paul's Orphanage in Pittsburgh closed. The *Times* reporter compared orphanages to daguerreotypes—"the memorabilia of another time."[42]

Institutional care suffered another crushing blow with the revelations in the 1970s that some child protective agencies were placing large numbers of children in out-of-state care under highly dubious circumstances. "There is in this country," wrote investigative reporter Kenneth Wooden in 1976, "a mushrooming multi-million-dollar industry that thrives on the interstate commerce of dependent and neglected children." Since the 1960s agencies and courts in at least 28 states had been sending thousands of children to private institutions elsewhere, mostly poor and racial minorities, who were supposedly "hard to place," "high risk," and "emotionally disturbed." Many of these institutions were reprehensible, trimming essential costs to increase profits. The Meridell Center in Texas was a notorious example. To cut expenses, it established an outdoor living program by which the children cooked their own food and made their own shelters. One boy in the program received no education for three years; two youngsters went six years with no schooling. The per diem expense per child was around $4, about one-sixth of the amount the center received from states.[43]

In 1973 a team of Illinois investigators finally exposed the plight of some five hundred children whom the state's Department of Child and Family Services had placed in Texas and failed to supervise. A devastating report, "An Illinois Tragedy: An Analysis of the Placement of Illinois Wards in the State of Texas," scandalized the state's child protective system. With great embarrassment, officials admitted that they did not know what had happened to around 55 of the children. Among the rest of the children whom the state brought back within its own borders, four were in coffins. "An Illinois Tragedy" summed up the situation bitterly: "Everyone is responsible. No one is or will be accountable. No one meant for it to happen. It just did. Too bad."[44]

Some people were equally disparaging of foster care during the early seventies and midseventies, even though it was more popular than institutional alternatives. The critiques reflected a mixture of concerns and politics, but they all pointed to the conclusion that foster care, in the words of Children's Defense Fund president Marian Wright Edelman, constituted nothing less than a "national disgrace." Some critics focused mainly on its threats to the rights of parents and children; others were more concerned about saving the biological family.[45]

The campaigns for equality had alerted many people on the political left to ways in which established groups trampled on the freedom of poor and powerless individuals. Influential scholarly works emphasized the theme of social control in human affairs. From this perspective, the history of child saving reflected less interest in rescuing children than in imposing dominant values on immigrants and the working class. The crusades of the anticruelty organizations and progressive reformers thus offered instructive examples about how "doing good" undermined civil liberties. The social control interpretation, as well as revelations about hideous conditions in institutions such as New York State's Willowbrook, helped to fuel a growing movement against arbitrary exercises of authority in many areas, including social welfare. This movement gained additional momentum in the seventies in reaction to the large number of unsubstantiated charges of child abuse and reports that white, middle-class child protective workers acted imperiously against weak, impoverished clients.[46]

This anti-statist, anti-interventionist persuasion also resonated in conservative circles. To people on the right, welfare institutions and child protective services symbolized big government and added to tax loads. Conservatives feared, moreover, that authority had conceded too much ground to the civil rights and other protest movements of the sixties, thereby undermining the role of parents and the integrity of America's families. In this context, efforts mounted to "recapture" the traditional family, an illusive goal because visions of that family typically drew more on myth than historical realities. By the late seventies, salvaging family values was a popular goal. McDonald's restaurants conducted a "family reunion" campaign and suggested activities that parents and their children could "have fun doing together." The head of the conservative Rockford Institute on the Family counseled that the proper response in a world gone awry was "*a turn toward home*." Republicans and Democrats alike scrambled to make that turn. President Jimmy Carter took office in 1977, for example, deploring "the steady erosion and weakening of our families," and pledging himself to reverse that trend.[47]

In that setting, criticism of foster care surfaced with a vengeance. Some critics pointed out that foster care was nothing but a "revolving door" for children, moving them from one place to another and wreaking all kinds of psychological and emotional damage on them at a time when they desperately needed a sense of commitment, security, and stability. This argument drew heavily from an influential collaborative study in 1973, *Beyond the Best Interests of the Child*, by psychoanalyst Anna Freud, attorney Joseph Goldstein, and pediatrician/psychiatrist Albert Solnit. In the midseventies Stanford law professor Michael Wald attacked the class-based nature of protective intervention, which tended to remove mainly poor and minority children from their families. On Capitol Hill and elsewhere, critics assailed foster care as unsafe, too expensive, and an unchecked arm of authoritarian welfare departments.[48]

In response to the attack on foster care, Congress passed the Adoption Assistance and Child Welfare Act in 1980. Its conceptual framework was that of "permanency planning," which meant simply that foster care should be a very temporary arrangement, lasting only until the child could be returned as quickly as possible to the biological family or moved to an adoptive home. According to the legislation, the federal government would provide 75 percent of the funds to help states effect a successful reunion of children and biological parents—a major goal—or, in hopeless cases, terminate parental rights and seek adoption. In special circumstances, if authorities had exhausted other efforts to secure adoptions, the law provided for adoption subsidies. No child was to enter foster care without a specific, deliberate plan in place, which social service agencies were to review every few months. In sharp contrast to the 1974 Child Abuse Prevention and Treatment Act, the philosophy behind the 1980 law was noninterventionist. As one scholar has pointed out, CAPTA "sought to protect children from child abuse" while the 1980 legislation was supposed "to protect them from foster care."[49]

In truth, however, permanency planning looked better on paper than in reality. For one thing, the government quickly backed off on the promised funding. According to the legislation, $3 billion would be available in 1981 and would gradually increase to $3.7 billion in 1985. But the new administration of Ronald Reagan, intent on reducing federal spending for social programs, cut the funding; the $2.8 billion granted in 1985 was less than the act had initially provided. Moreover, perhaps because of a lack of money, but certainly because of flaws within permanency planning itself, the system never really worked. After the number of children in foster care dropped fairly dramatically (from around 302,000 in 1979 to around 243,000 in 1982), the trend reversed. Studies showed that although children moved faster than before out of foster families, they typically did not stay long with the biological family to which they returned and were soon back in foster care again. The placement door still revolved.[50]

Nor was there any guarantee that abused children were better off back with their biological parents. One study concluded that abused children were five times more likely to be at risk in their own homes than with foster or adoptive families. To people who remembered New York City's sensational Roxanne Felumero case in 1969, such conclusions were no surprise. A judge had removed the three-year-old from her foster family and returned her to the mother and stepfather, both heroin addicts. The child's homecoming was brutal and brief. "I hit her lots of times," her stepfather confessed. "She was always wetting the bed." Several other addicts who visited the house found the child in frightening condition, her face so swollen from beatings that it appeared "two feet wide, you could hardly see her eyes." Another witness saw the girl's hand sticking out from beneath a blanket. "It moved a little." After she had been home 10 days, police found her battered body, weighted with rocks, at the bottom of the East River. Three years later, the well-publicized Lindquist case in Chicago revealed that a boy's biological parents had killed him after he returned to them from a foster home. Tragedies built upon tragedies: While some children unquestionably ended up in foster care unnecessarily, others remained very much at risk in their homes of origin. Donald Besharov guessed that in 1979 some 50,000 observable injuries went unreported.[51]

V

Adoption provided an alternative to foster care or to living in unsafe biological homes, but it was also in turmoil. Gloria and Doug Bates discovered one of the reasons firsthand. In April 1972 they read that the five-thousand member National Association of Black Social Workers (NABSW) had issued a major declaration: African American children should only be adopted by families of their race. According to the organization, the white parents who over the past decade had adopted around 20,000 black children were not equipped to help those children build a sense of racial pride and culture. Even worse, transracial adoptions were a "particular form of genocide." The NABSW statement stunned and depressed the Bates couple, who were white and had recently adopted two African American girls. Lynn, whom they adopted when she was four, had lived until then with white foster parents. (Her birth parents were in prison and ultimately abandoned her.) The foster father had tormented her by waving dead rats in her face and threatening to lock her in a closet with one of them. Liska, the other child, still bore visible scars from the severe abuse and neglect she had suffered at the hands of her biological parents during her first 18 months. She had also lived for several years with a white foster family before the Bateses adopted her. The Bateses, who already had two natural sons, believed they had built a kind and loving family—an opinion the girls shared. But after the Bateses read about the NABSW pronouncement, they agonized for a long time about whether they had in fact done their adoptive daughters a disservice.[52]

Two African American social workers hardly eased the Bateses' anxieties. They denied, for example, the usual argument that black parents were unwilling to adopt black children in foster care. Other factors were at work, they said, including an abiding African American distrust of the white-controlled social agencies that screened applications. Doug and Gloria Bates had themselves found the investigation process terribly intimidating and had struggled uncomfortably with questions about their finances, parenting abilities, and other quite personal matters. They could only imagine the additional grilling that prospective African American parents had to endure. Moreover, the social workers said, adoption costs were too high for many African American families. Additionally, state and private placement agencies did not try very hard to find black parents. Even after conceding the truth of the social workers' arguments, the Bateses suspected that if they had not adopted Lynn and Liska, the girls would still be living in "foster homes—*white* foster homes— waiting who knows how long for the state to find black adoptive parents for them." Doug and Gloria Bates decided ultimately that their decision to take custody of Lynn and Liska was correct.[53]

By the midseventies, however, other families increasingly found obstacles to transracial adoptions. In response to NABSW's proclamation, some states required same-race placement, and, by 1991, 77 percent of state and almost half of private agencies had unwritten understandings that enforced the same policy. In the context of advancing civil rights legislation, that policy was a curious anomaly, a throwback to the years before 1950. Since then the legal trend had been to break down discriminatory racial barriers. In that spirit, agencies in the sixties had finally relaxed their opposition to transracial adoption. But NABSW's 1972 statement reversed this brief development by rallying a diverse coalition of black nationalists, white segregationists, and adoption professionals who had historically assumed that biological sameness is crucial to families. An emerging result was what legal scholar Elizabeth Bartholet called "the numbers mismatch": In 1987, 37 percent of children in out-of-home placement were black (up from 34.2 percent five years earlier), but the bulk of families who wanted to adopt were white. Yet in 1986 NABSW adamantly reaffirmed "the position that Black children should not be placed with white parents under any circumstances." NABSW's members were certain that they acted in the best interests of African American children. Dissenters such as Bartholet nevertheless opposed policies that made children the property of any group—biological parents or racial communities. To what extent, wondered Bartholet and her allies, did children benefit from policies that delayed and often prevented their permanent placement in families that wanted them?[54]

That question also very much haunted adoption policies regarding Native American children. The policies of the federal and state governments toward Indians had long been shameful. For decades, those policies had included putting young Native Americans, for "civilizing" purposes, in boarding schools far removed from families and tribes. Indeed, by the 1970s an off-reservation Bureau of Indian Affairs Boarding School in Utah still housed more than 1,500 Navaho children. "This wholesale separation of Indian children from their families," as one legal scholar described it, occurred mainly in another form, however—one of placing them in foster or adoptive homes, almost always those of non-Indians. The psychological consequences for many of these children were injurious, according to Dr. Joseph Westermeyer, a leading authority on the subject. The children often developed a psychological condition that he dubbed the "apple syndrome"—red on the outside because of birth, but white on the inside because of a lack of contact with Native American culture. Studies between 1977 and 1979 revealed that one-third of non-Indian adoptive parents made little or no effort to introduce their Indian children to Native American culture.[55]

Placement statistics were indeed shocking. Between 1969 and 1974 states placed perhaps as many as 35 percent of Native American children in foster or adoptive care. In South Dakota, Native Americans comprised 7 percent of the juvenile population but provided 40 percent of the adoptions in 1967–68; in Wisconsin, Indian children were 1,600 percent more likely than non-Indians to suffer forced separation from their parents. "In 16 states surveyed in 1969," according to the head of the Association on American Indian Affairs, "approximately 85 percent of all Indian children in foster care were living in non-Indian homes." By 1978 over 90 percent of adopted Indian children were in the custody of non-Indian families. Such statistics helped to confirm what an important collection of essays in 1977 labeled as *The Destruction of American Indian Families*, and what many Native Americans attacked as cultural and legal "genocide." The figures attested also to the tendency of non-Indian child protective workers to misunderstand Native American culture, finding neglect or abandonment where it did not actually exist. Native Americans historically relied on an extended family, or kinship network, in which scores of relatives shared childrearing responsibilities. Significantly, no Indian language includes the words *orphan* or *adoption*.[56]

Several important court decisions in the seventies, along with the complex Indian Child Welfare Act of 1978, marked a turning point in the legal status of Native American children. The 1978 law came after a series of congressional investigations and was supposed to protect Indian families. Noting that there was no more vital resource for "the continued existence and integrity of Indian tribes than their children," the act established minimum federal standards to discourage the removal of children from Indian settings. "Where possible," according to the law, "an Indian child should remain in the Indian community." Tribal governments received virtually exclusive control over children on reservations and a kind of concurrent jurisdiction with states regarding off-reservation children. At the heart of the legislation was the belief that the best interest of Indian children rested with their relationships to their tribes. Without a tribe, the child lost his or her culture; without the child, the tribe lost a means to survive. As Mel Tonasket, president of the National Congress of American Indians told Congress, "When I look at our children, our Indian children, they are too few; but when one is taken away, that is too many." The act's defenders hailed an important beginning. In 1986, for example, authorities placed around 62 percent of Indian children with Indian families. Critics worried nevertheless that the legislation would in fact harm Indian children, either by subjecting them to endless legal proceedings or by keeping them in harmful living conditions.[57]

While issues of race and ethnicity increasingly influenced the politics of adoption, so did controversies about sealed records. A turning point in that controversy occurred in 1969, when Florence Ladden Fisher suffered an automobile crash. "I'm going to die," she thought, "and I don't know who I am." Years earlier Fisher had been adopted. Now, in her early forties, she was still searching for her "true identity." After her automobile accident she finally located her birth parents and, in 1971, started the Adoptees Liberty Association (ALMA), a support group for adoptees. Within a year, ALMA had more than one thousand members. "Whether you have a good or bad adoptive home," Fisher argued, "you have an identity crisis." ALMA's main goal was to open to all adoptees after age 18 the "sealed records" with information about their birth families. Opponents, including the Adoptive Parents Committee, countered angrily that the opening of such records would constitute an "invasion of privacy" on the part of either adoptive children or their birth parents.[58]

Contrary to myth, this sealed records battle was of rather recent origin. Until the post–World War II era, birth parents and adopted persons generally had access to case histories. A key reason was that a majority of adopted children came from birth mothers who had usually been married at the time of conception and who had relinquished their children, typically for reasons of poverty, after the youngsters were old enough to remember their biological families. By the end of the war, however, the demographics of adoption were rapidly changing. In 1944 the number of adoption petitions was triple that of 1934, and, largely because of momentary wartime romances, many of the children were illegitimate. Sealed adoption records quickly became the rule in all states, thereby providing "a bargain of silence," in the words of journalist Lincoln Caplan. "Confidentiality laws protected adoptees and birth parents from the shame of illegitimacy, and adoptive parents from the shame of infertility."[59]

Social workers endorsed the bargain of silence partly because popular psychoanalytic theories encouraged an unsympathetic view of unmarried mothers and of adopted persons who seemed "obsessed" with their biological roots. In 1955 a prominent psychiatrist who worked for the New England Home of Little Wanderers saw no reason to conclude that "a school age, neurotic, unmarried mother ... would gain by keeping her baby." Similarly, according to professional wisdom, adopted persons who wanted information about their birth parents were "very disturbed" and "sick." Such thinking, when combined with the changing backgrounds of adopted children and social workers' growing respect for confidentiality, influenced placement agencies to close their records. They did so despite the opposition of Jean Paton, who in 1953 opened the Life History Study Center in Philadelphia to help adoptees trace their roots. Paton's organization, Orphan Voyage, grew out of the center and pointed the way for Florence Ladden Fisher and others in the new adoption rights movement that emerged in the 1970s.[60]

"Adoptees grow up with a slave psychology," Fisher explained. Elizabeth Bartholet, herself an adoptive mother, understood such thinking. Sealed files containing the original birth certificate meant, in effect, that "for legal purposes the child is effectively reborn, with all legal and relational links to the past destroyed. The sealed records are supposed to ensure against any reconnection with that past." The push to open up files also came from birth parents, some of whom founded Concerned United Birthparents (CUB) in 1976. CUB's members resented the pressure they had been under to give up their babies and their subsequent inability to contact them. "As birth mothers, we were just used and thrown away," said one of the group's officers. In response to these various organizations that lobbied for open files, states altered adoption laws. The emerging consensus was that information bearing on matters such as health should be available to adoptive families and the adoptees. Disagreements on open records otherwise prevailed. Although a few states granted adult adoptees complete access to original birth records, by 1991 more than 30 others favored a mutual consent system that involved all parties: birth parents, adoptive parents, and adult adoptees. Some people even demanded eliminating adoption altogether, replacing it with guardianship arrangements that preserved legal and informational links with the birth family. One thing was clear, as Bartholet observed: The impassioned debate had put "the opposing advocates at each other's throats."[61]

Adding to these disputes about adoption were scandals regarding the awful fate of some adopted children because of slipshod procedures. The six children whom a Minnesota couple, Lois and Harold Jurgens, adopted in the sixties and early seventies were tragic examples. Despite a series of negative reports from psychiatrists and welfare department workers regarding Lois's emotional fitness to bear or raise children, the Jurgens gained custody in 1960 of a baby, Robert, and in early 1963 of one-year-old Dennis. Seven years after Dennis died amid suspicious circumstances in 1965, the Jurgens adopted four Kentucky siblings. A neighbor of the Jurgenses later admitted that he and his wife "couldn't believe" the abuse the children received. In retrospect, he said that he or someone should have intervened. "But that was the way of the neighborhood. You just minded your own business." In 1987, when Lois Jurgens finally went to jail for murdering Dennis more than 20 years earlier, the public learned what some people already knew: The Jurgens home had been an absolute hell for the children. After excruciating abuse, three-year-old Dennis had died. The other children had endured Lois's angry explosions, when she screamed, slapped, and beat them with a belt buckle and cedar board. Sometimes she thrashed the boys' bare bottoms with a metal pancake spatula or forced the adolescent girl to remove her panties, bend over, and receive a spanking in front of her younger brothers. Lois Jurgens also made the youngsters wash their own underwear on an old-fashioned scrubbing board and, if they did not get out all the stains, to wear the dirty shorts on their heads.[62]

For years, no one stepped in to protect the Jurgens' adopted children. Harold Jurgens, afraid of his wife, did nothing during her frequent tirades. Nor did help come from the neighbors, the child welfare system, or other authorities. Little Dennis lost his life. "This just didn't happen here, with this one boy," said medical examiner Michael McGee, who performed the autopsy on the child's exhumed body. "The difference in this case is that Dennis's blood cried out from the ground."[63]

VI

Discussions of such tragedies typically centered on the flaws of parents, especially their psychological shortcomings, rather than on larger social and economic issues. When, for example, pediatricians and radiologists "discovered" the battered child, they implicitly stamped it as a medical problem—indeed, as a "syndrome." Perhaps only the mystique of modern medicine could have so effectively and quickly removed traditional blinders against abuse. X-rays made the historic tendency to ignore the physical mistreatment of children more difficult; by finding evidence of multiple fractures, contusions, and subdural hematoma, doctors provided evidence of ongoing brutality and documented abuse as never before. The weakness of the medical model, however, was that it too had blinders.[64]

A prominent example was Kempe's speculation that abused children became abusive adults. "Child abuse is contagious," declared a prominent handbook as late as 1977. "If you caught it from your parents, you may give it to your kids." The supposition that abuse was a "disease," moving from one generation to another and creating a "cycle of violence," quickly dominated common and professional wisdom. Careful research showed, however, that the vast majority of abused and extremely neglected children (perhaps twothirds) did not become abusing or neglectful parents. Such findings suggested that the real question was what conditions shaped abusive situations. Those conditions were multiple and, as two well-known researchers insisted, "cannot be separated from the effects of poverty, stress, and social isolation"—factors that went beyond the medical model's emphasis on "aberrant parental characteristics."[65]

The medical model also helped to popularize the "myth of classlessness," which held that child abuse was no more characteristic of one social group than of another. There was nothing wrong, of course, with reminders that affluent families were not immune to violence; too often, accusations of poor parenting had fallen on only destitute families. In that regard, the first full-length television movie that dealt with the issue of battered children, "Mary Jane Harper Cried Last Night" (1977), was important because it showed that child abuse was more widespread than most people realized; wealthy families simply had more resources with which to hide their crimes. But by suggesting that child abuse, like any contagion, was "classless," and by emphasizing themes of individual sickness and treatment, the movie dramatized quite powerfully a medical model that was deeply flawed—a model that diverted attention from the substantial connections between, for example, poverty and abuse.

At the heart of the medical model was the assumption that child abuse was a pathology, an "illness" that needed therapeutic solutions. "In most cases," Kempe's pioneering 1962 article asserted, "some defect of character structure is probably present." The roots of child abuse, from this perspective, were psychological, not social. Like earlier casework strategies, the medical model emphasized individual weaknesses and their treatment. The way to deal with these weaknesses was through therapy or the removal of the child, a "parentectomy," as one of Kempe's colleagues described it.[66]

Largely by attributing child abuse to "sick" individuals rather than to larger social ills, the medical model struck a popular chord. In that regard, the "myth of classlessness" was appealing because it disassociated abuse and neglect from any economic context. Researchers who placed abuse in that context, and who demonstrated that violence against children was more common among lower income groups, in fact opened themselves to charges of class prejudice. Child protection advocates denied the relationship between poverty and child abuse because they did not want to endanger their cause by tying it to increasingly unpopular welfare measures. Walter Mondale thus emphasized during the 1973 Senate hearings that child abuse "is not a poverty problem." However, the medical model, as its critics argued from the early 1970s on, cut in another direction as well: It allowed the public to sympathize with abused children without assuming any responsibility for eliminating some of the circumstances of their suffering. Problems without social causes did not demand social solutions. Guilt and blame rest with "them"—bad parents—not with such factors as inadequate health care, discrimination, disintegrating slums, or economic dislocations. Larger social failures were, in sum, irrelevant, given the faults of neglectful, abusive parents.[67]

VII

As the decade of the 1980s approached, the battles over children's issues moved steadily onto a social and legal minefield. Subjects such as adoptions, foster care, welfare, the responsibilities of the state, and the role of child protective agencies were more and more volatile. The issue of abuse was especially explosive.

By the midseventies a serious legal debate was under way between advocates and opponents of "open definitions" of child maltreatment laws. Supporters of open-ended definitions, such as family law scholar Harry Krause, emphasized that flexible statutes were essential because they allowed individualized responses to specific, changing circumstances. On the other side, Stanford law professor Michael Wald worried that too much official discretion encouraged injustice, and that official good faith and wisdom were weak foundations upon which to build any child protective system.[68]

In 1977 the U.S. Supreme Court made one thing clear: The Constitution offered no protection against even severe corporal punishment in public schools. James Ingraham, a 14-year-old junior high school student, had received "at least twenty licks" with a wooden paddle across his buttocks. The principal had administered the punishment while two school administrators held Ingraham across a table. In court, during Ingraham's lawsuit, other students recounted similar incidents that had happened to them. One boy claimed that the principal had hit him with a belt as well as a paddle. In a five-to-four decision, the Supreme Court acknowledged that the system at Ingraham's school "was exceptionally harsh" but refused to extend constitutional protections "to traditional disciplinary practices in the public schools."[69]

Some groups worried nevertheless that the American family was in danger of losing its traditional disciplinary powers. Religious conservatives in particular feared that the rights revolution and social permissiveness were undermining parental authority. From their perspective, warnings against child abuse were much exaggerated and represented a bureaucratic assault on parental prerogatives and responsibilities.

James C. Dobson's bestseller, *Dare to Discipline* (1970), offered an early signal of this building reaction. Dobson, a self-described Christian Fundamentalist psychologist, believed that parents by nature were in a state of war with their children. "You have drawn a line in the dirt," he reminded parents, "and the child has deliberately flopped his big hairy toe across it. Who is going to win?" Parents must not only beat back such challenges but must "win decisively." Spanking was the best weapon to use against children under age 11. Not only was pain "a marvelous purifier," but "God created this mechanism as the child's best vehicle for instruction." According to Dobson, if the child cried too much after a spanking, he or she was simply trying "to punish the [parental] enemy" and needed "a little more of whatever caused the original tears." In *How to Rear Children* (1972), the Reverend Jack Hyles agreed: "*The spanking should be a ritual. . . .* He [the child] should not only dread the pain but the time consumed in the ordeal." If the spanking left marks, wrote Roy Lessin in *Spanking: Why? When? How?* (1979), the parent should find solace in knowing that "it is better for children to carry a few temporary marks on the outside than to carry within them areas of disobedience and wrong attitudes." After all, Lessin said, "Spanking is God's idea," and parents must not confuse it with child abuse. The popularity of such advice books provided notable evidence of the growing reaction to the idea of children's rights—"kiddie lib," as the *Conservative Digest* derisively called it.[70]

The fury of that reaction made some observers wonder how much Americans genuinely respected their children. "Do Americans Suddenly Hate Kids?" asked *Esquire* magazine in a mid-1970s "special report." A few years later *Ms.* magazine repeated the question: "Do Americans Hate Children?" Why, otherwise, did children constitute the nation's poorest group? How can one explain the fact that a greater percentage of American babies died at birth than did the infants of 15 other comparable countries? How does one account for the growing reluctance to fund children's nutrition programs? Journalist Letty Pogrebin, who attended part of the 1980 White House Conference on Children, noted that "parental frustration thickened the air." The nature of the conference was itself suggestive. Since 1909 presidents had convened these conferences roughly every 10 years to consider children's needs. In 1980, for the first time, what Pogrebin described as "a series of low-priority state meetings" replaced the one large gathering. At one of the meetings, she sensed a prevailing view among the parents, who fretted about their children's behavior and dress, that "they've lost their children and they don't know why."[71]

Popular culture mirrored their negative feelings with an outpouring of books and movies intimating that children were unlovable, untrustworthy, even evil and monstrous. "Children possessed by the devil are a growth industry," noted one reviewer. Examples proliferated: *Rosemary's Baby, The Exorcist, Children of Darkness, The Lucifer Child, The Firestarter, The Omen, Damien—Omen II.* Letty Pogrebin suspected that, deep down, "America is a nation fundamentally ambivalent about its children, afraid of and increasingly punitive toward its children."[72]

That combination of ambivalence, fear, and punitiveness did not bode well in the 1980s for the "discovery" of child sexual abuse. Debates over children and child protection soon heated up even more. From one angle, as accusations of sexual abuse reached epidemic proportions, children appeared more vulnerable than ever. From another angle, skeptics, asserting that many of the accusations were false, contended that the issue was really one of "sex accuse." On this subject, according to an investigative reporter: "one thing is clear: there *is* a war." But as adversaries faced off over issues such as sexual abuse, foster care, adoption, and AFDC, some observers suspected that the antagonists overlooked the best interests of the children—always a nebulous concept, but one that was increasingly politicized as well.[73]

8

Continuing Battles, Tragedies, Crisis: The 1980s and 1990s

$\mathbf{A}$s the twentieth century came to a close, anger, fear, and sensationalism marked debates regarding abused, neglected, and dependent children. Dramatic, highly publicized incidents cascaded upon a shocked and disbelieving public. The list of child abuse victims lengthened and some children gained attention only by dying. Joshua DeShaney survived, but his brain-damaged condition offered mute testimony to the limitations and failings of social services agencies. Trials of suspected sexual abuse tore communities apart, turned into media circuses, and left legacies of deep suspicion. Groups with different political agendas seized upon children's issues to advance a variety of causes. Foster care and adoption controversies erupted, pushing names such as "Baby Jessica" and "Baby Richard" onto the front pages. A backlash against welfare resulted in a full-scale assault on Aid to Families of Dependent Children. Suddenly there was even talk about bringing back orphanages.

Despite all the publicity that children's issues received, the plight of dependent, neglected, and abused children seemed only to worsen. One of several major studies in the 1990s about the growing numbers of endangered children sounded a "Code Blue," the medical term for emergency. As the politics of children's issues became increasingly nasty, and as the backlash against child saving gathered momentum, the living conditions of many children deteriorated. The chilling sagas of child victimization and suffering that pervaded the news were doubly sad. They attested to agonizing individual misery and grief and at the same time diverted attention from a deeper children's crisis, a crisis that was rooted in economically vulnerable families, decaying inner cities, and spreading poverty. The situation reminded one child welfare expert of scenes in a battlefront hospital: While rescuers frantically sorted out individuals who most desperately needed attention, the valiant acts of triage were limited to the immediate situation and a few victims—not the larger circumstances that brought them there and imperiled others.[1]

I

In 1985 authorities received two million reports of child abuse (30 per every 1,000 children); within seven years the number leaped to almost three million (45 per 1,000). From any angle, these rapidly escalating numbers were scary. If such abuse existed, it was unnerving. If it represented only the "tip of the iceberg," it was even more frightening. If many of the reports were untrue, they offered a sad commentary on Americans' veracity, sense of proportion, and susceptibility to hysteria.[2]

The reality of extensive, severe abuse was undeniable, given the grisly examples that filled the news. In 1983 six-year-old David Rothenberg became, in the words of one popular magazine, "a symbol of child abuse at its most extreme." While he slept in a motel room near Disneyland his father poured kerosene on him and then set him on fire. Despite burns over 90 percent of his body, he somehow survived, but with mutilated hands and a horribly disfigured face. In 1990 CBS television included him in a morning segment on abused, neglected, and dependent children.[3]

Eli Creekmore failed to survive his abuse. In September 1986 the three-year-old died in Everett, Washington, after his father kicked him to death. During his short life he had endured a number of beatings, and Child Protective Services (CPS) had removed him from his family several times. When he died of a ruptured intestine following a kick in the stomach, the state legislature moved into action, passing a package of child abuse legislation in the spring of 1987. According to the "homicide by abuse" law, death that resulted from a pattern of abuse constituted first-degree murder. Another law permitted CPS to interview children without their parents' permission, added child-care workers to the list of people mandated to report suspected abuse, and indicated that children's safety should receive priority over the protection of family units.[4]

Lisa Steinberg's death in 1987 triggered another outpouring of puzzlement, dismay, and procedures. Although an estimated four thousand youngsters died that year of physical abuse, Lisa captivated the media because, on paper, she enjoyed privileged conditions; her adoptive parents were white, well-to-do, college-educated professionals. Hedda Nussbaum, an editor of children's books at Random House, and Joel Steinberg, a criminal lawyer, demonstrated all too starkly the deception of respectable appearances. After illegally obtaining Lisa and then a toddler from two unfortunate single women, the couple proceeded to abuse the children dreadfully. Joel Steinberg, gregarious with friends and associates, pounded unmercifully on Nussbaum while inflicting excruciating beatings on Lisa. At age six, Lisa died after one beating too many, her body "a map of pain," in the words of reporter Joyce Johnson. Investigators found her 17-month-old neglected brother covered with excrement and attached by a string to a playpen. For weeks after Lisa's death, anonymous New Yorkers left flowers, notes, candles, and other memorials at the entrance of her apartment building. A television documentary following the media-dominated funeral claimed that her death would "*forever* change the way we look at child abuse." The New York City school system instituted training for all guidance counselors, teachers, and administrators in how better to identify it.[5]

Some observers worried about the effects that the soaring number of reported abuses were having on child protective agencies across the country. They disagreed sharply, however, on what those effects were. Defenders of CPS insisted that the reports were saving children but overwhelming a system that desperately needed more money; opponents argued that the reports, often unjustified, were creating what journalist Richard Wexler described as "a child-protective empire" that only made things worse.[6]

To underpaid workers with burgeoning caseloads, the only sensible strategy was to provide more help and better salaries. "A major part of the problem," argued Patricia Schene of the American Protective Association, "is that we've been taking these 22-year-old, wet-behind-the-ears zoology majors at best and putting them on the front lines in life-or-death situations." However accurate her assessment, there was little indication that a tax-resistant public favored higher CPS budgets. Washington State provided a prime example. Three years after Eli Creekmore's death had stirred the public's wrath, citizens overwhelmingly defeated a "children's initiative" that would have provided additional funds for children's services. By a two-to-one margin, voters rejected the proposal, which would have added one cent to the sales tax.[7]

CPS critics, coming from different political angles, worried that the agencies comprised runaway bureaucracies, which were too often insensitive to people's rights. Richard Wexler, a respected reporter, noted that at least half of the two million annual child abuse reports were demonstrably false. In many cases, they grew out of child custody or neighbors' disputes. But while Wexler objected to needless interventions in families, he did not put himself in the parents' rights camp. Instead, his major concerns were with seriously endangered children, whom an overextended and overreaching child protective network often did not help. He quoted one expert who said, "We went from doing nothing to trying to do everything." As a result, Wexler argued, CPS looked into so many marginal cases that it inadequately assisted children who were truly at risk. He objected also to the hasty removal of children from their homes. "There are a lot of Cap'n Hooks out there," he said of CPS workers who eagerly took youngsters from parents. As one of Wexler's sources said, "It's so much easier to just go ahead and yank the kids." In Wexler's estimation, "The war against child abuse has become a war against children."[8]

In 1985 the liberal *Progressive* magazine expressed alarm about the "invasion of the child savers." Wexler contributed one of the essays, arguing that CPS was destroying children in order to save them. In answer to the director of Ohio's CPS who claimed that she would "rather see a family disrupted than a bunch of dead children," Wexler responded, "Unfortunately, the laws tend to give us both." Neglect statutes had become so sweeping and so vague that, according to one attorney, they resembled broad fish nets that permitted "the fisherman to pick which he wants to keep and which to throw back. Social agencies proposed [the system] and social agencies love it." Reporting laws were equally flawed and, by feeding hysteria about abuse, pushed CPS workers in myriad directions. Child abuse was a serious problem, according to Wexler, but he objected to the "phony" solutions.[9]

Much of Wexler's portrait of invading child savers resonated with critiques by political conservatives. But, as his hard-hitting book *Wounded Innocents* (1990) subsequently showed, Wexler was no kindred spirit of the right. He favored redirecting energy and resources into preventive services that would help keep families together. When people wondered why someone did not save an abused child from dying, Wexler replied that they should "put their tax money where their mouths are."[10]

Conservatives, in contrast, worried mainly about government meddling in private family matters. "What's the difference between a children's rights activist and a pit bull?" asked the *National Review*. "Answer: You might get your child back from a pit bull." Parental rights advocate Mary Pride worried about a future in which "we get to keep our children only as a temporary favor that can be denied at any time." In her book *The Child Abuse Industry* (1985), she blamed an "anti-family climate" for encouraging the "institutional control of every citizen," replacing parents with bureaucrats, making children "fearful of their own loved ones," imposing a "family Marxism" that pitted "the parents (bosses) against the proletariat (children)," turning the state into "Superparent," and basically seeking "to eliminate child abuse by eliminating parents." Pride cited much of the same evidence that Wexler used, but whereas he blamed poverty for many children's problems, she targeted working mothers, day care, television, divorce, and "post-Christian parenting philosophies."[11]

In Pride's estimation, "phony child abuse prevention" confused real abuse with necessary corporal punishment. In her opinion, parents had "the biblical right to apply the 'rod of discipline' to an erring child's backside— e.g., spanking." On this issue, she had the support of a number of people, particularly several influential fundamentalist Christians. Echoing the recent advice of James Dobson and others, Richard Fugate and Larry Tomczak in the early 1980s emphasized that corporal punishment was crucial to parental authority in the face of youthful rebellion and willfulness. Fugate believed that the only option for the child should be "honorable, but unconditional surrender." According to Tomczak's book *God, the Rod, and Your Child's Bod* (1982), "Daddy always wins and *wins decisively*!" Spankings would leave red marks on the skin but, Tomczak wrote, "This is nothing to get upset about! These marks are only temporary," and far better than allowing "improper attitudes inside that can leave permanent scars in later life."[12]

The issue of corporal punishment very much complicated the debates over child abuse because the line between legally permissible discipline and illegal violence was sometimes fine. Most state child prevention acts specifically granted parents the right to spank their children, and no state forbade that practice. Studies revealed that by the 1990s spanking remained almost as common as oxygen in American families; virtually all parents hit their toddler children, over 90 percent spanked 3-year-olds, and more than 60 percent hit children ages 10 to 12. In the mideighties, 40 percent of 14-year-olds and 25 percent of 17-year-olds still received corporal punishment. Nor had the publicity about child abuse lowered the rate of parental spanking and hitting; between 1975 and 1985 the percentage did not change. "The virtuous violence," as critic Murray Straus labeled spanking, grew out of the deeply rooted assumptions regarding its effectiveness, the virtual universality of corporal punishment among children's experiences, the beliefs that families needed to produce orderly citizens, and the strong fundamentalist views among perhaps 28 percent of the public.[13]

Straus, the founder of the Family Research Lab at the University of New Hampshire, nevertheless sensed that public opinion was beginning to question ever so slightly the use of corporal punishment against children. The number of states that prohibited corporal punishment in public schools, for example, had grown from 4 in 1979 to 25 in 1993. Moreover, in 1992 the national Kiwanis organization urged the showing of a tape, "Spanking—What To Do Instead." That same year the Wisconsin legislature considered a bill to prohibit parents from using corporal punishment against children. Although the bill never got beyond a committee hearing, where the overwhelmingly hostile crowd carried signs such as "PADDLE LAWMAKERS," it was symbolically important and was reportedly the first such proposal to come before a state legislature.[14]

In mid-1993 the popular *Redbook* magazine printed words that Straus believed had been unthinkable in a mass-circulation forum only five years earlier. "Though spanking or slapping may halt misbehavior temporarily, over the long term physical punishment will backfire," the magazine advised. "A kid who's smacked doesn't learn self-control; he learns fear—and that it's okay for a bigger person to hit a smaller one." Columnist Ann Landers also had a change of heart about corporal punishment and urged parents not to hit their children. The antispanking message was hardly loud, but it was growing. "By consciously deciding not to inflict pain, not to cause suffering, not to coerce, and not to assault a child in the name of discipline," wrote historian Philip Greven in 1990, "we will be making choices that will enhance and sustain life, not deny it."[15]

In Straus's opinion, the United States was ready for another major step in the "moral passage" that had, over the decades, rendered the hitting of workers or of spouses illegal. "Children are next on the agenda," he wrote optimistically in 1994. Convinced that corporal punishment was harmful to individuals and society, he took heart in a Texas survey that showed a growing perception that hitting a child with a belt or wooden paddle constituted physical abuse. In 1978 only one-third of adults held that opinion; in 1991 half did. A more cynical interpretation would be that 50 percent of adult Texans still did not consider such punishment abusive.[16]

Surveys, statistics, and percentages invariably carried mixed messages. On the one hand, the rising number of abuse reports were encouraging: They suggested that more and more abusive situations were coming to light. On the other hand, of course, they provided discouraging evidence of widespread, perhaps even growing, cruelty. And to some individuals they were virtually meaningless, because so many reports (perhaps as many as 65 percent in 1986) were exaggerated or false.[17]

II

There were, however, strong hints that child abuse was even worse than the swollen statistics suggested. Every day perhaps as many as three child abuse deaths went undetected in the United States. That was the conclusion, in December 1990, of a stunning Pulitzer Prize–winning series of articles from the Gannett News Service. "I wish I had a nickel every time someone came into my office and said his kid fell down the stairs—and then you find out they live in a trailer," said one director of social services. A former medical examiner who specialized in children's deaths was convinced that child abuse deaths were "grossly underestimated." Another medical examiner agreed: "Children are being killed and just buried." The only way to stop this pattern was to investigate children's deaths more thoroughly. Autopsies sometimes revealed abuse when the outward signs were not visible. In a famous Ohio case in 1989, an autopsy discovered why three-year-old Matthew Peters vomited to death. The answer astounded community groups who had applauded the inspiring devotion of his mother, Judi Peters, who had stayed by his side day after day. She had killed him. The autopsy showed that Matthew died of poison that she had administered to him, even in the hospital. Judi Peters suffered from Munchausen syndrome by proxy, a personality disorder in which parents or guardians make their children sick, or fabricate symptoms, to gain attention for themselves.[18]

Although autopsies could expose secrets that children would otherwise carry to their graves, many officials performed them on a random basis that had less to do with the circumstances of deaths than with locales, budgets, and the social standing of the families. In most rural areas, elected coroners were typically funeral directors who were reluctant to offend local families by pressing for an autopsy. Moreover, many coroners were not truly qualified. "They can't even spell the things they have to put on the death certificates," said one medical examiner in Atlanta. Even conscientious and able coroners could only do so much within budget constraints. One quipped that, if he were going to commit a homicide, he would do it at the end of the year; by then there was insufficient money for an autopsy. But the failure to discover an abuse-caused death sometimes resulted in even greater tragedy. All too often, the siblings of a murdered child remained in the killer's custody. "It's just like leaving a child with a pit bull," said a former medical examiner.[19]

Such was the case with Diane Lumbrera, who apparently murdered seven children, six of them her own. Casual investigations had indicated that the deaths were accidental. In 1990 Lumbrera went to prison for killing her four-year-old and was under indictment for the six other murders. By then a number of states were considering mandatory autopsies in unexplained children's deaths. In some places "death review committees" investigated cases. Across the country, however, knowledge about dead children was often lacking. "We can tell you how many cars are sold in the last hour, but some states don't keep track of how many children are killed," complained an analyst with the National Committee for Prevention of Child Abuse.[20]

The extent of child abuse became more evident after the late 1970s when well-known individuals stepped forward with accounts of personal torment they had endured as children. In 1978, for example, country-western singer Hank Snow revealed that he had been an abused child and sponsored a sell-out concert to aid other victims. Snow and other celebrities helped to break what the daughter of famed actress Joan Crawford described as "the dam of denial" regarding child abuse. By bringing abuse out of the shadows, they legitimized its discussion.[21]

"It was something I had tried so hard to forget," said Florida senator Paula Hawkins in 1985, as she described her own fight against child abuse. A neighbor had sexually molested her when Hawkins was five years old. For years Hawkins brooded about the incident, which sensitized her to the many accounts she heard later about various kinds of child abuse. She had no doubt that "many abuse incidents are never reported."[22]

Movie star Robert Blake and former Miss America Marilyn Van Derbur could attest to that fact. In the 1990s Blake finally spoke out publicly about what had happened to him. He had suffered ferocious parental beatings with belts, wire and wooden hangers, and wooden spoons; spent days in a closet; was tied up like a dog and forced to eat off the floor; endured sexual abuse. Relatives knew what was happening, he recalled, but no one helped him. In

1991 Van Derbur revealed her own well-kept secret: "I stand before you an incest survivor," she told a group at the Kempe National Center in Denver. Her highly respected, millionaire father had sexually assaulted her again and again when she was a child.[23]

In 1992, 23 celebrities, including Desi Arnaz Jr., Gary Crosby, Angie Dickinson, and Cindy Williams, published short personal accounts in a book, *Wednesday's Children: Adult Survivors of Abuse Speak Out.* The anthology's editor was television star Suzanne Somers, who recalled a "terror-filled" childhood because of an alcoholic father who suffered attacks of " 'the means.' " In public, she had covered up what was happening by "putting on a happy face and acting as if everything were okay."[24]

Wednesday's Children referred to the words of a familiar poem that "Wednesday's child is full of woe"—a description that, to the surprise of many Americans, fit more people than they realized. Readers of Richard Rhodes's Pulitzer Prize–winning book on the atomic bomb had no idea, for example, that as a boy the author had lived for several years in a "concentration camp" kind of setting in which his stepmother beat, humiliated, starved him, and sometimes denied him access to the bathtub and toilet, while his father watched passively. In a painful memoir in 1990, Rhodes described how he and his older brother had "cowered, cringed, screamed, wrapped our poor heads protectively in our arms, danced the belt-buckle tango." Before the brothers found shelter at ages 11 and 13 at a private farm for wayward and abandoned boys, they almost died. Years later they were still trying to shake the emotional and psychological legacies of their torture. But "human beings are tough," he decided. "They take a lot of killing."[25]

Christina Crawford demonstrated the truth of that statement. In the bestselling *Mommie Dearest* (1978), she described the cruelty that her movie-star mother had inflicted on her. Subsequently, she wrote, spoke, and lobbied to expose the issue of child abuse. She bewailed the society's complicity in "household terrorism" by permitting "family members to be treated with more violence and less protection than is accorded prisoners of war under the terms of the Geneva Convention." Fear, she wrote, dominated abusive homes—fear of the violence that could erupt anytime, but also "fear born in the childhood experience of retribution for exposing the truth."[26]

These recollections suggested that considerable abuse and neglect occurred in unsuspected places and comprised well-hidden family secrets. Genie Clark, whose father had imprisoned her in a room for years, lived in what neighbors viewed "as the quietest family of all." And Dennis Jurgens, a fatal victim of his adoptive mother, encountered what child protective attorney Andrew Vachss described as "a modern horror story in which the monster wears a mask—the mask of normalcy."[27]

Some individuals protested that such descriptions imperiled the American family by making it seem a violent inferno. "No dogma," wrote conservative Mary Pride, "is more common in the child abuse camp than this: home is horrible." And liberal columnist Ellen Goodman warned about television talk shows that by the 1990s paraded "an unbroken stream of pathological families" across the screen. "If Norman Rockwell's Thanksgiving family were on the air," Goodman quipped sardonically, "grandpa would be a child molester, grandma a recovering drug abuser and the kids would bear sexually transmitted diseases. The abnormal is the norm."[28]

Yet, often out of sight, real abuse took its daily toll. "Two children die every week" in New York City, lamented TV reporter Bree Walker on the evening of Lisa Steinberg's funeral. "How can we ignore such numbers?"[29]

All too easily, it seemed. Within two months after Steinberg's funeral, at least 25 other New York City children had died of abuse, with virtually no public notice. One outraged journalist, Nat Hentoff, urged the press to do a better job of reporting what was happening. "The city's surge of grief for Lisa Steinberg hardly indicates a 'shared social responsibility' for the murdered children to come," he wrote angrily. Steinberg's case "was a singular event, singularly italicized in the press; but two months later, child abuse and neglect is no longer a pressing concern."[30]

If getting an accurate sense of the dimensions of the abuse problem was difficult and divisive, the challenge of dealing with it was equally anguishing and controversial. While some critics rebuked child protective agencies for being too intrusive and rushing to judgment, others protested that CPS was not responsive enough. There was disturbing evidence on both sides. Meanwhile, caseworkers were caught in the middle, wrestling with often-agonizing dilemmas, trying to answer the questions of how much risk the child faced at home and what dangers the child might encounter outside the home. Was the danger greater inside the family or in alternative care? Too often the appropriate answer was apparent only in retrospect, after wrong choices ended in tragedy.[31]

III

Joshua DeShaney could easily have wondered how much proof child protective services needed before they acted. In the early 1980s in Wisconsin, he had ended up in the hospital three times, once with a bruised body and genitals and with hair yanked from his scalp. Although authorities removed him briefly from his home, they soon returned him. During his caseworker's monthly visits, she duly noted evidence of ongoing brutality against him, including cigarette burns on his face. "I just knew the phone would ring some day and Joshua would be dead," she admitted. It did, and he was barely alive. The day after the caseworker visited his home but failed specifically to look in on him, he showed up again at the hospital. His father had beaten him into a coma. Not quite four years old, Joshua was left permanently and severely brain damaged. His mother, who had divorced the father (the custodial parent), sued the Winnebago County child-care officials for violating Joshua's constitutional rights, namely under the Fourteenth Amendment, which guarantees that "no state shall . . . deprive any person of life, liberty, or property without due process of law."[32] In 1989, by a six-to-three vote, the Supreme Court ruled that the Fourteenth Amendment was no protection in this instance. The due process clause, according to Chief Justice William Rehnquist's majority opinion, "was to protect people from the State, not to insure that the State protected them from each other." In other words, although the state could not arbitrarily deprive citizens of their Fourteenth Amendment rights, the state did not have "an affirmative obligation" to protect those rights from "harm through other means." Renquist argued that the state had not created the dangers that Joshua faced. The upshot of the decision, as one commentator observed, was that the state did not have a constitutional obligation to protect a child from abusive parents.[33]

"Poor Joshua!" protested Justice Harry Blackmun in an impassioned dissent. "Victim of repeated attacks by an irresponsible, bullying, cowardly and intemperate father, and abandoned by [social workers] who placed him in a dangerous predicament . . . and yet did essentially nothing. . . ." Blackmun considered the incident, and the Court's majority decision, to be "a sad commentary upon American life." Another dissenter, William Brennan, reasoned that the state had accepted responsibility for Joshua once child protective workers had identified his situation and, surely, Joshua had not been able to speak in his own behalf. Authorities had "effectively confined Joshua DeShaney within the walls of Randy DeShaney's violent home."[34]

DeShaney v. Winnebago County Department of Social Services placed in sharp relief the perplexities of dealing with child abuse. In this case, the child protective agency had not protected Joshua. There were nevertheless hazards in opening caseworkers to lawsuits for not removing children from homes. Such a decision, as Ellen Goodman noted, "would have tipped the scales further in the direction of 'rescuing' children from their parents. Do we want that?"[35]

However, the effort to keep children in their homes seemed futile when so little happened to make those homes safer. In 1990 seven New York City children died from beatings in families that the child protection system had already identified as abusive. One victim was five-year-old Adam Mann. His three older brothers had already been in and out of the hospital and foster care many times. Keith, for example, suffered a broken jaw, then a fractured skull. After a beating, Larry ended up in the hospital with a broken leg, and later with a broken arm. During a 16-month period, the caseworker stopped checking on the Manns because she thought their case now belonged to someone else and she was dealing with 60 to 70 others. At another point there was a two-year hiatus in the casework records. On March 6, 1990, Adam died from a beating so severe that it split his liver in half and broke virtually every bone in his body.

The Mann home proved deadly indeed, but foster care could be equally unsafe. The year of Adam's death, three other New York City children, whom child protective workers had removed from their parents, died from beatings in foster families. Adam's three brothers all suffered physical abuse at the hands of foster parents and other foster children. These situations were the backdrop against which a panel of child welfare experts in early 1992 recommended tougher monitoring of families with histories of child abuse, training for foster parents, and more experienced caseworkers. However, the city's budget crisis doomed the recommendations from the outset.[36]

As child welfare caseloads proliferated, agencies around the country groaned under the burden. In 1988 half of Dallas's caseworkers quit, indicating that they were simply worn down. Despite the textbook load of around 25 cases, social workers in Washington, D.C., in 1989 averaged more than 60 each. They handled that many, remarked one of them sadly, "by ignoring most of them." Another commented, "I don't go to work, I go to war. If we help a child, it's by accident." Because of a lack of desks, some Florida workers kept their files in their cars. In Illinois, where caseloads went up to 100 per caseworker, one worker said that even Mother Teresa would be doing a bad job. Caseworkers resembled someone with a finger in a dike, trying to hold off a sea of destitution, inadequate or no housing, unemployment, mental illness, and drug addiction, all of which contributed to abuse. "You go into a home and find the child abused, but you have nothing to work with to make life any better for these kids," complained one weary New York City caseworker. In Los Angeles, one worker said that the heavy load precluded real social work. "You can't go out and see ten children and just say hello and good-bye." A colleague added, "You just hold your breath and hope nothing will recur."[37]

In 1991 a national blue ribbon panel warned that the child protective system was "on the verge of collapse." Still, the victims kept coming. Among them was Tashia Shipley, who by the age of nine had been neglected, molested, physically and emotionally abused, and infected with the deadly virus that leads to AIDS. Her foster mother, who finally provided a good home for the dying girl, said bitterly that she wanted the head of the child protective system "to come here and look this child in the eyes so that when she dies . . . I know somebody who is a part of the system has this child's soul on their conscience."[38]

IV

In the 1980s, against this backdrop of recrimination, victimization, and overburdened child welfare agencies, an outbreak of sexual abuse cases created a furor. Until then, abuse reports had generally ignored the issue of sex. Accusations of sexual abuse started surfacing in the late 1970s and soon shook the foundations of the child protection and legal systems. Between 1975 and 1985 sexual abuse reports jumped from around 12,000 to more than 150,000. In 1976 they constituted 3.2 percent of all child abuse and neglect reports; by 1986 that figure had reached 16 percent. Significantly, too, whereas around 80 percent of the alleged perpetrators in general child abuse cases were parents or stepparents, in sexual abuse cases, 58 percent were non-parent relatives or people unrelated to the victim.[39]

Out of those statistics leaped the question of false accusation and victimization, raised by a series of sensational cases that prompted analogies with the infamous Salem witch trials, when the accusations of several girls had touched off a wave of hysteria that had claimed 20 lives and ruined many others. "SALEM, MASSACHUSETTS 1692. MANHATTAN BEACH, CALIFORNIA 1985," read a newspaper advertisement in the summer of 1985 as a trial for alleged sexual abuse at a day care center unfolded. Placed by friends of the defendants, the advertisement claimed that history was repeating itself: "In the 17th century, innocent lives were lost or ruined because of the false accusations of the infamous Salem witch hunts. In the 20th century, the same thing is happening again."[40]

Jordan, Minnesota, a small community that one writer compared to "Garrison Keillor's mythical hamlet, Lake Wobegon," became an early and prominent outpost in the raging controversies over sexually abused children. In September 1983 two 10-year-old girls in the Minneapolis suburb accused a 27-year-old trash collector of molesting them. As police interviewed other children about suspected sexual abuse, accusations spread. Within a few months the "Jordan sex case" was in the national news, implicating several dozen men and women, mostly parents and citizens with respectable reputations, with running a sex and torture ring that involved their own children. Lies, said the defendants. The trial divided the town into bitter factions as children recounted stabbings, decapitations, mutilations, ritualistic torture. Ultimately, however, a jury acquitted one couple of abusing their own and several neighborhood children; prosecutor Kathleen Morris dropped the charges against 21 other adults; and only the trash collector, a previously convicted child molester, went to prison. The governor's special commission to look into the matter concluded "that some of the cases could have been reasonably prosecuted." According to the commission, "Kathleen Morris did not respect the rights of the accused" and "did not see that the guilty were prosecuted." The public, seemingly forgetting the commission's inference that some abuse had indeed occurred, ultimately viewed Jordan as "that little town up in Minnesota where all the children lied."[41]

More immediately, however, allegations of sexual abuse swept the country. In one year, reports in Maine leaped 300 percent. In New York, according to *Newsweek* in mid-1984, "allegations of sexual abuse were spreading like an infectious disease." The Bronx district attorney moaned, "We're being inundated with complaints."[42]

One of the biggest scandals rocked the well-to-do California community of Manhattan Beach, outside Los Angeles. There, in August 1983, a massive sexual abuse case burst from accusations against six teachers and the aging owner of Virginia McMartin's Pre-School. In interviews that the prosecution conducted, as many as 350 children claimed that someone at the school had abused them, in some cases by raping and sodomizing them. Some children also recounted stories about the ritualistic killing of animals, drinking rabbits' blood, and going to the local cemetery to witness the exhuming and chopping up of bodies. The case dragged on for seven years, ending in mid-1990 after two trials produced no convictions and cost Los Angeles County $15 million. To many people, the McMartin case symbolized a system run amok and cast doubts on the veracity of children who charged sexual abuse.[43]

Similar "ritual abuse" cases reinforced that conclusion. In 1984 the Amirault family faced accusations of sexually abusing around 40 children, ages three to six, at the Fells Acres Day School in Malden, Massachusetts. During therapeutic interrogation, the children described a "magic room" torture chamber in which they drank urine and endured rape and molestation. Three of the Amiraults ended up in prison, victims, according to the *New Republic* a decade later, "of mass hysteria, fueled by panicky parents, vicious prosecutors, opportunistic therapists and a rapacious news media who showed no qualms about assuming guilt." In another day care mass-molestation case, Margaret Kelly Michaels also went to prison, convicted of 114 counts of assault, sexual abuse, and terroristic threats against 20 children, ages three to five, at the Wee Care Nursery School in Maplewood, New Jersey. Between 1983 and 1994 more than one hundred other sexual abuse cases involved child-care centers, and many included charges such as animal sacrifice. Ultimately, however, the cases may have comprised what the chief of the Manhattan District Attorney's sex crimes unit described as "the most flawed class of prosecutions ever." By the mid-'90s higher courts had overturned over a dozen verdicts, including those of Michaels and the Amiraults. Bitter, sad, and angry after five years in jail, Michaels sued the county and state. "It's about innocence," she said. "If they offered me a buck and an apology, I'd go away." But a parent of one of the alleged victims still insisted "that Kelly Michaels sexually molested my child, and I will believe that until the day I go to my grave."[44]

During the nineties, accusations of child sexual abuse took a new and highly controversial turn with the phenomenon of "repressed memories." When some adults, often through therapy, remembered abuse they had suffered years earlier, they touched off a series of media events and legal collisions. One of the most celebrated legal cases involved the recollections in 1989 of 28-year-old Eileen Liskers that her father had sexually abused her and had raped and murdered her eight-year-old friend. In 1990 a California jury convicted the man of first-degree murder. Over the next few years, the issue of repressed sexual abuse memories gained prominent attention in mass-circulation magazines, television talk shows, and TV movies (such as ABC's 1993 film, "Not in My Family"). "Americans are at a fever pitch over sex abuse these days," *Newsweek* reported in April 1993. A year later the noted psychiatrist Walter Reich referred to "these plague years of true and false memories of sexual abuse." By then, according to one estimate, more than three hundred civil cases involving repressed memories of sexual abuse were in the courts. In Napa, California, Gary Ramona successfully sued a therapist for planting ideas in the mind of his daughter, Holly, that had prompted her "flashbacks" about his alleged sexual abuse of her years earlier. In 1995 a court overturned the conviction of Eileen Liskers's father. *Newsweek*, commenting on a Massachusetts case that sprang from repressed memories, wondered if Americans "may be pushing too hard, too fast" regarding the problem of child sexual abuse.[45]

In an effort to explain the wave of personal revelations about abuse, as well as the huge public interest in such disclosures, some commentators identified a cultural bent toward "victimization." According to this explanation, many Americans saw themselves as victims of one kind of oppression or another, whether the reason was race, gender, class, big government, or ubiquitous social forces. Out of their sense of grievance came a willingness to identify with and support other victims. Some critics wondered whether America was not engaged in a kind of "blame game" and becoming a nation of whiners. "Blame you, blame them, blame everyone, but don't blame me. I'm just a victim," quipped journalist Scott Montgomery. In their quest for "victimhood" and instant sympathy, such Americans supposedly turned to support groups or empathized with others in pain.[46]

Attorneys increasingly used what law professor Alan Dershowitz called the "abuse excuse" to defend their clients. After Susan Smith drowned her two children in 1995, the defense attributed her conduct to the fact that her stepfather had sexually abused her for years. Although Smith was nevertheless convicted, several other juries were more forgiving. In California, a jury could not agree on a verdict regarding the Menendez brothers, who claimed that abuse had driven them to kill their parents. In 1992, however, in the first Washington State case to allow the "battered-child syndrome" as a defense, a jury convicted a youth of first-degree manslaughter, rather than second-degree murder, for his admitted shooting to death of his brutal stepfather. "Abuse is such a hot topic that it constitutes abuse even if you can't remember ever being abused," Rowland Nethaway of Cox News Service complained.[47]

V

By the mideighties the subject of child abuse had thus mobilized a powerful reaction among people who argued that wildly exaggerated charges were victimizing innocent parents. "Hug Your Kid, Go to Jail," quipped the conservative *American Spectator* in June 1985. Nine months earlier, a group of Minnesota citizens had formed Victims of Child Abuse Laws (VOCAL) in behalf of people "falsely accused of abusing children." Within four years, one hundred chapters existed in 40 states. As one member said, "Molestationmania has hit us, full force." Paul and Shirley Eberle, who toured the country in the mideighties warning about the "child abuse witch hunt," believed that child molestation was less of a problem than were corrupt authorities, including the " 'mental health professionals.' " The Eberles advised Americans to "reevaluate the Welfare State hierarchy and its 'social workers,' "—the real sources of child abuse. A Phoenix, Arizona, group, Parents Against Protective Services, shared that opinion. And in 1992 the False Memory Syndrome Foundation emerged, joining the chorus against therapists while offering support to parents who claimed they were blameless casualties of their children's mistaken memories.[48]

The appearance of such organizations revealed much about the growth of state intervention. State powers, according to one scholar, had never before "expanded so rapidly into the domain of the family." Traditionally, the targets of such intervention had been the poor and racial and ethnic minorities. But the growing anger of other groups indicated that they, too, felt increasingly vulnerable.[49]

Some of these groups hardly raised the level of debate, however. Marilyn Gunther, the founder of the Coalition of Concerned Citizens, an organization whose declared purpose was to defend unjustly accused individuals, argued that "there are a lot of people who sexually offend their own children who are excellent parents, despite that one little hangup. It's not as if they abuse them all the time." Men International, another organization, placed an advertisement in a VOCAL newsletter about a newly formed "Annihilation Team" whose objective was "to destroy false allegations. You can call it the 'A-Team' for short. We mean business."[50]

All of the storm and fury about the "witch hunts" had several adverse consequences. The macho posturing of the new "A-Team," VOCAL's hyperbole, and Gunther's incredible comment detracted from the real problem of false accusations. That problem especially affected parents of children who died of sudden infant death syndrome (SIDS), a mysterious affliction with no symptoms that claimed annually around five thousand seemingly healthy babies. When investigators discovered that some supposed SIDS victims were murder victims, authorities justifiably looked into SIDS cases. But for the vast majority of parents whose children had indeed died of SIDS, this additional scrutiny only compounded their anguish; grieving over a dead child, they now also had to deal with suspicions that they were killers.[51]

Some parents indeed suffered unfairly in the search for abuse, but the hysteria of sensational sexual abuse cases and the protests of groups such as VOCAL threatened to trivialize the abuse issue. When Albuquerque medical examiner Kris Sperry kept checking for evidence of abuse, a defense attorney accused him of seeing "child abuse in a peanut butter sandwich." Sperry, however, insisted that he was in the unique position of being able to "speak for a dead child who can't talk—and maybe never could." Andrew Vachss, an attorney who specialized in children's cases, noted that most of the backlash rhetoric focused on children who "fantasized" about sexual abuse. He served a reminder that there was another kind of evidence that was less easy to dismiss: "an X-ray of a child's broken bones."[52]

Vachss noted correctly that most of the backlash focused on cases of child sexual abuse, where investigators had sometimes used questionable means to elicit information from children. Studies showed, for example, that very small children "are phenomenally suggestible," as psychologist Richard Ofshe said. "They are very accommodating to adults. Their main problem is distinguishing reality from fantasy. A poorly trained interviewer seeking to elicit information on a particular subject can hardly fail to do it." For children, moreover, the trial process could be devastating—like "drop kick[ing] them into a system that turns them into hamburger," as one person said.[53]

All of the attention on false or questionable accusations threatened to obscure the gruesome reality of abuse. Large numbers of children felt its effects and suffered its consequences. "The lowest numbers one can reasonably come up with," wrote Richard Wexler, "still leave more than 1,100 children dead of abuse every year, 21,000 suffering major physical abuse, and more than 100,000 sexually abused."[54]

At bottom, the public fascination with "ritual abuse" and sexual molestation stories perhaps deflected anxieties, not only about the rising abuse statistics but also about the status and health of the American family. The truth was, of course, that most sexual mistreatment occurred inside the home. "Overwhelmingly," as Debbie Nathan observed in one of her award-winning essays on ritual abuse, "when children are molested, the culprits are fathers, stepfathers, mothers' boyfriends, brothers, and funny uncle types." In contrast, only 1.7 percent of reported child abuse singled out people, whether teachers or day care workers, who were salaried to care for children. Of that figure, a mere one-tenth reportedly involved sexual abuse; the rest included beatings and neglect. In that context, commentators such as Nathan, criminal defense lawyer Michael Snedeker, and journalist Lawrence Wright suspected that the scandals surrounding several child-care centers or schools were often a form of scapegoating. "We have given our children to strangers to rear, and it makes us uneasy and fearful," Wright speculated. In fact, those strangers jeopardized children far less than did a larger set of social problems, such as divorce, neglect, unsafe neighborhoods, and bad schools. Those problems helped to confirm fears about the vulnerability of families, fears that economic uncertainty and relentless consumerism only heightened. According to Nathan, "it seems that the weaker the family gets, the holier is its image." In that sense, the backlash represented an anguished cry of protest, but its targets were largely symbolic villains—strangers "out there." As Nathan summarized the concept: "If the private family is sacred, the public child-care center is profane."[55]

Precisely because the issue of child abuse was so tightly bound up with other concerns, the efforts to define it became increasingly politicized. The fight over abortion offered a prime example. Pro-life advocates argued that abortion was in itself one of the worst forms of child abuse and that it contributed to additional maltreatment by diminishing the value of children. Pro-choice advocates countered that unwanted children were particularly susceptible to abuse. "Birth abuse," according to one book, was "the unconscionable giving birth to unwanted babies." By the mid-1980s, some people were finding other forms of child abuse, ranging from the lyrics of rock music to circumcision and "fetal abuse" from drugs and alcohol. The American Cancer Society featured advertisements that showed a pregnant woman smoking. "Some People Commit Abuse Before Their Child Is Even Born," read the caption. And while feminists linked child abuse with wife battering, their New Right adversaries located greater threats to children from outside the home.[56]

In an important sense the issue of child abuse—especially that of sexual abuse—had become what child welfare expert Duncan Lindsey dubbed a "red herring," an arresting topic that diverted attention from more fundamental and deeper problems. He and others regretted that the abuse issue now dominated child welfare work and discussions. By commanding so much attention, the horrific incidents and sensational trials ultimately overshadowed the underlying poverty and other devastating social ills that jeopardized millions of American children. And given the shifting political mood of the late twentieth century, there was little chance that those ills would receive much consideration.[57]

VI

Welfare, always suspect, became an increasingly popular political target. Attacks against it intensified during the Reagan administration, which was determined to cut back on domestic government services and taxes, to let market forces deal with social problems, and to halt a perceived "breakdown of the American family." To resurgent conservative forces, that breakdown had resulted from the rights revolution, which had encouraged women to leave the home for careers and jobs, fostered demands for more and more welfare, and elevated permissiveness over parental authority. "The federal government should not fund missionaries who would war on the traditional family or on local values," asserted Gordon Humphrey, a conservative Republican from New Hampshire. In that spirit, Senator Paul Laxalt of Nevada, a staunch Reagan loyalist, had in 1979 introduced a Family Protection bill that would have ended federal spending for child abuse prevention. Laxalt's bill failed, but the ideas behind it survived. In 1992 the Washington State Republican campaign platform advocated an end to child abuse investigations.[58]

Conservatives particularly criticized Aid to Families of Dependent Children (AFDC), which to them symbolized the welfare state, the collapse of the independent family, and the decline of morality—"households headed by a mother dependent upon public charity," as a 1986 report to Reagan put it. Reagan himself had long made welfare fraud a major theme in his political career and administration. When the topic of welfare came up, aides knew, as top staffer Michael Deaver later said, that he would invariably "tell the story of the Chicago welfare queen next"—a favorite Reagan story about a woman who had been convicted in 1977 of welfare fraud. When the topic of poverty surfaced occasionally at White House "issues luncheons," Reagan tended to talk mainly about reducing the federal government's role and cutting spending. During his first administration, cuts in AFDC and programs such as school lunches and subsidized housing resulted in a decline of almost 8 percent in the federal benefits that went to households with incomes under $10,000. In contrast, households with more than $40,000 lost no federal aid. "When all was said and done," according to Reagan biographer Lou Cannon, "it was in fact the 'weak clients' who had the weakest claims upon the Reagan administration and Congress." By the end of the 1980s, the retrenchment on welfare was having significant effects on the poor. For example, an Illinois family of three received only $367 a month from AFDC—47 percent of what was necessary for basic needs. Nationally, at the beginning of 1993, the state median for AFDC and food stamps together was only $652—70 percent of the poverty threshold. These figures had particularly disturbing implications for children, a rising percentage of whom (one of four under age six in 1989) lived in poverty.[59]

VII

By the 1990s the developing consensus across the political spectrum in favor of reduced federal budgets and family restoration reinvigorated talk about adoption. Members of both political parties hailed it as an answer to many social problems, including those of unwed teen mothers (who, in 1991, gave birth to 36,000 babies) and youngsters whose families were disintegrating. Yet, as *Newsweek* indicated in 1994, "Adoption as an institution has never been in such turmoil." Storms that had been building around adoption issues such as sealed records and race continued to rage, and ugly conflicts broke out between birth and adoptive parents as well as over questions of whether homosexual couples could adopt children, and how "open" the adoption process should be.[60]

In the push for greater openness, some young, unwed mothers were set-ting the terms, approving the adoptive parents and often maintaining contact with the children. Opposition to open adoptions hardened in 1980, when William Pierce of the National Committee for Adoptions launched a relent-less campaign. On popular television talk shows and elsewhere, he made the case against what he viewed as a form of "malpractice." Open adoption, in his and the committee's opinion, was "an untried, untested mutation of an institution that has worked for large numbers of people for decades."[61]

Although some studies confirmed his view that traditional adoptions had worked well, others disagreed. Clinical psychologist David Kirschner, for example, identified an "adopted child syndrome," whose symptoms included antisocial tendencies and law-breaking. In 1986 Kirschner testified as a defense witness for 14-year-old Patrick DeGelleke, who had killed his adop-tive parents in a fire. Kirschner's precedent-setting use of the adopted child syndrome resulted in a minimum sentence for DeGelleke, who was convicted of arson and second-degree murder. "Suddenly," complained one irate adop-tive mother, "a defense testimony for one child had turned into an indictment of an entire group of children." But among the defenders of the adopted child syndrome was Betty Jean Lifton, whose *Lost and Found: The Adoption Expe-rience* (1988) became a kind of bible to many adoptees.[62]

Hampering careful research on the syndrome, or what Lifton preferred to call "cumulative adoption trauma," however, was the fact that no one knew how many adoptees existed in the United States. Closed records accounted in large part for the imprecise numbers, but so did independent adoptions, which by the 1990s constituted perhaps as many as one-third of adoptions. Many of these adoptions were unregulated. "Baby selling," or the illegal sale of children, had grown increasingly profitable, drawing as much as $50,000 per child. "The opportunists are leaving us idealists gasping for breath," lamented a leading advocate of open adoptions.[63]

Meanwhile, opposition to transracial adoptions continued, despite the success of the civil rights movement in lowering racial barriers throughout much of American life. Still under pressure from certain groups, particularly the influential National Association of Black Social Workers (NABSW), place-ment agencies moved gingerly on the issue, typically seeking racially matched adoptions. By the 1980s, San Francisco was the site of Black Adoption Fairs, a strategy to help move African American children out of temporary emer-gency placements with middle-class white families in such places as the Napa Valley. White foster parents would dress up the children and put them on dis-play—"like a dog show," complained one foster mother who dreaded taking the four-year-old whom she had raised since he was a baby. "When I came home I cried," reported another woman. "It's just like a big slave market." Angry at the racial barriers that prevented whites from adopting the children, some of these foster parents turned to the courts, arguing that the children's best interests rested with "bonding," not "racial matching." To officials in San

Francisco's Department of Social Services Adoption Unit, however, these "Napa Nannies" seemed naive. Love alone was insufficient "in a racist, sexist, homophobic culture," argued the Adoption Unit's supervisor. Dr. Farris Page, the black psychologist at the city's Children's Home Society, agreed. "All the love, attention, and bonding" in themselves, she said, could not prepare black children who lived with white families for the real world.[64]

In Fort Wayne, Indiana, social workers believed they had handled the situation of one African American girl quite admirably. When she was an infant in 1989, they had placed her as quickly as possible in a stable foster home with Sandy and Don Kintz, who were white. After searching for two and one-half years for an adoptive black family, the social workers found Audrey and Frank Mace. The Kintzes by then wanted to adopt the girl themselves but now had to relinquish her to the Maces. "No bonding mattered," Sandy Kintz said angrily. "It was the race." Bitter, the Kintzes brought an antidiscrimination case to the Office of Civil Rights (1 of 27 such cases in early 1993) and joined the National Coalition to End Racism in America's Child Care System, a group of mostly white foster parents fighting racial and ethnic discrimination in child placements. "You yank kids around because they're black or because they're Hispanic, does that teach kids anything positive about being black or being Hispanic?" asked the coalition's president, Carol Coccia. Audrey Mace had a different perspective. Delighted that her adopted three-year-old daughter had in a few months adjusted happily to her new surroundings, Mace indicated that she did not oppose "a black child going into a white home . . . but let their own race be a priority first."[65]

Senator Howard Metzenbaum tried to provide guidelines for such cases. As a strong civil rights advocate who personally repudiated bans against transracial adoptions, the Ohio Democrat introduced in 1993 a Multiethnic Placement Act denying federal funds to any agency that made race its only factor in adoptive placements. By the time Metzenbaum's proposal became law, however, it prohibited only undue delays in adoption in order to find racial matches, and it hedged on transracial adoptions by conceding simply that they "may be a preferable alternative" to foster care. Although the bill received support from the Children's Defense Fund, the *New York Times*, and prominent African Americans such as Jesse Jackson, it evoked substantial opposition, especially from a group of 30 prestigious law professors who argued that race should not be a factor in adoptions.[66]

Among the group was Harvard law professor Randall Kennedy, an African American who believed that Metzenbaum's proposal violated the spirit of the civil rights movement by implicitly judging transracial placements as less desirable than racial matches. Moreover, according to Kennedy, the bill failed to recognize the demographics of a growing adoption crisis. Between 1986 and 1992, of the 450,000 children under state care, around 100,000 were eligible for adoption; 40 percent of that number were African American. On an average, children as a whole waited two years and eight months until adoption; black children typically waited more than five years. Any search for a racial match entailed a delay, during which the child stayed in a "limbo of parentlessness." Although Metzenbaum thought his bill served the best interests of the child, Kennedy argued that it would make many dependent children "orphans of separatism."[67]

After the act's passage in late 1994, Metzenbaum was incensed when people emphasized that the law allowed agencies to "consider" issues of race and ethnicity. "That was not intended by the legislation, and completely misses the point of the law," he insisted, noting that his goal was to help white parents adopt black children. But Mary Beth Style, vice president of the National Council for Adoption, blamed Metzenbaum's "flawed" legislation itself for creating interpretive problems.[68]

In March 1995 Republicans, who had recently captured Congress, responded to racial questions in adoptions with a new toughness. As part of a proposed welfare reform package, the House of Representatives approved legislation to deny all federal child protection money to any state that delayed a minority adoption in order to seek a minority family. "No other misdeed by a state could invite such harsh punishment," wrote *Washington Post* reporter Barbara Vobejda, "not even ignoring child abuse." Republican backers claimed they were determined to dislodge minority children from foster care. Critics attacked this "sledgehammer" approach to a difficult social problem.[69]

Native American children were not immune to questions of race in adoptions. In 1993 a controversial case involving a four-year-old Native American boy was tried in the courts. The boy's father was an Oglala Sioux, but the non-Indian mother had never married him and did not live with him. She surrendered the boy at birth to Karla and Leland Swanson, who proceeded to adopt him. But the Oglala Tribe intervened, under the provisions of the Indian Child Welfare Act, when it learned of the adoption. The boy's Sioux aunt and uncle on the Pine Ridge Reservation in South Dakota wished to adopt him. An Idaho trial judge ruled that the 1978 act did not apply in this case because the boy was not enrolled with the tribe. However, in 1993, the Idaho Supreme Court overruled that decision, agreeing with the tribe that technicalities could not circumvent the 1978 act. The U.S. Supreme Court refused to hear the Swansons' appeal.[70]

If the best interests of the child seemed highly debatable within the politics of transracial adoption, they were equally murky during emotionally wrenching legal battles between adoptive and biological parents of the same race. In August 1993 the print media and television featured dramatic pictures of attorneys taking a sobbing, two-and-a-half-year-old "Baby Jessica" from the only parents she had ever known: Jan and Roberta DeBoer, who had raised her since birth and planned to adopt her. Cara Clausen, her unmarried biological mother, had surrendered her at birth, after naming a man as the father and getting his consent to release the baby. When Daniel Schmidt, the real father, discovered he was the biological father, he went to court to reclaim the girl. His legal claim, which the Iowa and Michigan courts upheld, was that he had not relinquished his parental rights. The DeBoers contended unsuccessfully that they, as Jessica's nurturers and the only parents she knew, should be able to keep her. Much of the public was aghast when the tearful child was removed from the DeBoers amid a stampede of print and TV journalists.[71]

"The much-battered idea of adoption as a happily-ever-after answer . . . took another hit this week," wrote Chicago reporter Joan Beck. "But then the law cares more about legal technicalities and biological ties than it does about 2-year-olds." Beck wondered when adoption laws would "work in the best interests of vulnerable children instead of treating them as property to be handed out on the basis of adult 'rights.' " Columnist Ellen Goodman also questioned laws that cared "too much about parents' rights and not enough about children. . . . the law has sent a toddler packing. They call this justice. I wonder what Jessica . . . will call it." Cartoonist Mike Luckovich portrayed adoptive and biological parents as basketball teams; between them stood a referee (the courts) ready to throw a child into the air and saying, "Jump ball. . ."[72]

A cartoonist's rendering of the plight of children caught in late-twentieth-century custody battles between biological and adoptive parents. Courtesy Mike Luckovich and Creators Syndicate.

In May 1995, in a virtual replay of what had happened to "Baby Jessica," the biological father of "Baby Richard" took his son from distraught adoptive parents. The tearful four-year-old boy reached back desperately for his adoptive family to rescue him. "Monster," shouted some neighbors and onlookers at the biological parent, Otakar Kirchner. The biological mother had told Kirchner that his child was dead and then placed the infant for adoption. Like Daniel Schmidt, he argued successfully that he had not surrendered his parental rights.[73]

Similar but less-publicized cases confirmed that adoption was in the midst of troubled times. In Arizona in mid-1994, another natural father found out about his previously unknown child and won a custody suit. In Vermont, an adoptive mother and biological father agreed to share legal custody of "Baby Pete," a nine-month-old child, thus making it an open adoption. Such openness met with criticism: "Many experts," according to the *New Yorker*, "fear that this openness, which often includes full identification of everyone involved, and sometimes even visitation rights, may confuse children about who their psychological parents are."[74]

Pressures grew to devise adoption laws that would ease the custody conflicts that were breaking out, even though subsequent reports on the progress of "Baby Jessica" and "Baby Richard" were somewhat reassuring. The day after Kirchner took the boy from his adoptive parents, Richard was apparently already adjusting. *Newsweek* pictured a smiling three-year-old girl on its cover with the words, "She's Not Baby Jessica Anymore." After a year with the Schmidts, she seemed contented and happy. Shortly thereafter, the DeBoers adopted a baby boy, after having gone through a long period of mourning and entering therapy. In the meantime, the DeBoer Committee for Children's Rights expanded into 36 states and claimed two thousand members. Its purpose was to protest against and publicize what seemed to be unfair custody rulings.[75]

In 1994 a legal battle over a gay couple's right to adopt a child detonated yet another explosion of nationwide publicity and marshaled forces on both sides. At the center of the custody fight was Gailen Brandt, who was three years old when the 18-month court fight started in 1993. His teenage single mother had given him up when he was two. He drifted through a series of abusive and neglectful foster care placements until Ross and Luis Lopton, Seattle bankers, provided him with a caring home and then sought to adopt him. At that point his birth mother, by then married, a recovering alcoholic, and a Christian, contested the Loptons' move, asking the courts to reverse her decision to relinquish her parental rights. "Living with a gay couple is not what I want for my child," she said, appearing on television talk shows. Conservative Christian groups rallied to her cause as part of their campaign against gay rights. They took heart from a 1993 Virginia case in which a judge had taken a two-year-old from his lesbian mother and given him to his grandmother, on grounds that the mother's life was "immoral." Conservatives introduced a bill before the Washington state legislature that would have prohibited adoptions by homosexuals—legislation that, according to one Seattle reporter, already existed in six states. The Loptons, in turn, founded a gay and lesbian family adoption support group. Ultimately, in late 1994 a King County Superior Court ruled that the Loptons could adopt Gailen. "I'm living here forever," the boy said happily. But conservatives continued to seek support for an anti-gay statewide initiative that would prevent gays and lesbians from becoming adoptive or foster parents.[76]

Meanwhile, each month in Washington State alone, according to a representative of the Children's Home Society, "between 500 and 800 special needs children wait[ed] to be placed in adoption in permanent families." The much-publicized legal fights and controversies over adoption hardly helped to relieve that kind of situation. Adoption needed something other than praise from politicians to get through a rough, contentious era.[77]

Passage in 1996 of a $5,000 federal tax credit to defray the costs of adoption seemed mainly to reflect the power of what columnist Katha Pollitt dubbed an "adoption fantasy." Finding homes for healthy babies was relatively easy. The real challenge was how to place children who had special needs because of their age or physical and emotional problems. Those adoption realities raised questions about the public priorities that underlay the new tax credit. Pollitt wondered why a poor baby who was apparently not worth "$64 a month, or $768 a year, in government support if he stays in his family of origin," could suddenly be "six times more valuable once he joins a supposedly better-ordered household." The *Washington Post* guessed that the tax credit would cost the U. S. Treasury some $2 billion in seven years—an amount that the government, given its pressing budget problems, might better use to help children who were poor and had special needs.[78]

Efforts to equate "adoption and apple pie," in Pollitt's words, were clearly fraught with difficulty. In 1994 the parents of a much-touted "Celebration Family" that included 79 adopted children went on trial for manslaughter. As parents of Oregon's largest family, Dennis and Diane Nason had even appeared on the CBS television program *60 Minutes* in 1984. There and elsewhere, they had enjoyed a reputation as a heroic couple who adopted children who often had mental or physical handicaps. But in mid-1992, complaints from some of the children triggered investigations. One detective found bedrooms that stank of urine and feces. Some of the children described how the Nasons had beat them with boards and belts and had even used electric cattle prods on them. One adopted daughter, by then age 27, accused Dennis Nason of having sexually abused her. Claiming innocence, the Nasons insisted that the anti-child-abuse forces had targeted them in a crusade to deny parents the right to discipline their children. They had the backing of Family PAC, a group that opposed child protective services' meddling in family matters.[79]

VIII

While adoption forces contended with a range of issues, children were affected as the foster care system struggled with sheer numbers, child protective services strained under growing pressures, and policies to reunify families (a goal of the 1980 "permanency planning" legislation) drew criticism. Within three years the number of children placed in foster homes had jumped 29 percent, from 280,000 in 1986 to 360,000 in 1989. By 1994 that number was 430,000; in New York City alone, the figures had shot up from 16,240 in 1984 to 50,518 a decade later. Parental drug use was a chief cause of the increase. "We have an epidemic of crack-cocaine babies," warned a Washington State resident who was engaged in child care. "We can't get people to take some of these kids." Finding foster parents was increasingly expensive, costing the nation $6 billion annually by the midnineties. The quality of care varied from abominable to impressive. A new and much-praised New Mexico program for problem placements was reportedly excellent, but very expensive—$182 daily per child ($82 going to specially trained foster parents, and the rest to cover support services such as therapy). Founded in late 1992 and receiving state money, the All Faiths Treatment Foster Care program was small but offered children such as 10-year-old Clark perhaps their last hope to live with a family. During the prior seven years, Clark had been through 22 placements, including some abusive foster homes, emergency shelters, and even a psychiatric hospital.[80]

The swelling ranks of dependent, neglected, and abused children placed enormous pressure on Child Protective Service agencies around the country. "It's maddening to work here," sighed a director of Washington State's Children's Service's programs. The escalation of child abuse reports provided a crucial source of distress, but the demands of trying to reunify families also took a toll.[81]

According to some skeptics, the movement to reunify families rested on the same simplistic assumption that years earlier had informed Charles Loring Brace's placing-out movement: namely, that family life was the answer to child dependency. Although the idea made a good slogan, it was wrapped in complexities. One complexity involved what kind of family life was at issue. In 1991 Illinois judges wrestled with that complicated problem when they considered the fate of seven-year-old Sarah, whom the courts had removed as a baby from her drug-addicted mother and placed with foster parents Joseph and Marjorie Procopio. The mother subsequently claimed that she was rehabilitated and wanted her child back. Sarah, who had never known her mother, begged to remain with the Procopios. A juvenile court judge nevertheless decided that a reunited family best served the interests of the child. A panel of Illinois Appellate judges who reexamined the case disagreed. Sarah, the panel declared, was "a helpless child caught in the quagmire of the bureaucratic maze which we mistakenly call our child-welfare system." For the moment, the judges ruled that Sarah should at least be able to see the Procopios while living with her mother and awaiting another custody hearing.[82]

Further complicating the issue of family reunification was the continuing disrepair of large numbers of birth families. In mid-1993, the fate of three-year-old Joseph Wallace illustrated this problem. After Illinois's Department of Child and Family Services and the Juvenile Court returned him to his home, his mother hanged him with an electrical cord. The legislature promptly began to consider a law that would elevate "the child's best interest" over keeping a family together. By 1996 one of the leading advocates of family preservation programs, Richard Gelles, had concluded that the goals of protecting children and saving the family unit were in basic conflict.[83]

IX

Amid these colliding issues and a growing child welfare crisis, a cry went up to "bring back the orphanage," as recommended by Judge Lois Forer in a 1988 *Washington Monthly* essay. That advice flowed from her growing discouragement, after 50 years as an attorney and judge, about what was happening to children. She noted that many adoptions ended unhappily. And she agreed with a colleague who said, "We're sending kids home to bad circumstances because foster care is such a terrible alternative." After she discovered that a number of adults had better memories of orphanages than of foster care, Forer concluded that "government should provide safe permanent homes for all these countless children who are living at risk." Such homes needed to have well-trained, highly qualified, closely monitored professional staffs. Dozens of positive responses to her article from people who had lived in foster homes and orphanage care reinforced her views regarding government-sponsored children's homes.[84]

Several other individuals began calling for small group-care facilities as a supplement to the existing alternatives of adoption, foster care, and home preservation, which were buckling under the sheer numbers of children and, in many cases, not working well. As dependent, neglected, and abused children poured into protective custody, the nation had to devise solutions. New York senator Daniel Patrick Moynihan predicted in 1989 that the proliferation of no-parent children because of drugs would likely force the reestablishment of orphanages. Two years later journalist Penelope Lemov noted that orphanages were already returning because there were no alternatives. But the orphanage she described was small and had a dozen or fewer children under the care of highly trained professionals. In 1993 Illinois state senator Judy Baar Topinka proclaimed that her state "will have orphanages." She and some of her colleagues who wanted state-supported institutions to provide long-term care for needy children were responding to several scandals, including the murder of Joseph Wallace and the discovery of 19 children in utter destitution in a Chicago apartment. "I've lost my patience," Topinka said. "Kids are being killed, tortured, starved, abandoned."[85]

Conservatives such as writer Charles Murray and Speaker of the House Newt Gingrich also championed orphanages, but their agenda differed from that of individuals such as Forer. Murray and Gingrich wanted primarily to smother the welfare state and penalize illegitimacy. In a 1993 article in the *Wall Street Journal,* Murray summed up ideas he had been discussing for some time. He described illegitimacy as "the single most important social problem of our time" and advocated an end to welfare. In his opinion, by cutting off AFDC, food stamps, and other forms of welfare, the government would put pressure on young unmarried women either not to have children or to relinquish them. Murray hoped that the smaller children would find adoptive homes; orphanages could take care of older children who were not adopted. "I am not recommending Dickensian barracks," he emphasized. "Those who find the word 'orphanages' objectionable may think of them as 24-hour-a-day preschools."[86]

Gingrich picked up on Murray's ideas. In mid-1994, he proposed ending welfare payments to unwed teenage mothers and telling them, "We'll help you with foster care, we'll help you with orphanages, we'll help you with adoption," but not with money to keep your illegitimate child. Later that year, the Republicans captured both houses of Congress for the first time in half a century. They did so with the Gingrich-inspired "Contract for America," which had called for halting welfare and replacing federal regulations with market solutions. Gingrich endorsed a Republican welfare reform bill that would stop payments to women under 21 and instead use that money to operate "a boarding school or a group home" for the children of unwed mothers. He envisioned a time in which a poor, unwed mother, who might otherwise abandon her infant, would call an 800 number and say to herself, "Here are people who want children to take care of, and I don't have to dump them in a trash Dumpster." When First Lady Hillary Clinton dubbed his idea "unbelievable and absurd," he urged her and other critics to see the movie *Boys' Town,* the 1938 film about Father Flanagan's famous home in Nebraska for boys. "The Orphanage," *Newsweek* asked on its December 12, 1994, cover: "Is It Time to Bring It Back?"[87]

Significantly, several popular movies in the 1990s hinted that a new image of the orphan was taking shape, one that allowed public distancing from tragedy and suffering. *Home Alone,* a record-grossing comedy about an eight-year-old boy whose family accidentally abandons him, set the tone. The boy, Kevin, represented a substantial departure in popular culture from the familiar portraits of abandoned children, from Oliver Twist to Little Orphan Annie, that had long evoked sympathy. As journalist Kay Hymowitz observed, Kevin "is savvy, cool, and devilishly resourceful. Nothing in his demeanor suggests need or demands pity." Unlike the traditional helpless

The return of the orphanage as a proposed solution during the late-twentieth-century debate over welfare policy. © 1994, Newsweek, Inc. All rights reserved. Reprinted by permission. Photo courtesy of Caufield & Shook Collection, University of Louisville Photographic Archives.

orphan who exuded innocence, Kevin and his 1990s counterparts (in movies such as *Problem Child* and *Problem Child II*) were "designer orphans," typically with access to a range of consumer goods, radiating "a polished veneer of wise-cracking, hip irony," and capable of cruel tricks. "Instead of evoking pity," stated Hymowitz, "they absolve adults of their indifference and neglect." Although such films implicitly acknowledged the existence of abuse and neglect, they wrapped such subjects in humor. When one father advises his son, "Don't trust anyone," the son asks, "Not even your own father?"

A cartoonist's rendering of House Speaker Newt Gingrich's proposal to reform welfare policies by reintroducing orphanges. Courtesy Milt Priggee/Spokesmen-Review.

"Especially your own father," is the reply. "I miss Mommy," cries the youngest child in *Don't Tell Mom the Babysitter's Dead*. His older siblings stare at him incredulously. Hymowitz suspected that "Hollywood's new orphans" allowed audiences to swallow in laughter "their bitter fatalism about family life run amok."[88]

Within that interpretive context, the backlash against repressed memories of sexual abuse looked like another form of cultural distancing from family horrors. As the media focused on the theme of false accusations, commentators often intimated that alleged victims simply sought attention and sympathy. This shift in opinion suggested that testimonials about sexual abuse amounted to little more than a fad. Such opinion implicitly diminished the awful reality of child sexual abuse. Some critics of the trend surmised that it provided the public with a way of making more manageable the terrifying facts of molestation, incest, and unwanted sexual contact. A *Los Angeles Times* poll in 1985 discovered that 22 percent of Americans had suffered child sexual abuse. Even *Newsweek*'s much more conservative estimate that 1 in 10 girls under 14 had been sexually abused was hardly reassuring. By the 1990s, the backlash against false memories specifically, and accusations of sexual abuse generally, contained suggestions of a kind of public denial, ironically reminiscent of the "Never tell" advice that haunted most victims of abuse.[89]

Epilogue

In late November 1995, the ghastly fate of six-year-old Elisa Izquierdo in a ravaged section of New York City forced the nation's child welfare system once again into the national spotlight. The crushing blow to the head that killed her followed months of terror during which her mother forced her to eat feces and mopped the floor with her head. One police officer claimed that he had not seen a worse case of child abuse in his 22 years on the force. In her last tortured weeks, Elisa suffered sexual abuse and endless beatings, but no one came to her rescue. Most neighbors who heard her pathetic screams did nothing, and the several who called the authorities got no response. "A Shameful Death," declared *Time* magazine on its cover: "Let down by the system, murdered by her mom, a little girl symbolizes America's failure to protect its children."[1]

The wave of sympathy for Elisa Izquierdo was certainly understandable, but some observers wondered once again why the public rage was so selective. In 1987 Lisa Steinberg's brutal death at the hands of her adoptive father had stirred a similar firestorm of publicity about children at risk. Yet the subsequent deaths of some seven hundred other children in New York City alone as a result of abuse or neglect had barely made the news, until the killing of Izquierdo. It was puzzling indeed that the fate of millions of children who lived each day in social and economic conditions as hopelessly pathetic as Elisa's failed to galvanize a massive public uproar. "It's almost a cliché now to say that we only pretend to care about children, so obvious has become our vast social neglect," wrote journalist Katha Pollitt. That record of neglect and abuse constituted nothing less than the "nation's shame," in the words of Secretary of Health and Human Services Donna Shalala.[2]

Shalala's words reverberated across the past. In the wake of a tragedy such as Izquierdo's—for example, after the revelations in 1874 concerning Mary Ellen Connolly's ordeal, or following the discovery in the 1960s of the "battered child"—various groups had forced the issue of child protection to the forefront. They had in notable instances directed child welfare strategies

down particular paths by mobilizing other citizens, influencing private and public policies, and even obtaining legislation. Thus Hannah Stillman and her friends had established the Boston Female Orphan Asylum in 1800, thereby helping to lay the institutional ground in the nineteenth century for hundreds of orphanages, houses of refuge, and almshouse nurseries. By the mid-1800s, antipathy for such institutions had prompted Charles Loring Brace and others to champion the alternatives of foster care and home placement. Private organizations, including the Societies for the Prevention of Cruelty to Children, initially dominated efforts in behalf of dependent and endangered children, but by the late 1800s state officials were increasingly active in dealing with children at risk. In the 1930s, the federal government took the lead, at first by reshaping earlier mothers' pensions programs into Aid for Dependent Children, and later by passing such laws as the 1974 Child Abuse Prevention and Treatment Act.

Invariably, however, these evolving children's policies were intertwined with highly charged issues regarding the roles of families and government. Moreover, bursts of interest in children's causes typically gave way to periods of public apathy, until a crisis or shocking incident again galvanized a response. When attempted solutions proved expensive, the public and policymakers characteristically settled for symbolic and rhetorical answers, ones that separated matters of child dependency, neglect, and abuse from their most common social and economic root: poverty and its attendant consequences.

By the 1990s study after study showed connections between child abuse and low income—evidence that hardly facilitated a consensus on policy. People suspicious of social welfare programs were inclined to perceive such findings as additional proof that the poor were a breed apart, largely responsible for their own sorry predicament. On the other hand, advocates of a social safety net tended to disassociate abuse from social class, in order to shield child protection programs from the stigma of unpopular welfare programs. As a result of these tendencies, poverty, and its accompanying miseries, continued to wreak havoc on the lives of helpless youngsters. In that regard, Katha Pollitt correctly identified the nation's "vast social neglect" as the major threat to children. Sadly, almost inexorably, that overwhelming social failure took a staggering toll.[3]

By the mid-1990s the renewed interest in children and the debates over child welfare issues were thus welcome. "Family preservation" policies, for example, desperately needed rethinking, despite their wide appeal. The arguments of family preservation advocates such as the Homebuilders, an influential organization headquartered in Washington State, were logical and persuasive: Rather than removing endangered children from their biological families, child welfare programs should seek to "remove the risk" in those homes so that the children could remain with their natural families. The Adoption Assistance and Child Welfare Act of 1980 favored such a goal but was mainly a

paper commitment. In 1993 child advocacy groups such as the Children's Defense Fund successfully enlarged that commitment by pushing into law the Family Preservation and Support Program (FPSP) of the Omnibus Budget Reconciliation Act. The legislation provided $930 million for five years that the federal government could offer states, on a three-to-one matching basis, to fund services that would help families keep their children at home.[4]

Although family preservation had become a favored response to child dependency, neglect, and abuse, skeptics justifiably worried about it. For one thing, it was not as innovative as its champions suggested; it harkened back a century earlier to the flawed efforts of socially upstanding "friendly visitors" who worked voluntarily with the poor. Modern family preservationists had, in the words of several leading child welfare scholars, simply "sanitized 'friendly visiting' by creating a secular and professionalized version of it." Trying to improve on past strategies was not inherently misguided, of course, but some of the main reasons for such efforts were troubling. Family preservation appealed to some groups mainly as a cheap alternative to the soaring costs of foster care. These fiscal concerns did not bode well for what organizations such as the Homebuilders and the Children's Defense Fund had in mind: providing extensive family services. Conservative defenders of the home not only disliked such services but also interpreted family preservation mainly as a way to sanctify parental authority.[5]

Ideology easily obscured the fact that family preservation was a risky venture for many children and, for an Elisa Izquierdo, calamitous. The courts had returned Elisa to a mother whose long history of drug abuse, emotional instability, and cruelty were a matter of record. Columnist Murray Kempton raged that the child welfare system's "philosophical preference for the monster parent as caretaker was founded not on concern for family values but for budgetary costs."[6]

Although family preservation policies demanded scrutiny, so did the longtime alternatives of foster care and adoption. There were far too many disasters such as the one in 1989 when foster parents subjected a nine-year-old Los Angeles boy to beatings, sodomizing, burned genitals, and, finally, drowning. Adoptions hardly guaranteed safer environments, and sometimes turned children into helpless pawns in contests involving race, gender, confidentiality, and competing custody claims.[7]

The crescendo of talk about helping children was problematic at best, as the passage of major welfare reform legislation in 1996 starkly demonstrated. The law President Bill Clinton signed on August 22 abolished the 60-year-old AFDC program, set a five-year cap on welfare benefits, required most recipients to work within two years, and provided federal block grants to states to establish their own programs (which could, for example, include harsher work requirements). Clinton's decision to support such legislation sparked a fierce political reaction, much of it from people who otherwise usually supported the president. "Shame! Shame! Shame!" chanted several hundred demonstrators outside the White House. "This act will leave a moral blot on his presidency and on our nation that will never be forgotten," charged one of Clinton's close friends, Marian Wright Edelman of the Children's Defense Fund. Senator Daniel Patrick Moynihan (D-NY) warned that, "in our confusion, we are doing mad things."[8]

The repeal of AFDC had its defenders, of course. Representative E. Clay Shaw Jr. (R-FL), a key sponsor, hailed it as "probably . . . the most important piece of legislation in this half-century"—legislation that would "rescue millions of Americans out of a corrupt welfare system." House Majority Leader Newt Gingrich (R-GA) asserted that the president had nothing less than "an absolute moral obligation to sign this bill." Senator Phil Gramm (R-TX) praised the reform measure for rescuing children from an old system that "bred child abuse and neglect." Clinton himself had doubts, however, observing that the legislation "throws the dice on the future without knowing the consequences." Some individuals who worried that the law was flawed nevertheless judged the welfare system so awful that, in the words of journalist Mickey Kaus, "it's worth taking some risks to end it."[9]

Critics countered that throwing the dice, or taking risks, on children's lives made for terrible policy. "Poor Children: The Guinea Pigs of Welfare Reform," read one headline. According to an estimate of the Urban Institute, the new law would increase the number of children in poverty by more than one million. Senator Moynihan described the legislation as "the most brutal act of social policy since Reconstruction," a "monstrous political deception," and "an obscene act of social regression." Fearing for the worst, Moynihan argued against "a fearsome assumption," namely "that the behavior of certain adults can be changed by making the lives of their children as wretched as possible." The law "is mean," complained Rep. John Lewis (D-GA). "It is base. It is downright lowdown." Several critics believed that society, in its efforts to deal with a host of social problems, was scapegoating the nine million children who benefited from AFDC, which consumed less than 1 percent of the federal budget. One columnist spotted a sad irony in that situation. "If an individual brutalizes a child, the crime scene can be dusted for fingerprints," wrote Norman Solomon. "But no fingerprints are available when the social order routinely brutalizes children." Moynihan was perhaps most prophetic. "So you've come to do welfare reform," he had told assistant secretary of Health and Human Services David T. Ellwood in 1993. "I'll look forward to reading your book about why it failed this time."[10]

Moynihan's pessimism was entirely understandable given the questions that haunted child welfare policy at the end of the twentieth century. What, for example, was supposed to happen to the more than 460,000 children whom authorities by 1995 had already removed from families because of abuse and neglect? If AFDC supposedly encouraged single mothers to have more children, what of the fact that, as sociologist Ruth Sidel pointed out, "in no state do welfare benefits plus food stamps bring recipient families up to the poverty line"? How did members of Congress, as they tried to shift responsibility from the federal government to the states, deal with the fact that between 1980 and 1992, as a major study revealed, "real state spending on AFDC per poor family declined by 31 percent"? Some politicians saw the 1996 welfare reform bill as providing an opportunity for even more cuts at the state level. "In my own state," said Colorado's Democratic governor Roy Romer, "there are some legislators who are saying, 'Now we have a chance to cut welfare spending all off.' " If parents, often single mothers, lost welfare checks because they were not working, what would happen to their children (whose average age in 1993 was 7.4 years)? If the mother worked, who would take care of her children? Were there not contradictions between criticizing women who left the home to work and chastising them—welfare mothers—for not working? According to the Children's Defense Fund in 1995, proposals to revise and cut AFDC with time limits, work requirements, and additional eligibility restrictions would end assistance to an estimated four million poor children. What would happen to them? In that regard, as columnist Murray Kempton remarked, the "most systematic form of child abuse," and one that differed little from the physical violence in housing projects, was "the sort practiced in the chambers of Congress and the offices of state budget directors."[11]

If orphanages again became popular, who would pay for them? At the end of 1994, welfare, housing, Medicaid, and food stamps cost around $16,000 for a family of three; a quality residential center for abused and neglected children cost at least $30,000 per child annually (and from $40,000 to $48,000 at Boys' Town); foster care was more than $15,000 per year per child. "If even a quarter of an estimated 1 million children who would be cut loose under [House Speaker Newt] Gingrich's plan ended up in orphanages," reported *Time* magazine, "the additional cost to the public would be more than $8 billion," a genuine "budget buster." There might be cheaper kinds of institutional care, of course, but it would resemble the "warehousing" of hundreds of children that had given orphanages a bad name in the first place. As historian David Rothman said, "When custody meets care, custody always wins."[12]

Columnist Katha Pollitt suspected that the talk about restoring orphanages was in fact a smoke screen. The objective was less to resurrect orphanages than to cultivate the view that children with living parents were in fact " 'orphans' just because those parents are young, female, unmarried and poor. We are thus also being taught to see those women as having no rights and nothing to contribute—as being, in effect, dead. . . ."[13]

Legislation to abolish welfare and to make it a workfare program had huge implications for dependent children. "Like horror stories? Forget Stephen King," advised one newspaper in a 1995 editorial on how "child-care issues haunt society." The editorial asked who would watch the children if government forced welfare mothers back into the workforce after two years. "If you don't have a good answer to that question," the editors wrote, "you'll soon have a crisis on your hands that will make the trillion-dollar national debt look like child's play." Marian Wright Edelman described the congressional assault on welfare policies as "really quite evil." How, she wondered, could anyone in 1996 justify cutting the proposed $250 billion "from programs for poor children, poor families, disabled children—and it's not even to balance the budget! It's to give a two-hundred-and-forty-five-billion-dollar tax cut to the non-needy."[14]

Despite all the talk about helping children, they were, as usual, mere puppets in larger political, social, and ideological struggles. "If patriotism is the last resort of the scoundrel," wrote columnist Ellen Goodman, "talking about children can be the last hiding place of skulduggery." Only a few years before, in the early 1980s, politicians had rallied to the issue of "missing children," a label that summoned up images of strangers abducting youngsters—actually a rare occurrence. As the search for missing children intensified, inspiring at one point the strategy of printing their pictures on milk cartons and shopping bags, liberal and conservative politicians alike embraced the cause. The non-controversial issue was, as one congressional aide admitted, "the apple pie of the eighties."[15]

There was little that was "apple pie" about most children's issues, however. In 1993, according to chilling figures from the Children's Defense Fund (CDF), the child poverty rate was higher than it had been in 30 years; 15.7 million children, including 27 percent of all American children under age three, lived in poverty. Moreover, the number of confirmed cases of child maltreatment (out of almost three million reported instances) exceeded one million. Half of those confirmed cases entailed, in the words of the CDF, "neglect, often deprivation of necessities, as opposed to physical or sexual abuse." Of the additional cases, 22.3 percent involved physical abuse; 13.6 percent, sexual abuse; 5.1 percent, emotional abuse; and 9.1 percent "other." Additional bad news came from a study predicting that, by the year 2000, the AIDS epidemic would leave between 72,000 and 125,000 motherless children.[16]

Yet campaigns for justice too often stopped at the age barrier. Hard-won gains for women, for example, made wife-beating a crime—no matter what the husband's culture, religion, race, ethnicity, or economic status. By the 1990s the time to confer such protections on children was long overdue. By defining child abuse as criminal behavior, society would allow law enforcement authorities to deal with violence while freeing child welfare agencies to help families who faced overwhelming social and economic pressures. The political backlash appeared to doom such changes, however, particularly when some commentators dismissed the issue of domestic violence as nothing but "one of the left's favorite big lies" to advance antifamily strategies. By century's end, efforts were thus under way to define child neglect and abuse in the narrowest terms. In 1996 in Washington State, for instance, legislators debated a bill to demarcate child abuse as actions that inflicted "physical injury that causes or creates a substantial risk of death," or that resulted in "protracted" injury or disfigurement or in a damaged bodily organ. The bill's sponsor, whom Child Protective Services had earlier investigated for spanking a foster child with a Ping-Pong paddle and a wooden spoon, insisted that he simply wanted to protect parents from false accusations.[17]

Over generations, the history of child dependency, neglect, and abuse in the United States remained anything but uplifting. In the tragic DeShaney case, Justice Harry Blackmun wondered who spoke for Joshua. A bigger question was who spoke for all the other homeless, deprived, battered, and impoverished children? As the twentieth century ended, that question, and the answer to it, grew increasingly urgent.

Chronology

1601	The Elizabethan Poor Law, with considerable implications for dependent children, consolidates measures of assistance to needy citizens.
1618	The Virginia Company sends one hundred poor children as apprentices to the Virginia colony.
1641	Massachusetts enacts the *Body of Liberties*, protecting "the liberties of children" but also prescribing the death penalty for unruly youths.
1646	Massachusetts amends the *Body of Liberties*, underwriting parental authority with the state's power, yet also protecting children from "unnatural severitie."
1658	Maryland enacts county court system to oversee orphans' assets and, by implication, to appoint guardians for dependent children who need them.
1663	Maryland requires guardians to oversee orphans according to their income and status; most poor children would be indentured.
1675	Massachusetts General Court establishes tithingmen to inspect families and ensure, among other things, that families are not neglecting the proper rearing of children.
1729	Ursuline nuns establish orphanage in New Orleans, the first orphan asylum in what would become the United States.
1738–1739	German Lutherans open short-lived Ebenezer orphanage outside Savannah, Georgia, and a few months later George Whitefield establishes the Bethesda Orphan House nearby—the first orphanages in the British colonies in North America.

1790   Charleston, South Carolina, establishes first public orphanage in the United States.

1800   Boston Female Asylum opens.

1809   The first public decision to challenge the prevailing rights of fathers, *Prather v. Prather*, in South Carolina, awards child's custody to the mother rather than the abusive father; a new legal doctrine—"the best interests of the child"—begins to emerge.

1813   In *Commonwealth v. Addicks*, a Pennsylvania court articulates a "tender years" doctrine, tilting child custody cases in favor of mothers.

1820   Philadelphia Children's Asylum, the second public orphanage in the United States, opens for poor, dependent whites under age 10.

1822   Society of Friends opens the Shelter for Colored Orphans, Philadelphia's first private children's charity for African Americans.

1825   New York House of Refuge opens the first U.S. institution for delinquent children; like subsequent houses of refuge, it also accepts neglected, abused, and dependent children.

1835   Philadelphia Children's Asylum closes; city's new Blockley Almshouse accepts dependent children.

1838   *Ex Parte Crouse* upholds right of the state to remove children from "incompetent" parents and to place the children in institutions.

1851   Massachusetts passes landmark "Act to Provide for the Adoption of Children," the first formalized adoption law in the United States.

1853   Charles Loring Brace founds the New York Children's Aid Society (NYCAS).

1854   NYCAS starts its "orphan trains," implicitly instituting a free foster care system.

1862   Hebrew Orphan Asylum opens, ultimately housing more than 1,700 children.

1863   White rioters destroy New York City's Colored Orphan Asylum.

          Catholics found the New York Catholic Protectory, one of the nation's largest orphanages, sheltering almost 2,200 children in 1885 alone.

1866   Ohio establishes a system allowing counties to impose taxes to support asylums for needy children.

1872   Charles Loring Brace publishes *The Dangerous Classes of New York*, helping to popularize foster care.

1874   The New York Society for the Prevention of Cruelty to Children is organized.

Michigan opens its State Public School for Dependent and Neglected Children at Coldwater.

1875   New York state passes a "Children's Law," prohibiting the commitment of children to poorhouses.

1880   Massachusetts starts plan to board dependent children in private homes—paid foster care—and expands the plan two years later.

1883   Martin Van Buren Van Arsdale establishes the Illinois Children's Home and Aid Society, launching the Home Society movement.

1886   Boston Children's Aid Society hires Charles Birtwell, who works to preserve families and to use foster home placement as a last resort and, if possible, as a temporary means to help restore child to own family.

1899   Chicago Juvenile Court is founded, the first of its kind.

1907   The *Delineator* magazine, edited by Theodore Dreiser, launches its "Child Rescue Campaign," opposing orphanages and boosting the home-placing movement.

1909   First White House Conference on Dependent Children emphasizes the importance of home life and says that children should not be removed from families solely for reasons of poverty.

1911   Mothers' (or widows') pension programs begin, initially in Jackson County, Missouri, and then in Illinois where the legislature enacts the first statewide plan.

1912   Congress establishes the U.S. Children's Bureau.

1929   New York Children's Aid Society terminates its "orphan trains."

1935   Title IV of the Social Security Act establishes Aid for Dependent Children (ADC).

1953   Jean Paton initiates an adoption rights movement by opening the Life History Study Center to help adoptees trace their roots.

1954   Vincent DeFrancis of the American Humane Association conducts first national survey on the subjects of child abuse and neglect.

1957   The Children's Bureau issues first major statement from a federal agency that states that child abuse deserves national attention.

1961   C. Henry Kempe and colleagues conduct a symposium on "The Battered-Child Syndrome" at the American Academy of Pediatrics' annual meeting.

1962   *Journal of the American Medical Association* publishes essay by Kempe et al., on "The Battered-Child Syndrome," and advances shocking estimate of the number of children who die because of abuse.

Following up on temporary legislation of a year earlier, the Public Service Amendments change ADC to Aid to Families of Dependent Children (AFDC)—with an emphasis on family rehabilitative social services—end "suitable home" criteria, provide federal assistance to two-parent families in which unemployment results in income below the poverty line, and make funds available for foster care.

1967   In *In re Gault* the Supreme Court faults the logic of institutionalization in the 1838 *Crouse* case and, by ruling that the juvenile court system had denied a boy's basic procedural rights, advances the idea that children, like adults, should be protected by the Bill of Rights.

Congress amends AFDC by shifting focus from "social services" to "workfare," requiring individuals with children over age six to register for work and training.

1968–1969   The Supreme Court bans the man-in-the-house rule within AFDC, and then abolishes state residency requirements.

1969   The Nixon administration proposes a Family Assistance Plan to replace the existing welfare bureaucracy with direct cash payments to poor families.

1971   Adoptees Liberty Association (ALMA) forms as a support group for adoptees and as an opponent of "sealed records."

1972   National Association of Black Social Workers declares that only African American families should adopt children of their race.

1973   Children's Defense Fund is founded.

A new Senate subcommittee on children holds hearings on child abuse.

1974   Congress passes the Child Abuse Prevention and Treatment Act (CAPTA), establishing National Center on Child Abuse and Neglect and providing financial assistance for prevention and treatment programs.

1977   In *Ingraham v. Wright*, the Supreme Court rules that the Constitution offers no protection against corporal punishment in public schools.

1978   Indian Child Welfare Act discourages removal of Indian children from Indian settings and recognizes the jurisdictional salience of tribal courts in Native American child welfare issues.

Christina Crawford's best-selling *Mommie Dearest* helps to popularize the issue of child abuse by showing that it is not limited to poor families.

1980   Adoption and Assistance and Child Welfare Act endorses permanency planning and limits use of foster care.

1989   Supreme Court rules in *DeShaney v. Winnebago County Department of Social Services* that the state has no constitutional obligation to protect children from abusive parents and, thus, that child welfare officials were not responsible for the permanent disabling of three-year-old Joshua by his father.

1990   Marjie Lindstrom and Rochelle Sharpe publish series of Pulitzer Prize-winning essays on undetected child abuse deaths.

1993   The Omnibus Budget Reconciliation Act includes a Family Preservation and Support Program, a five-year federal commitment to strengthening families and reducing out-of-family placement of children.

1994   Congress passes Multiethnic Placement Act, prohibiting undue delays in adoption in order to find racial matches.

1995–1996   Congress debates welfare reform legislation to end AFDC and provide block grants to states to administer; on August 22, 1996, President Clinton signs the welfare bill.

Notes

Introduction

1. Qtns., Ruthie Bolton, *Gal: A True Life* (New York: Harcourt Brace, 1994), 49; Anthony G. Johnson, *A Rock and a Hard Place: One Boy's Triumphant Story* (New York: Crown, 1993), 4.

2. See, e.g., Joel Best, *Threatened Children: Rhetoric and Concern about Child-Victims* (Chicago: University of Chicago Press, 1990), and Barbara J. Nelson, *Making an Issue of Child Abuse* (Chicago: University of Chicago Press, 1984), for insightful discussions of the formation of issues.

3. Robert Bremner, *Children and Youth in America: A Documentary History*, vol. 2 (Cambridge: Harvard University Press, 1971), 247; Timothy A. Hacsi, " 'A Plain and Solemn Duty': A History of Orphan Asylums in America" (Ph.D. diss., University of Pennsylvania, 1993), 90 ("virtual").

4. Children's Defense Fund, *The State of America's Children Yearbook, 1995* (Washington, D.C.: Children's Defense Fund, 1995), 13 (stat.).

5. Nelson, *Making an Issue of Child Abuse*, 15 (Gelles); Best, *Threatened Children*, 112 (stuff).

6. Duncan Lindsey, *The Welfare of Children* (New York: Oxford University Press, 1994), 3 (qtn.).

7. Richard Wexler, *Wounded Innocents: The Real Victims of the War Against Child Abuse* (Buffalo: Prometheus Books, 1990), 45 ("tragedy"); Murray A. Straus, *Beating the Devil Out of Them: Corporal Punishment in American Families* (New York: Lexington Books, 1994), 173; John Demos, *Past, Present, and Personal: The Family and the Life Course in American History* (New York: Oxford University Press, 1986), 69.

8. On the Carver case, see, e.g., Bonnie Harris, "Uncle Tells Police He Killed Niece," *Spokesman-Review,* 17 June 1995: A1, 9; Jim Lynch and Gita Sitaramiah, "Rachel's Life Was Filled with Fear and Abuse," ibid., A1, 8; Jim Lynch, "California Took Rachel, Sister from Mom's Home," ibid., 30 June 1995: A1, 5; Lynch, "Children's Deaths Spur Community Action," ibid., 27 August 1995: A1, 9 (qtn.).

Chapter 1

1. Mary A. Mason, *From Father's Property to Children's Rights* (New York: Columbia University Press, 1994), xii (property); Elizabeth Pleck, *Domestic Tyranny: The Making of American Social Policy against Family Violence from Colonial Times to the Present* (New York: Oxford University Press, 1987), 8 (Coke); John M. Johnson, "Symbolic Salvation: The Changing Meanings of the Child Maltreatment Movement," *Studies in Symbolic Interaction* 6 (1985): 292 (rule); Jeanne M. Giovannoni and Rosina M. Becerra, *Defining Child Abuse* (New York: Free Press, 1979), 31.
2. See, e.g., Judith Areen, "Intervention Between Parent and Child: A Reappraisal of the State's Role in Child Neglect and Abuse Cases," *The Georgetown Law Journal* 63 (March 1975): 894–96; Michael B. Katz, *In the Shadow of the Poorhouse: A Social History of Welfare in America* (New York: Basic Books, 1986), 13–14; Walter I. Trattner, *From Poor Law to Welfare State,* 2d ed. (New York: Free Press, 1979), 10–12.
3. Joseph M. Hawes, *The Children's Rights Movement: A History of Advocacy and Protection* (Boston: Twayne, 1991), 2; Giovannoni and Becerra, *Defining Child Abuse,* 36–39.
4. Carole Shammas, "Anglo-American Household Government in Comparative Perspective," *The William and Mary Quarterly* 52 (January 1995): 104–9 (qtn., 104), 115–20, 124–26.
5. Qtns. in Robert Bremner, *Children and Youth in America,* vol. 1 (Cambridge: Harvard University Press, 1970), 7–8, and Grace Abbott, ed., *The Child and the State,* vol. 1 (Chicago: University of Chicago Press, 1938), 189; Mason, *From Father's Property to Children's Rights,* 32 (father); E-mail communications, E. Wayne Carp and J. Douglas Deal, 25 August 1995, H-State@MSU.EDU.
6. Ross W. Beales Jr., "The Child in Seventeenth-Century America," in *American Childhood: A Research Guide and Historical Handbook,* ed. Joseph M. Hawes and N. Ray Hiner (Westport, Conn.: Greenwood Press, 1985), 18–20; Darrett B. and Anita H. Rutman, *A Place in Time: Middlesex County, Virginia, 1650–1750* (New York: Norton, 1984), 114–19 (qtn., 119).
7. Lois Green Carr, "The Development of the Maryland Orphans' Court, 1654–1715," in *Law, Society, and Politics in Early Maryland,* ed. Aubrey C. Land, Lois Green Carr, and Edward C. Papenfuse (Balti-

more: Johns Hopkins University Press, 1977), 41–56 (qtn., 56); Rutman, *A Place in Time*, 116–18.

8. Trattner, *From Poor Law to Welfare State*, 23; Abbott, *The Child and the State*, 189; John Demos, *A Little Commonwealth: Family Life in Plymouth Colony* (New York: Oxford University Press, 1970), 104 (qtn.).
9. See, e.g., Areen, "Intervention Between Parent and Child," 902; Henry Thurston, *The Dependent Child* (New York: Columbia University Press, 1930), 10, 15–16 (Love), 18.
10. Thurston, *The Dependent Child*, 10, 17 (qtn.).
11. Bremner, *Children and Youth in America*, vol. 1, 123–24; Mason, *From Father's Property to Children's Rights*, 36.
12. Bremner, *Children and Youth in America*, vol.1, 125.
13. See, e.g., Thurston, *The Dependent Child*, 17; Grace Abbott, *The Child and the State,* vol. 2 (Chicago: University of Chicago Press, 1938), 3; Kristine E. Nelson, "The Best Asylum: Charles Loring Brace and Foster Family Care" (D.S.W. diss., University of California, Berkeley, 1980), 21–22. Rutman, *A Place in Time*, 138, shows how Benjamin Davis, e.g., moved through several indentures.
14. Carr, "The Development of the Maryland Orphans' Court," 50; Alan D. Watson, "Orphanage in Colonial North Carolina: Edgecombe County as a Case Study," *North Carolina Historical Review* 52 (1975): 106 (qtn.), 108, 113.
15. Marcus W. Jernegan, *Laboring and Dependent Classes in Colonial America, 1607–1783* (Chicago: University of Chicago Press, 1931), 165–70; Rutman, *A Place in Time*, 128–29; Mason, *From Father's Property to Children's Rights*, 34–35 (Harper); Watson, "Orphanage in Colonial North Carolina," 106–08.
16. Lawrence W. Towner, "The Indentures of Boston's Poor Apprentices: 1734–1805," *Proceedings of the Colonial Society of Massachusetts* 43 (February 1962): 424.
17. Clifford K. Shipton, *Isaiah Thomas: Printer, Patriot and Philanthropist, 1749–1831* (Rochester, N.Y.: Leo Hart, 1948), 2–4.
18. On the importance of the Body of Liberties, see Hawes, *The Children's Rights Movement*, 4–5; Pleck, *Domestic Tyranny*, 21–22 ("the first American reform against family violence"); and John R. Sutton, *Stubborn Children: Controlling Delinquency in the United States, 1640–1981* (Berkeley, Calif.: University of California Press, 1988), which describes the stubborn child statute as "the first statute of its kind in North America, and probably in the modern world" (11). Mason, *From Father's Property to Children's Rights*, 36 (Franklin and Fowler).
19. Mason, *From Father's Property to Children's Rights*, 4; Bremner, *Children and Youth in America*, vol.1, 28; Giovannoni and Becerra, *Defining Child Abuse*, 39–40, 51. Also, Abbott, *The Child and the State*, vol. 1, 212–13.

20. Shammas, "Anglo-American Household Government," 111–12.
21. Edmund S. Morgan, *The Puritan Family,* rev. ed. (New York: Harper & Row, 1966), 103–8; John Demos, *Past, Present, and Personal: The Family and The Life Course in American History* (New York: Oxford University Press, 1986), 78, 84 (qtn.); Philip Greven, *Spare the Child: The Religious Roots of Punishment and the Psychological Impact of Physical Abuse* (New York: Knopf, 1991), 48–49 (re: scriptures); Pleck, *Domestic Tyranny,* 27 (Plymouth), 28.
22. Pleck, *Domestic Tyranny,* 27.
23. Wilma King, *Stolen Childhood: Slave Youth in Nineteenth-Century America* (Bloomington: Indiana University Press, 1995), 31 (worms), 69, 93–98; Eugene Genovese, *Roll, Jordan, Roll: The World the Slaves Made* (New York: Pantheon, 1974), 509–12.
24. Pleck, *Domestic Tyranny,* 29 (minister); Andrew Billingsley and Jeanne M. Giovannoni, *Children of the Storm: Black Children and American Child Welfare* (New York: Harcourt Brace Jovanovich, 1972), 23–24.
25. Bremner, *Children and Youth in America,* vol. 1, 267–68; Abbott, *The Child and the State,* vol. 2, 4 (qtn.), 7.
26. Abbott, *The Child and the State,* vol. 1, 202.
27. David J. Rothman, *The Discovery of the Asylum: Social Order and Disorder in the New Republic* (Boston: Little, Brown, 1971), 36–42; Abbott, *The Child and the State,* vol. 2, 4.
28. Timothy A. Hacsi, " 'A Plain and Solemn Duty': A History of Orphan Asylums in America" (Ph.D. diss., University of Pennsylvania, 1993), 27.
29. Clyde Buckingham, "Early American Orphanages: Ebenezer and Bethesda," *Social Forces* 26 (March 1948): 312–13.
30. Ibid., 313–21 (319 re: time); Abbott, *The Child and the State,* vol. 2, 28–29 (re: souls); Hacsi, " 'A Plain and Solemn Duty,' " 28; Bremner, *Children and Youth in America,* vol. 1, 271–75; Samuel X. Radbill, "Children in a World of Violence: A History of Child Abuse," in *The Battered Child,* 4th ed., ed. Ray E. Helfer and Ruth S. Kempe (Chicago: University of Chicago Press, 1987), 6 (abuse). "In 1902," according to Buckingham, p. 321, the orphanage "contained one hundred and twenty-five boys."
31. Hacsi, " 'A Plain and Solemn Duty,' " 28–29.
32. On changing perceptions see, e.g., Constance B. Schulz, "Children and Childhood in the Eighteenth Century," in Hawes and Hiner, *American Childhood,* 62–63, 84, 88–89; Karin Calvert, *Children in the House: The Material Culture of Childhood, 1600–1900* (Boston: Northeastern University Press, 1992), 51–52, 55–61, 87–88; Bremner, *Children and Youth in America,* vol. 1, 131–32. On the roots of foster care and adoption see, e.g., Schulz, "Children and Childhood in the Eighteenth Century," 65; Stephen B. Presser, "The Historical Background of the American Law of Adoption," *Journal of Family Law* 11 (1971): 459; Mason, *From Father's Property to Children's Rights,* 24.

Chapter 2

1. Susan L. Porter, "The Benevolent Asylum—Image and Reality: The Care and Training of Female Orphans in Boston, 1800–1840" (Ph.D. diss., Boston University, 1984), 203–4.

2. Rachel B. Marks, "Institutions for Dependent and Delinquent Children: Histories, Nineteenth-Century Statistics, and Recurrent Goals," in *Child Caring: Social Policy and the Institution*, ed. Donnell M. Pappenfort, Dee M. Kilpatrick, and Robert W. Roberts (Chicago: Aldine Publishing Co., 1973), 51 (qtns.).

3. Qtn. in Kristine E. Nelson. "The Best Asylum: Charles Loring Brace and Foster Family Care" (D.S.W. diss., University of California, Berkeley, 1980), 68.

4. Chief Justice William Tilghman, in *Commonwealth vs. Addicks* (Pa. 1813), qtd. in Michael Grossberg, *Governing the Hearth: Law and the Family in Nineteenth-Century America* (Chapel Hill: University of North Carolina Press, 1985), 239; Mary Ann Mason, *From Father's Property to Children's Rights: The History of Child Custody in the United States* (New York: Columbia University Press, 1994), 49; see also, 82.

5. Qtns. from *In re Mitchell* (Ga. 1836) and *State v. King* (Ga. 1842) in Peter W. Bardaglio, "Families, Sex, and the Law: The Legal Transformation of the Nineteenth-Century Southern Household" (Ph.D. diss., Stanford University, 1987), 203–04.

6. William G. McLoughlin, "Evangelical Childrearing in the Age of Jackson: Francis Wayland's Views on When and How to Subdue the Willfulness of Children," *Journal of Social History* 9 (Fall 1975): 20–43.

7. Dwight qtd. in Elizabeth Pleck, *Domestic Tyranny: The Making of American Social Policy Against Family Violence from Colonial Times to the Present* (New York: Oxford University Press, 1987), 40.

8. Pleck, *Domestic Tyranny*, 41 (manuals), 43 (Child qtn.); Bardaglio, "Families, Sex, and the Law," 286–87 (Tennessee).

9. Teacher in Pleck, *Domestic Tyranny*, 44; minister in McLoughlin, "Evangelical Childrearing in the Age of Jackson," 30; Eliot in Kirk Jeffrey, "The Family as Utopian Retreat from the City," *Soundings* 55 (Spring 1972): 21.

10. Bardaglio, "Families, Sex, and the Law," 129–31, 144–45.

11. Joan Gittens, *Poor Relations: The Children of the State in Illinois, 1818–1990* (Urbana: University of Illinois Press, 1994), 16 (re: Illinois); Marilyn I. Holt, *The Orphan Trains: Placing Out in America* (Lincoln: University of Nebraska Press, 1992), 33 (re: Kansas).

12. Robert Bremner, *Children and Youth in America: A Documentary History*, vol. 2 (Cambridge: Harvard University Press, 1970), 269–70.

13. See esp. Karin Calvert, *Children in the House: The Material Culture of Early Childhood, 1600–1900* (Boston: Northeastern University Press, 1992), 104–10 (qtns. 104–5, 108).

14. Gittens, *Poor Relations,* 16–17 (re: Illinois).

15. Dickens qtd. in Barbara Berg, *The Remembered Gate: Origins of American Feminism* (New York: Oxford University Press, 1978), 43.

16. Qtn., David Grimsted, "Rioting in Its Jacksonian Setting," *American Historical Review* 77 (April 1972): 374–75.

17. Alcott and school comm qtns., Stanley K. Schultz, *Culture Factory: Boston Public Schools, 1789–1860* (New York: Oxford University Press, 1973), 60, 68.

18. Judith A. Dulberger, "Refuge or Repressor: The Role of the Orphan Asylum in the Lives of Poor Children and Their Families in Late-Nineteenth Century America" (D. A. diss., Carnegie-Mellon University, 1988), 15 (Yates); Michael B. Katz, *In the Shadow of the Poorhouse: A Social History of Welfare in America* (New York: Basic Books, 1986), 23 (Burroughs); Walter I. Trattner, *From Poor Law to Welfare State,* 2d ed. (New York: Free Press, 1979), 53 (Mass.).

19. Katz, *In the Shadow of the Poorhouse,* 12.

20. David J. Rothman, *The Discovery of the Asylum: Social Order and Disorder in the New Republic* (Boston: Little, Brown, 1971), 189 ("noble").

21. Priscilla F. Clement, *Welfare and the Poor in the Nineteenth-Century City: Philadelphia, 1800–1854* (Rutherford, N.J.: Fairleigh Dickinson University Press, 1985), 119.

22. Ibid., 120–22.

23. Ibid., 119–23 (Phila.); Katz, *In the Shadow of the Poorhouse,* 26 (Charleston); Bremner, *Children and Youth in American History,* vol. 1, 640 (NYC); Ruth Shackelford, "To Shield Them from Temptation: 'Child-Saving' Institutions and the Children of the Underclass in San Francisco, 1850–1910" (Ph.D. diss., Harvard University, 1991), 14 (Boston); Ronald B. Taylor, *The Kid Business* (Boston: Houghton Mifflin, 1981), 76 (NY investigation); Trattner, *From Poor Law to Welfare State,* 54 (critics).

24. Eric C. Schneider, *In the Web of Class: Delinquents and Reformers in Boston, 1810s–1930s* (New York: New York University Press, 1992), 45; Bremner, *Children and Youth in America,* vol. 1, 644 (visitor).

25. House of Refuge qtn., Rothman, *Discovery of the Asylum,* 210. On *Crouse,* see Christine Stansell, *City of Women: Sex and Class in New York, 1789–1869* (Urbana, Ill.: University of Illinois Press, 1987), 215; Grossberg, *Governing the Hearth,* 266–68, and Michael Grossberg, "Children's Legal Rights? A Historical Look at a Legal Paradox," in

Children at Risk in America: History, Concepts, and Public Policy, ed. Roberta Wollons (Albany: State University of New York, 1993), 117.

26. John R. Sutton, *Stubborn Children: Controlling Delinquency in the United States, 1640–1981* (Berkeley: University of California Press, 1988), 45, 65, 75 (qtn.), re: statutorial inclusion of neglected children.

27. Schneider, *In the Web of Class*, 77 (McConnell); Shackelford, "To Shield Them," 40–43; 1858 study in Nelson, "The Best Asylum," 151.

28. Qtns., "folds," in Sutton, *Stubborn Children*, 75; supts. in Rothman, *Discovery of the Asylum*, 231–34.

29. Bruce W. Bellingham, " 'Little Wanderers': A Socio-Historical Study of the Nineteenth Century Origins of Child Fostering and Adoption Reform" (Ph.D. diss., University of Pennsylvania, 1984), 153–54 (NYC orphan); Shackelford, "To Shield Them," 19–20 (Bridewell).

30. Schneider, *In the Web of Class*, 45–50.

31. Shackelford, "To Shield Them," 30–32; Bremner, *Children and Youth*, 641.

32. Clement, *Welfare and the Poor*, 121, 125–26.

33. Ibid., 121, 127–28.

34. Ibid., 128–31; Shackelford, "To Shield Them," 28–29.

35. Clement, *Welfare and the Poor*, 121, 128, 131–40.

36. Timothy A. Hacsi, " 'A Plain and Solemn Duty': A History of Orphan Asylums in America" (Ph.D. diss., University of Pennsylvania, 1993), 32–45 (stats., 32); 188 (Cincinnati). Six orphanages were founded before 1800; 14 more between 1800 and 1820.

37. Porter, "The Benevolent Asylum," 62–66, 108–10.

38. Ibid., 123; qtns. in Henry W. Thurston, *The Dependent Child* (New York: Columbia University Press, 1930), 55–56.

39. Porter, "The Benevolent Asylum," 121 (qtn.), 129–30, 167–80.

40. Patricia Clement, "Children and Charity: Orphanages in New Orleans, 1817–1914," *Louisiana History* 27 (Fall 1986): 140, 347–49; Porter, "The Benevolent Asylum," 12–13, 53, 200–1, 352.

41. Porter, "The Benevolent Asylum," 200–1, 251, 271–72, 281–83, 328 (manager's qtn.).

42. Ibid., 202–5, 267–68; examples of the Henderson girls and Sophia Hyde, 217–18, 238–39.

43. Rothman, *Discovery of the Asylum*, 39–40 (re: moral orphans).

44. Peter C. Holloran, *Boston's Wayward Children: Social Services for Homeless Children, 1830–1930* (Rutherford, N.J.: Fairleigh Dickinson University Press, 1989), 41 (Boston), 43 (Hale), 74 (St. Vincent).

45. Paul Boyer, *Urban Masses and Moral Order in America, 1820–1920* (Cambridge: Harvard University Press, 1978), 43 (ASSU); Rothman, *Discovery of the Asylum*, 229 (Child); Thurston, *The Dependent Child*, 47 (Scriptures).

46. Thurston, *The Dependent Child*, 40–53; Hacsi, " 'A Plain and Solemn Duty,' " 193 (re: half-orphans).
47. Dulberger, "Refuge or Repressor," 94–95.
48. Clement, *Welfare and the Poor*, 123–25; Cecile P. Frey, "The House of Refuge for Colored Children," *Journal of Negro History* 66 (Spring 1981): 10–12; Holloran, *Boston's Wayward Children*, 141 (supt.'s qtn.).
49. Clement, *Welfare and the Poor*, 122, 129.
50. Frey, "The House of Refuge for Colored Children," 13–14, 18.
51. Hyman Bogen, *The Luckiest Orphans: A History of the Hebrew Orphan Asylum of New York* (Urbana: University of Illinois Press, 1992), 59, 61.
52. Ibid., 62.
53. Ibid., 64 (NYC); Gittens, *Poor Relations*, 18 (Chicago).

Chapter 3

1. See copy of frontispiece in Bruce Bellingham, "Waifs and Strays: Child Abandonment, Foster Care, and Families in Mid-Nineteenth-Century New York," in *The Use of Charity: The Poor on Relief in the Nineteenth-Century Metropolis*, ed. Peter Mandler (Philadelphia: University of Pennsylvania Press, 1990), 132. The drawing was also popularized in the August 1873 *Harper's New Monthly Magazine*; see Marilyn I. Holt, *The Orphan Trains: Placing Out in America* (Lincoln: University of Nebraska Press, 1992), illustration #2.
2. See, e.g., Bruce Bellingham, "The 'Unspeakable Blessing': Street Children, Reform Rhetoric, and Misery in Early Industrial Capitalism," *Politics and Society* 12 (1983): 300.
3. Bushnell qtn., Kristine E. Nelson, "The Best Asylum: Charles Loring Brace and Foster Family Care" (D.S.W. diss., University of California, Berkeley, 1980), 128; Brace qtns., ibid., 131, and Paul Boyer, *Urban Masses and Moral Order in America, 1820–1920* (Cambridge: Harvard University Press, 1977), 104.
4. Christine Stansell, *City of Women: Sex and Class in New York, 1789–1869* (Urbana: University of Illinois Press, 1987), 194–97.
5. Nelson, "The Best Asylum," 134–40.
6. Ibid., 140–42, 147–48; statistics in Stansell, *City of Women*, 198.
7. See Nelson, "The Best Asylum," esp. 143–44, 161; Holt, *Orphan Trains*, 43 (re: stats.); also Boyer, *Urban Masses and Moral Order*, 97; Stansell, *City of Women*, 212–14 (re the women's projects).
8. Nelson, "The Best Asylum," 160 and (re: girls) 178–79; Boyer, *Urban Masses and Moral Order*, 97–99.
9. Stats. in Ruth Shackelford, "To Shield Them from Temptation: 'Child-Saving' Institutions and the Children of the Underclass in San Francisco, 1850–1910" (Ph.D. diss., Harvard University, 1991), 94, and Mary Ann Mason, *From Father's Property to Children's Rights* (New York: Columbia University Press, 1994), 79.

10. Holt, *Orphan Trains*, 33, 43–45, 82–83 (re: Brace and Williams); Peter Holloran, *Boston's Wayward Children: Social Services for Homeless Children, 1830–1930* (Rutherford, N.J.: Fairleigh Dickinson University Press, 1989), 41–44 (re: the Mission).

11. See, e.g., Mason, *From Father's Property to Children's Rights*, 78–79 (Brace qtn.); Shackelford, "To Shield Them," 94 (Brace qtn.), 98, 107n; also Joan Gittens, *Poor Relations: The Children of the State in Illinois, 1818–1990* (Urbana: University of Illinois Press, 1994), 32.

12. Stansell, *City of Women*, 202; Mason, *From Father's Property to Children's Rights*, 78; Nelson, "The Best Asylum," 96–97, 259–60 (Brace qtn., 165); Shackelford, "To Shield Them," 91–92.

13. Peter W. Bardaglio, "Families, Sex, and the Law: The Legal Transformation of the Nineteenth-Century Southern Household" (Ph.D. diss., Stanford University, 1987), 262–65, including qtns. from the Ark. decision, *Morrill v. Kennedy* (1860); Michael Grossberg, *Governing the Hearth: Law and the Family in Nineteenth-Century America* (Chapel Hill: University of North Carolina Press, 1985), 260–64.

14. Qtn. from NYCAS 1859 report in Shackelford, "To Shield Them," 91.

15. See Joseph Ben-Or, "The Law of Adoption in the United States: Its Massachusetts Origins and the Statute of 1851," *The New England Historical and Genealogical Register* 130 (Oct. 1976): 266; Bardaglio, "Families, Sex, and the Law," 306–11.

16. Jamil S. Zainaldin, "The Emergence of a Modern American Family Law: Child Custody, Adoption, and the Courts, 1796–1851," *Northwestern University Law Review* 73 (1979): esp. 1068–86.

17. See ibid., 1042n (re: the law); Grossberg, *Governing the Hearth*, 268, 271–72; Bardaglio, "Families, Sex, and the Law," 312–20.

18. Stephen B. Presser, "The Historical Background of the American Law of Adoption," *Journal of Family Law* 11 (1971): esp. 471, 474, 479; Bellingham, "Waifs and Strays," 150; Holt, *Orphan Trains*, 105 (re: New England Home); Nelson "The Best Asylum," 184, 190 (Brace qtns.).

19. Mason, *From Father's Property to Children's Rights*, 79; Nelson, "The Best Asylum," 334–35 (family).

20. Nelson, "The Best Asylum," 158–59, 163–65, 184, 203, 209; Holt, *Orphan Trains*, 47.

21. Holt, *Orphan Trains*, 47–48; Nelson, "The Best Asylum," 166; Boyer, *Urban Masses and Moral Reform*, 102.

22. Nelson, "The Best Asylum," 160.

23. Shackelford, "To Shield Them," 103–04 (re: sponsors).

24. Stansell, *City of Women*, 198–202.

25. Ibid., 193–94.

26. Bellingham, " 'Unspeakable Blessing,' " 309.

27. Qtns. in Richard Wexler, *Wounded Innocents: The Real Victims of the War Against Child Abuse* (Buffalo: Prometheus Books, 1990), 33 (stupid, scum, cleanliness); Bellingham, " 'Unspeakable Blessing,' " 313–14 (1864 rpt).

28. See Bellingham, " 'Unspeakable Blessing,' " 303–6, 323–25.

29. Brace qtn. in Bellingham, " 'Unspeakable Blessing,' " 315; stats. in Bellingham, "Waifs and Strays," 130–36.

30. Bellingham, "Waifs and Strays," 136–43.

31. Bruce Bellingham, "Institution and Family: An Alternative View of Nineteenth-Century Child Saving," *Social Problems* 33 (Dec. 1986): S45–46.

32. Ibid., S46–47.

33. Stansell, *City of Women*, 210–11.

34. Qtns. in Nelson, "The Best Asylum," 160–61, 327; Shackelford, "To Shield Them," 126, 129.

35. Nelson, "The Best Asylum," 212–14.

36. Holt, *Orphan Trains*, 74–75.

37. Ibid., 103–04.

38. See ibid., 110–11, and Kristine E. Nelson, "Child Placing in the Nineteenth Century: New York and Iowa," *Social Service Review* 59 (March 1985): 108.

39. New York Juvenile Asylum broadside in Holt, *Orphan Trains*, photo #8.

40. Ibid., 60–61.

41. Qtns., ibid., 39, 50.

42. Hastings Hart, "Placing Out Children in the West" (1884), reprinted in *Care of Dependent Children in the Late Nineteenth and Early Twentieth Centuries*, ed. Robert H. Bremner (New York: Arno Press, 1974), 145 (charity worker); Nelson, "The Best Asylum," 169 (the grandfather and the hymns); Wexler, *Wounded Innocents*, 36 (display and muscles); other examples in Holt, *Orphan Trains*, 49–50, 52.

43. Holt, *Orphan Trains*, 108, 113.

44. Harry Colwell, "A New York Orphan Comes to Kansas," *Kansas History* 8 (Summer 1985): 110–23.

45. Ibid., 115–16.

46. Hart, "Placing Out Children in the West," 147 (Minnesota); Wexler, *Wounded Innocents*, 36 (godawfulnest); other examples in Holt, *Orphan Trains*, 139.

47. Shackelford, "To Shield Them," 99 (Kansas); Hart, "Placing Out in the West," 147 (Minnesota).

48. Shackelford, "To Shield Them," 122–29 (Brace qtn., 129), 539 (supt.); Holt, *Orphan Trains*, 128–30. See, however, Wexler, *Wounded Innocents*, 35: "Evidence of child stealing can be inferred from the records of Brace's Children's Aid Society itself."

49. Shackelford, "To Shield Them," 133 (Brace), 487 (Dooley); Wexler, *Wounded Innocents*, 35 (Guardian Society).
50. Nelson, "The Best Asylum," 226 (qtn.); Hyman Bogen, *The Luckiest Orphans: A History of the Hebrew Orphan Asylum of New York* (Urbana: University of Illinois Press, 1992), 63 (stat.).
51. Nelson, "The Best Asylum," 233–35; Holt, *Orphan Trains*, 121–22; Shackelford, "To Shield Them," 144–51; Robert H. Bremner, *Children and Youth in American History*, vol. 2 (Cambridge: Harvard University Press, 1971), 292 (re monument).
52. Richard A. Meckel, "Protecting the Innocents: Age Segregation and the Early Child Welfare Movement," *Social Service Review* 59 (September 1985): 469; Lyman P. Alden, "The Shady Side of the 'Placing-Out System' " (1885), reprinted in Bremner, *Care of Dependent Children in the Late Nineteenth and Early Twentieth Centuries*, 201–10.
53. Holloran, *Boston's Wayward Children*, 51–61; Shackelford, "To Shield Them," 106–11 (qtn., 109); Gary R. Anderson, "Charles Birtwell," in *Biographical Dictionary of Social Welfare in America*, ed. Walter I. Trattner (Westport, Conn.: Greenwood Press, 1986), 95–97.
54. Presser, "Historical Background of the American Law of Adoption," 479, 486–87.
55. Holt, *Orphan Trains*, 69–71, 136–37; A. Blake Brophy, *Foundlings on the Frontier: Racial and Religious Conflict in Arizona Territory, 1904–1905* (Tucson: University of Arizona Press, 1972).
56. Qtns. in Nelson, "The Best Asylum," 192.

Chapter 4

1. Statistics in Timothy A. Hacsi, " 'A Plain and Solemn Duty': A History of Orphan Asylums in America" (Ph.D. diss., University of Pennsylvania, 1993), 335–36; Stephen Lazoritz, "Whatever Happened to Mary Ellen?" *Child Abuse and Neglect* 14 (1990): 144–45, 147–48.
2. Lela B. Costin, "Unraveling the Mary Ellen Legend: Origins of the 'Cruelty' Movement," *Social Service Review* 65 (June 1991): 204.
3. Ibid., 204–06.
4. Ibid., 215.
5. Ibid., 207–09; Lazoritz, "Whatever Happened to Mary Ellen?," 148 (re: Mary Ellen's later condition and memories).
6. Barbara Nelson, *Making an Issue of Child Abuse: Political Agenda Setting* (Chicago: University of Chicago Press, 1984), 67 (Fox).
7. Lazoritz, "Whatever Happened to Mary Ellen?," 145–47.
8. Costin, "Unraveling the Mary Ellen Legend," 209–15, is good on these trends.
9. Stanton qtn. in Elizabeth Pleck, *Domestic Tyranny: The Making of American Social Policy against Family Violence from Colonial Times to the Present* (New York: Oxford University Press, 1987), 59; Linda Gor-

don, *Heroes of Their Own Lives: The Politics and History of Family Violence* (New York: Viking Penguin, 1988), 57, 80.

10. Elizabeth B. Clark, " 'The Sacred Rights of the Weak': Pain, Sympathy, and the Culture of Individual Rights in Antebellum America," *Journal of American History* 82 (Sept. 1995): 463–93 (qtn., 490).

11. Gordon, *Heroes of Their Own Lives*, 34; Pleck, *Domestic Tyranny*, 78 (re: Abbott); letter qtd. in Costin, "Unraveling the Mary Ellen Legend," 213.

12. Pleck, *Domestic Tyranny*, 72.

13. Ibid., 76 (qtn.).

14. Pleck, *Domestic Tyranny*, 69, 80.

15. See esp. ibid., 79–82.

16. Gordon, *Heroes of Their Own Lives*, 29–31.

17. Qtns. in Pleck, *Domestic Tyranny*, 72 (Wright), and Joseph Hawes, *The Children's Rights Movement: A History of Advocacy and Protection* (Boston: Twayne, 1991), 21–22.

18. Gordon, *Heroes of Their Own Lives*, 20, 28, 37–41; Pleck, *Domestic Tyranny*, 83 (Mass. qtn.).

19. Gordon, *Heroes of Their Own Lives*, 47.

20. Pleck, *Domestic Tyranny*, 83–85.

21. Gordon, *Heroes of Their Own Lives*, 48, 51–52 (MSPCC qtn.); Sherri Broder, "Informing the 'Cruelty': The Monitoring of Respectability in Philadelphia's Working-Class Neighborhoods in the Late Nineteenth Century," *Radical America* 21 (July-August 1987): 43 (qtn.).

22. Gordon, *Heroes of Their Own Lives*, 28; re: labor, Broder, "Informing the 'Cruelty,' " 36–37.

23. Broder, "Informing the 'Cruelty,' " 43 (1892 qtn.); law and stat. in Mason P. Thomas, Jr., "Child Abuse and Neglect Part I: Historical Overview, Legal Matrix, and Social Perspectives," *The North Carolina Law Review* 50 (February 1972): 311; Gordon, *Heroes of Their Own Lives*, 28 (qtn. re: report); Ruby Takanishi, "Childhood as a Social Issue: Historical Roots of Contemporary Child Advocacy Movements," *Journal of Social Issues* 34 (1978): 18 (game).

24. Nanette Schorr, "Foster Care and the Politics of Compassion," *Tikkun* 7 (May/June 1992): 21.

25. Gordon, *Heroes of Their Lives*, 294–97; also Gordon, "Child Abuse, Gender, and the Myth of Family Independence: A Historical Critique," *Child Welfare* 64 (May-June 1985): esp. 218–19.

26. Broder, "Informing the 'Cruelty,' " 37–45.

27. Pleck, *Domestic Tyranny*, 86–87.

28. Hacsi, " 'A Plain and Solemn Duty,' " 71 (stat.).

29. Marilyn I. Holt, *The Orphan Trains: Placing Out in America* (Lincoln: University of Nebraska Press, 1992), 74 (stats.); Hacsi, " 'A Plain and Solemn Duty,' " 94 (qtn.).

30. Hacsi, " 'A Plain and Solemn Duty,' " 70; Hyman Bogen, *The Luckiest Orphans: A History of the Hebrew Orphan Asylum of New York* (Urbana: University of Illinois Press, 1992), 56; Joan Gittens, *Poor Relations: The Children of the State of Illinois, 1818–1990* (Urbana: University of Illinois Press, 1994), 25–26 (Illinois).

31. Judith Areen, "Intervention Between Parent and Child: A Reappraisal of the State's Role in Child Neglect and Abuse Cases," *The Georgetown Law Journal* 63 (March 1975): 905n (qtn.), 907; also, Judith A. Dulberger, "Refuge or Repressor: The Role of the Orphan Asylum in the Lives of Poor Children and Their Families in Late-Nineteenth Century America" (D.A. diss., Carnegie-Mellon University, 1988), 17–19.

32. Hasci, " 'A Plain and Solemn Duty,' " 71, 73–76, 202–3; Robert H. Bremner, *Children and Youth in America: A Documentary History*, vol. 2 (Cambridge: Harvard University Press, 1971), 265–66 (Thomas Asylum).

33. Dulberger, "Refuge or Repressor," 25–26 (numbers); Hasci, " 'A Plain and Solemn Duty,' " 72, 88, 109; Marian J. Morton, "Homes for Poverty's Children: Cleveland Orphanages, 1851–1933," *Ohio History* 98 (Winter-Spring 1989): 12 (parents).

34. Viviana A. Zelizer, *Pricing the Priceless Child: The Changing Social Value of Children* (New York: Basic Books, 1985), 173–74 (qtn.); Sherri Broder, "Child Care or Child Neglect? Baby Farming in Late-Nineteenth-Century Philadelphia," *Gender and Society* 2 (June 1988): 128–32, 139–42.

35. Broder, "Child Care or Child Neglect?," 132–45.

36. Hasci, " 'A Plain and Solemn Duty,' " 88–93; also Dulberger, "Refuge or Repressor," 47.

37. Dulberger, "Refuge or Repressor," 187–248; qtns., 179, 193, 196, 201, 235; 237 (boarding school). See also many fascinating letters reprinted in Judith Dulberger, *"Mother Donit fore the Best": Correspondence of a Nineteenth-Century Orphan Asylum* (Syracuse: Syracuse University Press, 1996), 23–110. Kenneth Cmiel, *A Home of Another Kind: One Chicago Orphanage and the Tangle of Child Welfare* (Chicago: University of Chicago Press, 1995), 10–11, 14–15, 21–22, 53, 92, also emphasizes that orphan asylums provided temporary care for children of the poor.

38. Gittens, *Poor Relations*, 23.

39. Stats. in Dulberger, "Refuge or Repressor," 21; 94–95 (re: Albany asylum).

40. Qtns. in Gary E. Polster, *Inside Looking Out: The Cleveland Jewish Orphan Asylum, 1868–1924* (Kent, Ohio: Kent State University Press, 1990), 95, 137; Bogen, *The Luckiest Orphans*, 82 (crumbs); Josephine Shaw Lowell, "Report on the Institutions for the Care of Destitute Children of the City of New York," in *Care of Dependent Children in the Late Nineteenth and Early Twentieth Centuries*, ed. Robert H. Bremner (New York: Arno Press, 1974), 197 (Protectory).

41. Hacsi, " 'A Plain and Solemn Duty,' " 126 (qtn.), and esp. 45–50 (re: muted form of social control).

42. Qtns. in Dulberger, "Refuge or Repressor," 50–51; also Hacsi, " 'A Plain and Solemn Duty,' " 50; Polster, *Inside Looking Out*, esp. 54–57, 90–99, 201.

43. Bogen, *The Luckiest Orphans*, 68–69 (qtn.), 85–93; Polster, *Inside Looking Out*, 31, 200 (qtn.).

44. Qtns. in Dulberger, "Refuge or Repressor," 258–60, 293; Polster, *Inside Looking Out*, 190; Bogen, *The Luckiest Orphans*, 19–21 (Bauer).

45. Polster, *Inside Looking Out*, 99–100 (Wirpel qtn.), 149; figures in Reena S. Friedman, *These Are Our Children: Jewish Orphanages in the United States, 1880–1925* (Hanover, N.H.: Brandeis University Press, 1994), 23, 67; Bogen, *The Luckiest Orphans*, 151.

46. Bogen, *The Luckiest Orphans*, 102–03, 109; Polster, *Inside Looking Out*, 48.

47. Bogen, *The Luckiest Orphans*, 106; Polster, *Inside Looking Out*, 157.

48. Bogen, *The Luckiest Orphans*, 106 (Baar), 83–84 (warden); Polster, *Inside Looking Out*, 159 (bed wetters).

49. Stats. in Lowell, "Report on the Institutions for the Care of Destitute Children of the City of New York," 232, 235.

50. Gittens, *Poor Relations*, 21–22, 24.

51. For a convenient summary of these approaches, see Homer Folks, *The Care of Destitute, Neglected, and Delinquent Children* (New York: Macmillan, 1902), 82–162.

52. Hacsi, "A Plain and Solemn Duty,' " 81.

53. See R. S. Patterson and Patricia Rooke, "The Delicate Duty of Child Saving: Coldwater, Michigan, 1871–1896," *Michigan History* 61 (Fall 1977): 195–219; Folks, *Care of Destitute, Neglected, and Delinquent Children*, 94–95.

54. See esp. Ruth Shackelford, "To Shield Them from Temptation: 'Child-Saving' Institutions and the Children of the Underclass in San Francisco, 1850–1910" (Ph.D. diss., Harvard University, 1991), 220–24.

55. Third and Fifth Annual Reports of the Board of State Charities of Massachusetts, 1867 and 1869, in Grace Abbott, *The Child and the State*, vol. 2 (1938; reprint, New York: Greenwood Press, 1968), 36–40; Shackelford, "To Shield Them," 201–8.

56. Zelizer, *Pricing the Priceless Child*, 184–86.

57. Shackelford, "To Shield Them," 209, 212.

58. Ibid., 212.

59. Ibid., 214 (N.J.); Zelizer, *Pricing the Priceless Child*, 189.

60. Hacsi, " 'A Plain and Solemn Duty,' " 82, 85–86.

61. Michael Grossberg, "Children's Legal Rights? A Historical Look at a Legal Paradox," in *Children at Risk in America: History, Concepts, and*

Public Policy, ed. Roberta Wollons (Albany: State University of New York Press, 1993), 120.

62. Richard A. Meckel, "Protecting the Innocents: Age Segregation and the Early Child Welfare Movement," *Social Service Review* 59 (September 1985): 455–72 (qtn., 466).

63. Peter W. Bardaglio, "Families, Sex, and the Law: The Legal Transformation of the Nineteenth-Century Southern Household" (Ph.D. diss., Stanford University, 1987), 244–46 (stats.), 268 (qtn.), 268–69 (Tenn.), 270–71 (Texas), 276–78.

64. Bardaglio, "Families, Sex, and the Law," 287–89 (Ark.), 295–99 (blacks); Rebecca Scott, "The Battle Over the Child: Child Apprenticeship and the Freedmen's Bureau in North Carolina," *Prologue* 10 (Summer 1978): 101–13; Wilma King, *Stolen Childhood: Slave Youth in Nineteenth-Century America* (Bloomington: Indiana University Press, 1995), 151–54 (Fields, 151).

65. Bardaglio, "Families, Sex, and the Law," 148–66.

66. Ibid., 344; Freund in Michael Grossberg, *Governing the Hearth: Law and Family in Nineteenth-Century America* (Chapel Hill: University of North Carolina Press, 1985), 281.

67. Shackelford, "To Shield Them," 230–33 (stats, 230).

68. Stat. in Catherine Ross, "Society's Children: The Care of Indigent Youngsters in New York City, 1875–1903" (Ph.D. diss., Columbia University, 1977), iv.

69. Ellen Key, *The Century of the Child* (New York: G. P. Putnam, 1909).

Chapter 5

1. Qtns. in Robert H. Bremner, *Children and Youth in America: A Documentary History*, vol. 2 (Cambridge: Harvard University Press, 1971), 358, 365.

2. LeRoy Ashby, *Saving the Waifs: Reformers and Dependent Children, 1890–1917* (Philadelphia: Temple University Press, 1984), 14; re: neglect, Linda Gordon, *Heroes of Their Own Lives: The Politics and History of Family Violence* (paper ed., New York: Penguin Books, 1988), 21, 84, 117–18. Kenneth Cmiel, *A Home of Another Kind: One Chicago Orphanage and the Tangle of Child Welfare* (Chicago: University of Chicago Press, 1995), 40, 59–64, 207n, warns against seeing "a progressive takeover" and emphasizes that "there were powerful limits to change."

3. Ashby, *Saving the Waifs*, 4 (Lindsey), 7 (Riis); Leonard Benedict, *Waifs of the Slums and Their Way Out* (New York: Revell, 1907), 23 (Atkinson).

4. See, e.g., Linda Gordon, *Pitied But Not Entitled: Single Mothers and the History of Welfare, 1890–1935* (New York: Free Press, 1994), 31.

5. Qtns. in Ashby, *Saving the Waifs*, 83, 85 (poem).

6. Robert Wiebe, *The Search for Order, 1877–1920* (New York: Hill & Wang, 1967), 113 (Addams); Reena S. Friedman, *These Are Our Children: Jewish Orphanages in the United States, 1880–1925* (Hanover, N.H.: Brandeis University Press, 1994), 62 (Abbott).

7. Qtns., Joan Gittens, *Poor Relations: The Children of the State in Illinois, 1818–1990* (Urbana: University of Illinois Press, 1994), 37 (Hurley); *Juvenile Court Record* (August 1910): 6 (fault).

8. *Juvenile Court Record* (December 1911): 15; see also Elizabeth Pleck, *Domestic Tyranny: The Making of American Family Policy against Family Violence from Colonial Times to Present* (New York: Oxford University Press, 1987), 129.

9. Re: Baker, Peter Holloran, *Boston's Wayward Children: Social Services for Homeless Children, 1830–1930* (Rutherford, N.J.: Fairleigh Dickinson University Press, 1989), 205–8, 213, 219.

10. Qtns. in Ashby, *Saving the Waifs*, 158 (Lindsey); David Rothman, "Doing Good," in Willard Gaylin, Steven Marcus, and David Rothman, *Doing Good: The Limits of Benevolence* (New York: Pantheon, 1978), 78–79.

11. Qtn. in W. David Wills, *Homer Lane: A Biography* (London: George Allen and Unwin, 1964), 81.

12. Mary Ann Mason, *From Father's Property to Children's Rights* (New York: Columbia University Press, 1994), 102 (Cook County); Pleck, *Domestic Tyranny*, 131 (Boston and nation).

13. Gittens, *Poor Relations*, 40–41.

14. Ashby, *Saving the Waifs*, 69–70, 76.

15. Ibid., 85–87.

16. Figures in Hyman Bogen, *The Luckiest Orphans: A History of the Hebrew Orphan Asylum of New York* (Urbana: University of Illinois Press, 1992), 158, 163.

17. Sandra M. Stehno, "Foster Care for Dependent Black Children in Chicago, 1899–1934" (Ph.D. diss., University of Chicago, 1985), 15–50; Sandra M. O'Donnell, "The Care of Dependent African-American Children in Chicago: The Struggle Between Black Self-Help and Professionalism," *Journal of Social History* 27 (Summer 1994): 764–65. For a discussion of "fosterage and extendedness" as central to "the non-western, African heritage of African-Americans," see Andrew T. Miller, "Looking at African-American Families" (Ph.D. diss., University of Pennsylvania, 1991).

18. Qtns. in Ashby, *Saving the Waifs*, 28, 95–98.

19. Ibid., 95; Richard Wexler, *Wounded Innocents: The Real Victims of the War Against Child Abuse* (Buffalo: Prometheus Books, 1990), 37 (NY).

20. Gary E. Polster, *Inside Looking Out: The Cleveland Jewish Orphan Asylum, 1868–1924* (Kent, Ohio: Kent State University Press, 1990), 95–96 (Newmark), 138–39 (Gelder), 159 (Dahlberg and Wolfenstein).

21. Ibid., 96–97.

22. Henry W. Thurston, *The Dependent Child* (New York: Columbia University Press, 1930), 71–76.
23. Ibid., 82–84.
24. Nurith Zmora, *Orphanages Reconsidered: Child Care Institutions in Progressive Era Baltimore* (Philadelphia: Temple University Press, 1994), 75–79; Friedman, *These Are Our Children*, 182 (love).
25. Zmora, *Orphanages Reconsidered*, 164.
26. Mabel Potter Daggett, "The Child without a Home," *Delineator* (October 1907): 505–10; Daggett, "Where 100,000 Wait," ibid. (November 1908): 773–76, 858–61.
27. Grace Abbott, *The Child and the State*, vol. 2 (1938; reprint, New York: Greenwood Press, 1968), 143–51; Marilyn I. Holt, *The Orphan Trains: Placing Out in America* (Lincoln: University of Nebraska Press, 1992), 139–40 (ages).
28. Ashby, *Saving the Waifs*, 38–40.
29. Ibid., 50, 59, 63; on the WCHS, Pat Hart, "Prelude to Adoption: Child Relinquishment in Washington State, 1896–1915," unpublished draft ms. from her forthcoming Ph.D. diss. (Washington State University).
30. Ashby, *Saving the Waifs*, 44, 47–50, 54–58.
31. Qtns., ibid., 38, 54.
32. Stats in Judith A. Dulberger, "Refuge or Repressor: The Role of the Orphan Asylum in the Lives of Poor Children and Their Families in Late-Nineteenth-Century America" (D. A. diss., Carnegie-Mellon University, 1988), 26–27; Timothy A. Hacsi, " 'A Plain and Solemn Duty': A History of Orphan Asylums in America" (Ph.D. diss., University of Pennsylvania, 1993), 159.
33. See esp. R. R. Reeder, "Good Citizens from Institutional Children," *Charities* (15 August 1903):147–54, and Reeder, *How Two Hundred Children Live and Learn* (New York: Charities Publication Committee, 1909), 194–200.
34. Ashby, *Saving the Waifs*, 170–205.
35. On Freeville, see Jack M. Holl, *Juvenile Reform in the Progressive Era: William R. George and the Junior Republic Movement* (Ithaca, N.Y.: Cornell University Press, 1971).
36. Qtns., Ashby, *Saving the Waifs*, 19 (George), 29 (Bradley).
37. LeRoy Ashby, " 'Recreate This Boy': Allendale Farm, the Child and Progressivism," *Mid-America* 58 (January 1976): 31–53 (qtns., 47, 51).
38. Friedman, *These Are Our Children*, 68 (HSGS); Dulberger, "Refuge or Repressor," 119–20 (Albany); Polster, *Inside Looking Out*, 178 (CJOA).
39. See Hacsi, " 'A Plain and Solemn Duty,' " chap. 6; Friedman, *These Are Our Children*, 55–93 (qtn., 84–85).
40. Friedman, *These Are Our Children*, 85 (Sharlitt); Polster, *Inside Looking Out*, 174 (Girick).

41. Hacsi, " 'A Plain and Solemn Duty,' " 159 (stat.); Friedman, *These Are Our Children*, 69–70. See also Cmiel, *A Home of Another Kind*, 59–63.
42. Qtns., Thurston, *The Dependent Child*, 72; Friedman, *These Are Our Children*, 38, 83, 183 (Kirschner).
43. Zmora, *Orphanages Reconsidered*, 207 (1910 stat.); Hacsi, " 'A Plain and Solemn Duty,' " 132 (qtn.).
44. Gordon, *Pitied But Not Entitled*, 37 (qtn.); Molly Ladd-Taylor, *Mother-Work: Women, Child Welfare, and the State, 1890–1930* (Urbana: University of Illinois Press, 1994), 136, 140.
45. Richmond in Richard A. Meckel, "Protecting the Innocents: Age Segregation and the Early Child Welfare Movement," *Social Service Review* 59 (September 1985): 471; other qtns. in Ashby, *Saving the Waifs*, 25.
46. Qtn., Philip Davis, *Street-Land: Its Little People and Big Problems* (Boston: Small, Maynard, 1915), 14.
47. Nanette Schorr, "Foster Care and the Politics of Compassion," *Tikkun* 7 (May/June 1995): 19.
48. Qtn., Ladd-Taylor, *Mother-Work*, 33.
49. Michael Katz, *In the Shadow of the Poorhouse: A Social History of Welfare in America* (New York: Basic Books, 1986), 127 (Mack); Ladd-Taylor, *Mother-Work*, 145 (Lindsey).
50. Abbott, *The Child and the State*, 250 (Mass.); Gordon, *Pitied But Not Entitled*, 56.
51. Abbott, *The Child and the State*, 250–51 (Mass.); Gordon, *Pitied But Not Entitled*, 62–63.
52. Qtn. in Hastings Hart, "The Care of the Dependent Child in the Family" (1909), reprinted in *Care of Dependent Children in the Late Nineteenth and Early Twentieth Centuries*, ed. Robert H. Bremner (New York: Arno Press, 1974), 465; Gordon, *Pitied But Not Entitled*, 27, 38.
53. 1909 qtn., Ladd-Taylor, *Mother-Work*, 137.
54. See, e.g., ibid., 156 (Pa.); Gordon, *Pitied But Not Entitled*, 46; Wexler, *Wounded Innocents*, 38.
55. Christopher Howard, "Sewing the Seeds of 'Welfare': The Transformation of Mothers' Pensions," *Journal of Policy History* 4 (1992): 196; Gordon, *Pitied But Not Entitled*, 48; Ladd-Taylor, *Mother-Work*, 149.
56. Ladd-Taylor, *Mother-Work*, 157.
57. Ibid., 152–54.
58. Ibid., 150.
59. Leroy H. Pelton, *For Reasons of Poverty: A Critical Analysis of the Public Child Welfare System in the United States* (New York: Praeger, 1989), 15–16.
60. Ibid., 10 (Porterfield); Abbott, *The Child and the State*, 250 (Mass.). Also, Howard, "Sowing the Seeds of 'Welfare,' " 200.

61. Lynn Musselwhite and Sandra Quinn-Musgrove, "Kate Barnard, Pro-
    gressivism, and Indian Children" (paper, Southwestern Social Science
    Association Annual Meeting, New Orleans, 20 March 1993).
62. N. Ray Hiner, "Children's Rights, Corporal Punishment, and Child
    Abuse: Changing American Attitudes, 1870–1920," *Bulletin of the
    Menninger Clinic* 43 (1979): 240–44.
63. Mary Ann Mason, *From Father's Property to Children's Rights* (New
    York: Columbia University Press, 1994), 86; Ladd-Taylor, *Mother-
    Work*, 204 (Lathrop.)
64. Dulberger, "Refuge or Repressor," 27 (re: 1923); Abbott, *The Child
    and the State*, 237 (1921); Ladd-Taylor, *Mother-Work*, 159 (qtn.), 166
    (Ohio); Gordon, *Pitied But Not Entitled*, 63.
65. Gittens, *Poor Relations*, 47–49.
66. Stenho, "Foster Care for Dependent Children in Chicago," 45, 77–78,
    86; Ashby, *Saving the Waifs*, 217 (qtn.).

Chapter 6

1. James Borchert, *Alley Life in Washington: Family, Community, Religion, and Folklife in the City, 1850–1970* (Urbana: University of Illinois
   Press, 1980), 154.
2. Marilyn I. Holt, *The Orphan Trains: Placing Out in America* (Lincoln:
   University of Nebraska Press, 1992), 162–78.
3. Ibid., 178–79 (England); Henry Thurston, *The Dependent Child* (New
   York: Columbia University Press, 1930), 207–14.
4. "Lifetime" TV segment, 8 September 1994.
5. Richard Wexler, *Wounded Innocents: The Real Victims of the War
   Against Child Abuse* (Buffalo: Prometheus Books, 1990), 36 (Panzers);
   "Lifetime" TV segment.
6. Holt, *Orphan Trains*, 181 (qtn.).
7. Martin Wolins and Irving Piliavin, *Institutions or Foster Family: A Century of Debate* (New York: Child Welfare League of America, 1964),
   37 (stat.).
8. Thurston, *The Dependent Child*, 204–7; Joan Gittens, *Poor Relations:
   The Children of the State in Illinois, 1818–1990* (Urbana: University of
   Illinois Press, 1994), 49–50.
9. Thurston, *The Dependent Child*, 216–17, 239–40.
10. Ibid., 219–21.
11. Hyman Bogen, *The Luckiest Orphans: A History of the Hebrew Orphan
    Asylum of New York* (Urbana: University of Illinois Press, 1992), 188–90.
12. Elizabeth Pleck, *Domestic Tyranny: The Making of American Social Pol-
    icy against Family Violence from Colonial Times to the Present* (New
    York: Oxford University Press, 1987), 131 (stat.); Nurith Zmora,
    *Orphanages Reconsidered: Child Care Institutions in Progressive Era
    Baltimore* (Philadelphia: Temple University Press, 1994), 20, 28, 187

(re: Baltimore's HOA); Marian J. Morton, "Homes for Poverty's Children: Cleveland's Orphanages, 1851–1933," *Ohio History* 10 (Winter-Spring 1989): 15.

13. Pleck, *Domestic Tyranny*, 145–50; Joseph M. Hawes, *The Children's Rights Movement: A History of Advocacy and Protection* (Boston: Twayne, 1991), 54–55, 58–63.

14. Leroy H. Pelton, *For Reasons of Poverty: A Critical Analysis of the Public Child Welfare System in the United States* (New York: Praeger, 1989), 16–17; Morton, "Homes for Poverty's Children," 6, 12, 15–16 (Cleveland).

15. Howard W. Hopkirk, *Institutions Serving Children* (New York: Russell Sage Foundation, 1944), 41; Thurston, *The Dependent Child*, 218 (qtn. re: survey), 225–32.

16. Thurston, *The Dependent Child*, 238.

17. Ibid., 232–33.

18. Ibid., 236 (stats.); Grace Abbott, *The Child and the State*, vol. 2 (1938; reprint, New York: Greenwood Press, 1968), 279–80.

19. Thurston, *The Dependent Child*, p. 236.

20. *White House Conference on Child Health and Protection, 1930*, sec. 4, "Dependent and Neglected Children," Report of the Committee on Socially Handicapped—Dependency and Neglect (New York: Appleton-Century, 1933), 4–7, 17–28, 35.

21. Marshall B. Jones, "Crisis of the American Orphanage, 1931–1940," *Social Service Review* 63 (December 1989): 625.

22. Hopkirk, *Institutions Serving Children*, 1, 23, 37–38; Jones, "Crisis of the American Orphanage," 622–24 (Carstens, 623); Art Buchwald, *Leaving Home: A Memoir* (1993; paperback ed., New York: Ballantine Books, 1995), 48, 55. Hopkirk noted that the 1933 census report's official figure of 102,577 children in foster homes did not account for "personal arrangements." His guess was that the number exceeded 120,000.

23. Jones, "Crisis of the American Orphanage," 613, 624–25; Abbott, *The Child and the State*, 14 (Ohio); Elizabeth Glidden, *The Baby Fold: An Investment in Humanity* (Normal, Ill.: The Baby Fold, 1992), 58 (supt.); *Texas' Children: The Report of the Texas Child Welfare Survey* (Austin: University of Texas Press, 1938), 311. See also Kenneth Cmiel, *A Home of Another Kind: One Chicago Orphanage and the Tangle of Welfare* (Chicago: University of Chicago Press, 1995), 105–9.

24. Bogen, *The Luckiest Orphans*, 221; Morton, "Homes for Poverty's Children," 21–22.

25. Bogen, *The Luckiest Orphans*, 217–18, 225.

26. Ibid., 221–22; Buchwald, *Leaving Home*, 50–53, 63.

27. Bogen, *The Luckiest Orphans*, 218–19, 225–26, 232, 239.

28. Glidden, *The Baby Fold*, 52–56.

29. Gary E. Polster, *Inside Looking Out: The Cleveland Jewish Orphan Asylum, 1868–1924* (Kent, Ohio: Kent State University Press, 1990), 196; Reena S. Friedman, *These Are Our Children: Jewish Orphanages in the United States, 1880–1925* (Hanover, N.H.: Brandeis University Press, 1995), 190–91, 279; LeRoy Ashby, *Saving the Waifs: Reformers and Dependent Children, 1890–1917* (Philadelphia: Temple University Press, 1984), 204–5.

30. Emma O. Lundberg, *Unto the Least of These: Social Services for Children* (New York: Appleton-Century-Crofts, 1947), 309–10.

31. Winifred Bell, *Aid to Dependent Children* (New York: Columbia University Press, 1965), 6–10, 14; Christopher Howard, "Sowing the Seeds of 'Welfare': The Transformation of Mothers' Pensions, 1900–1940," *Journal of Policy History* 4 (1992): 202 (state figures); Linda Gordon, *Pitied But Not Entitled: Single Mothers and the History of Welfare, 1890–1935* (New York: Free Press, 1994), 185. In 1930 the African American population in the United States was around six million, 5 percent of the general population. U. S. Bureau of the Census, *Historical Statistics of the United States: Colonial Times to 1957* (Washington, D.C.: Bureau of the Census, 1960), 9.

32. Gordon, *Pitied But Not Entitled*, 183–285, is excellent on the political climate, assumptions, and battles behind the Social Security Act.

33. Ibid., 254–56.

34. Ibid., 259 (re: Bureau); Edwin F. Witte, *The Development of the Social Security Act* (Madison, Wis: University of Wisconsin Press, 1962), 164.

35. Gordon, *Pitied But Not Entitled*, 91, 102–5, 256 (Abbott qtn., 105).

36. Ibid., 189 (stat.), 204–5; 270 (Hopkins); Josephine Brown, *Public Relief, 1929–1939* (New York: Henry Holt & Co., 1940), 308–12.

37. Gordon, *Pitied But Not Entitled*, 263–64, 277 (wording).

38. See Gordon, *Pitied But Not Entitled*, esp. 158, 172–75, 179–81, 270–71; Gittens, *Poor Relations*, 57 (qtns.); Blanche D. Coll, *Safety Net: Welfare and Social Security, 1929–1979* (New Brunswick, N.J.: Rutgers University Press, 1995), 103.

39. Gordon, *Pitied But Not Entitled*, 145–50.

40. Bell, *Aid to Dependent Children*, 22; Howard, "Sowing the Seeds of 'Welfare,' " 212–14; Lela B. Costin, *Two Sisters for Social Justice: A Biography of Grace and Edith Abbott* (Urbana: University of Illinois Press, 1983), 224 (Lenroot); other qtns. in Gordon, *Pitied But Not Entitled*, 273, 277–78, but see also 91, 282, 284.

41. See, e.g., James T. Patterson, *America's Struggle Against Poverty, 1900–1980* (Cambridge: Harvard University Press, 1981), 67–71; Bell, *Aid to Dependent Children*, 46 (La.); Gordon, *Pitied But Not Entitled*, 275.

42. Roy Lubove, *The Struggle for Social Security, 1900–1935* (Cambridge: Harvard University Press, 1968), 109; Bell, *Aid to Dependent Children*, 34–35 (supervisor qtn.).

43. Gittens, *Poor Relations*, 57–58 (Illinois and Lindley); stats. in Leroy H. Pelton, *For Reasons of Poverty* (New York: Praeger, 1989), 17, and Howard, "Sowing the Seeds of 'Welfare,' " 215.

44. Howard, "Sowing the Seeds of 'Welfare,' " 216–19.

45. Pelton, *For Reasons of Poverty*, 18 (stat.).

46. Gordon, *Pitied But Not Entitled*, 185; William M. Tuttle Jr., *"Daddy's Gone to War": The Second World War in the Lives of America's Children* (New York: Oxford University Press, 1993), 69–90 (latchkey kids)—Hoover qtn., 70; *White House Conference, 1930*, 23.

47. Lela B. Costin, "Cruelty to Children: A Dormant Issue and Its Rediscovery, 1920–1960," *Social Service Review* 66 (June 1992): 189–91; Paul G. Anderson, "The Origin, Emergence, and Professional Recognition of Child Protection," *Social Service Review* 63 (June 1989): 234.

48. Pleck, *Domestic Tyranny*, 150–61.

49. Ibid., 161.

50. Tuttle, *"Daddy's Gone to War,"* 79; Pleck, *Domestic Tyranny*, 155 (supervisor).

51. Wexler, *Wounded Innocents*, 218 (stat.).

52. Linda T. Austin, *Babies for Sale: The Tennessee Children's Home Adoption Scandal* (Westport, Conn.: Praeger, 1993), 46–47.

53. Richard W. Carlson, "The Long Goodbye," *The Washington Post National Weekly Edition* (16–22 August 1993): 28.

54. Hopkirk, *Institutions Serving Children*, 5, 11–12, 16; Gittens, *Poor Relations*, 50–51.

55. Pelton, *For Reasons of Poverty*, 17 (stat.); Bell, *Aid to Dependent Children*, 63 (amount).

56. Bell, *Aid to Dependent Children*, 54, 57, 60; *Life*, 26 July 1948.

57. Bell, *Aid to Dependent Children*, 57–58, 60–68, 210n21. See also Coll, *Safety Net*, 176–79, 210–16.

58. Bell, *Aid to Dependent Children*, 85–89; Mimi Abramovitz, *Regulating the Lives of Women* (Boston: South End Press, 1988), 324 (investigations).

59. Bell, *Aid to Dependent Children*, 137–39.

60. Ibid., 91.

61. Marian J. Morton, *And Sin No More: Social Policy and Unwed Mothers in Cleveland, 1855–1990* (Columbus, Ohio: Ohio State University Press, 1993), 63–64. Rickie Solinger, *Wake Up Little Susie: Single Pregnancy and Race Before* Roe v. Wade (New York: Routledge, 1992), esp. 149–58, 165–67, is insightful on how these changing views influenced postwar adoption of illegitimate babies.

62. Viviana Zelizer, *Pricing the Priceless Child: The Changing Social Value of Children* (New York: Basic Books, 1985), 189–96. Fifty-nine percent of adoptees in 10 major states, according to a Children's Bureau study in the 1930s, were illegitimate. See Lincoln Caplan, *An Open Adoption* (Boston: Houghton Mifflin, 1990), 36.

63. Zelizer, *Pricing the Priceless Child*, 190 (1934 stat.), 192–93, 262 (qtns.); Glidden, *The Baby Fold*, 70 (Chicago). Solinger, *Wake Up Little Susie*, chap. 5, discusses the "mandate" (158, postwar stat., qtn.).
64. Abbott, *Children of the State*, 20 (licensing stat.); Glidden, *The Baby Fold*, 69–74.
65. Austin, *Babies for Sale*, 1, 53–54, 71, 83–87, 93–96, 122–23.
66. Ibid., 110, 124. See also Solinger, *Wake Up Little Susie*, 175–86.
67. Abramovitz, *Regulating the Lives of Women*, 319 (stat.).

Chapter 7

1. Frances Fox Piven and Richard A. Cloward, *Regulating the Poor: The Functions of Public Welfare* (New York: Random House, 1971), 183 (ADC stat.).
2. Terry H. Anderson, *The Movement and the Sixties: Protest in America from Greensboro to Wounded Knee* (New York: Oxford University Press, 1995), 71 (qtn.).
3. Herbert J. Gans, "The 'Equality' Revolution," *The New York Times Magazine* (3 November 1968). On the importance of the "rights revolution," see James T. Patterson, *Grand Expectations: The United States, 1945–1974* (New York: Oxford University Press, 1996), esp. vii, 385, 452–53, 562–92, 637–48, 671–73.
4. Michael Grossberg, "Children's Legal Rights? A Historical Look at a Legal Paradox," in *Children at Risk in America: History, Concepts, and Public Policy*, ed. Roberta Wollons (Albany: State University of New York Press, 1993), 127 (qtn.), 128; Joseph M. Hawes, *The Children's Rights Movement: A History of Advocacy and Protection* (Boston: Twayne, 1991), 107–8, 113.
5. Hawes, *The Children's Rights Movement*, 115–16.
6. Grossberg, "Children's Legal Rights?" 132 (Carnegie); Alan Sussman, *The Rights of Young People: A Basic ACLU Guide to a Young Person's Rights* (New York: Avon, 1977), 13.
7. Grossberg, "Children's Legal Rights?," 130–32.
8. Bruce Hafen, "Children's Liberation and the New Egalitarianism: Some Reservations about Abandoning Children to Their 'Rights,' " *Brigham Young University Law Review* 2 (1976): 605–58; Grossberg, "Children's Legal Rights?," 111–12 (Grundy).
9. Mimi Abramovitz, *Regulating the Lives of Women* (Boston: South End Press, 1988), 326 (qtn.), 327; Piven and Cloward, *Regulating the Poor*, 140n.
10. James T. Patterson, *America's Struggle Against Poverty, 1900–1980* (Cambridge: Harvard University Press, 1981), 78–114, 126–27, 137, 169–70.
11. Ibid., 129–32; Winifred Bell, *Aid to Dependent Children* (New York: Columbia University Press, 1965), 235n26.

12. Bell, *Aid to Dependent Children*, 149; Patterson, *America's Struggle Against Poverty*, 130.

13. Abramovitz, *Regulating the Lives of Women*, 331; Patterson, *America's Struggle Against Poverty*, 131–33; Bell, *Aid to Dependent Children*, 149, 171.

14. Gilbert Y. Steiner, *Social Insecurity: The Politics of Welfare* (Chicago: Rand McNally, 1966), 46 (ounce qtn.); Patterson, *America's Struggle Against Poverty*, 133 (other qtns.).

15. Piven and Cloward, *Regulating the Poor*, Source Table 1 (stat.).

16. Patterson, *America's Struggle Against Poverty*, 106 (survey), 135–40; Piven and Cloward, *Regulating the Poor*, 262 (qtn.), 269–70, 287–305.

17. Guida West, *The National Welfare Rights Movement: The Social Protest of Poor Women* (New York: Praeger, 1981), 294 (NYC); Piven and Cloward, *Regulating the Poor*, 320–30.

18. Patterson, *America's Struggle Against Poverty*, 107–8 (Mitchell); Joan Gittens, *Poor Relations: The Children of the State of Illinois, 1818–1990* (Urbana: University of Illinois Press, 1994), 62 (problem); Abramovitz, *Regulating the Lives of Women*, 334–35 (stats., Long, Reagan).

19. West, *The National Welfare Rights Movement*, 291–92; Sar A. Levitan and Robert Taggart, *The Promise of Greatness* (Cambridge: Harvard University Press, 1976), 51.

20. West, *The National Welfare Rights Movement*, 296; Piven and Cloward, *Regulating the Poor*, 308–9 (Court qtn.).

21. Robert H. Bremner, *Children and Youth in American History*, vol. 3 (Cambridge: Harvard University Press, 1972), 520; Stephen Ambrose, *Nixon: The Triumph of a Politician, 1962–1972* (New York: Simon & Schuster, 1989), 124 (crap); H. R. Haldeman, *The Haldeman Diaries* (1994; paper ed., New York: Berkley Books, 1995), 66 (blacks).

22. Ambrose, *Nixon*, 291–94; Haldeman, *Haldeman Diaries*, 218.

23. John Morton Blum, *Years of Discord: American Politics and Society, 1961–1974* (New York: Norton, 1991), 176; Abramovitz, *Regulating the Lives of Women*, 341 (1972); Patterson, *America's Struggle Against Poverty*, 157–70; qtn., 160.

24. Andrew Billingsley and Jeanne M. Giovannoni, *Children of the Storm: Black Children and American Child Welfare* (New York: Harcourt Brace Jovanovich, 1972), 62–63.

25. Mary Ann Mason, *From Father's Property to Children's Rights* (New York: Columbia University Press, 1994), 154–55; West, *The National Welfare Rights Movement*, 331.

26. Mason, *From Father's Property to Children's Rights*, 154–55.

27. Elizabeth Pleck, *Domestic Tyranny: The Making of American Social Policy against Family Violence from Colonial Times to the Present* (New York: Oxford University Press, 1987), 165–66.

28. Barry Siegel, *A Death in White Bear Lake* (1990; paper ed., New York: Bantam Books, 1991), 202–9.

29. Ibid., 209–10; Pleck, *Domestic Tyranny*, 170.

30. Siegel, *A Death in White Bear Lake*, 211; Pleck, *Domestic Tyranny*, 170; Hawes, *The Children's Rights Movement*, 100; Stephen J. Pfohl, "The 'Discovery' of Child Abuse," *Social Problems* 24 (February 1977): 310, 318–21; John M. Johnson, "Symbolic Salvation: The Changing Meanings of the Child Maltreatment Movement," *Studies in Symbolic Interaction* 6 (1985): 296.

31. Pleck, *Domestic Tyranny*, 168; Pfohl, "The 'Discovery' of Child Abuse," 320; Paul G. Anderson, "The Origin, Emergence, and Professional Recognition of Child Protection," *Social Service Review* 63 (June 1989): 241 (LC).

32. Russ Rymer, *Genie: An Abused Child's Flight from Silence* (New York: HarperCollins, 1993), 6–22.

33. Duncan Lindsey, *The Welfare of Children* (New York: Oxford University Press, 1994), 93 (Fla.).

34. Pleck, *Domestic Tyranny*, 176.

35. Mary Ann Jimenez, "Permanency Planning and the Child Abuse Prevention and Treatment Act: The Paradox of Child Welfare Policy," *Journal of Sociology and Social Welfare* 17 (September 1990): 55, 59, 61.

36. Johnson, "Symbolic Salvation," 290 ("math"); Lindsey, *The Welfare of Children*, 93; Leroy H. Pelton, *For Reasons of Poverty: A Critical Analysis of the Public Child Welfare System in the United States* (New York: Praeger, 1989), 29–33.

37. Joel Best, *Threatened Children: Rhetoric and Concern about Child-Victims* (Chicago: University of Chicago Press, 1990), 66–69 (pamphlet, 69).

38. Arlene Skolnick, "The Limits of Childhood: Conceptions of Child Development and Social Context," *Law and Contemporary Problems* 39 (Summer 1975): 41 (report); Johnson, "Symbolic Salvation," 294–99 (Katz, 295).

39. Pleck, *Domestic Tyranny*, 177–78 (re: the law); Richard Wexler, *Wounded Innocents: The Real Victims of the War Against Child Abuse*, (Buffalo: Prometheus Books, 1990), 12, 16, 18.

40. Alfred Kadushin, "Institutions for Dependent and Neglected Children," in *Child Caring: Social Policy and the Institution*, ed. Donnell M. Pappenfort et al. (Chicago: Aldine, 1973), 161 (re: 1958); Wexler, *Wounded Innocents*, 218–19 (ratios); Pelton, *For Reasons of Poverty*, 6. Pelton's estimates (6, 21–22) of more than five hundred thousand by the midseventies include children in all kinds of substitute care, including institutions.

41. *New York Times*, 26 December 1974; Kadushin, "Institutions for Dependent and Neglected Children," 145, 149–54, 164.

42. Elizabeth Glidden, *The Baby Fold: An Investment in Humanity* (Normal, Ill.: The Baby Fold, 1992), 104–9; Linda Amster, "Orphanages Vanishing for a Lack of Orphans," *New York Times*, 26 December 1974: 1, 67.
43. Kenneth Wooden, *Weeping in the Playtime of Others: America's Incarcerated Children* (New York: McGraw-Hill, 1976), 182–186 (qtn., 182).
44. Ibid., 192–93; also, Gittens, *Poor Relations*, 80.
45. Michael Mushlin, "Unsafe Havens: The Case for Constitutional Protection of Foster Children from Abuse and Neglect," in *Child, Parent, & State: Law and Policy Reader*, ed. S. Randall Humm et al. (Philadelphia: Temple University Press, 1994), 190 (Edelman).
46. See David J. Rothman, "The State as Parent," in *Doing Good: The Limits of Benevolence*, ed. Willard Gaylin et al. (New York: Pantheon, 1978), 69–96.
47. On the "recapture" effort, see, e.g., Stephanie Coontz, *The Way We Never Were: American Families and the Nostalgia Trap* (New York: Basic Books, 1992), (qtn., 92); Gilbert Y. Steiner, *The Futility of Family Policy* (Washington, D.C.: Brookings Institution, 1981), 3 (Carter).
48. Hawes, *The Children's Rights Movement*, 103–4; Pleck, *Domestic Tyranny*, 179–80; Jimenez, "Permanency Planning and the Child Abuse Prevention and Treatment Act," 64–66.
49. On the "permanency planning movement," see Pelton, *For Reasons of Poverty*, 79–98; Jiminez, "Permanency Planning and the Child Abuse Act," 69 (qtn.); also Gittens, *Poor Relations*, 76–78. According to Richard J. Gelles, *The Book of David: How Preserving Families Can Cost Children's Lives* (New York: Basic Books, 1996), 93, "experts and advocates generally consider [the 1980 act] the most significant legislation in the history of child welfare."
50. Lindsay, *The Welfare of Children*, 65–66; Jimenez, "Permanency Planning and the Child Abuse Act," 68; Pelton, *For Reasons of Poverty*, 6–7 (stats.), 81–83. Pelton cautions that the numbers are imprecise because of "methodological and definitional differences."
51. R. Barth and M. Berry, "Outcomes of Child Welfare Services Under Permanency Planning," *Social Services Review* 61 (1987): 71–89; Vincent J. Fontana, *Save the Family, Save the Child* (New York: Dutton, 1991), 1–2 (Felumero); Gittens, *Poor Relations*, 68–69, 249 (Lindquist); Mushlin, "Unsafe Havens," 208 (Besharov).
52. J. Douglas Bates, *Gift Children* (New York: Ticknor & Fields, 1993), 30–32, 77–79, 94; Elizabeth Bartholet, *Family Bonds: Adoption and the Politics of Parenting* (Boston: Houghton Mifflin, 1993), 94–95 (qtn.).
53. Ibid., 94–100, and passim.
54. Bartholet, *Family Bonds*, 60, 86–117, 242, 244.
55. Wooden, *Weeping in the Playtime of Others*, 183 (re: Navaho); Manuel P. Guerrero, "Indian Child Welfare Act of 1978: A Response to the

Threat to Indian Culture Caused by Foster and Adoptive Placements of Indian Children," *American Indian Law Review* 7 (1979): 53; Lynn K. Uthe, "The Best Interests of Indian Children in Minnesota," ibid., 17 (1992): 252–53.

56. Guerrero, "Indian Child Welfare Act of 1978," 52–53 (stats.), 56 (language); Uthe, "The Best Interests of Indian Children in Minnesota," 242; Linda A. Marousek, "The Indian Child Welfare Act of 1978: Provisions and Policy," *South Dakota Law Review* 25 (Winter 1980): 99–100, for additional statistics re: the midseventies; Steven Unger, ed., *The Destruction of American Indian Families* (New York: The Association of American Indian Affairs, 1977); Gaylene J. McCartney, "The American Indian Child-Welfare Crisis: Cultural Genocide or First Amendment Preservation," *Columbia Human Rights Law Review* 17 (Fall-Winter 1975–76): 529–51.

57. On the cases and the legislation, see Guerrero, "Indian Child Welfare Act of 1978," 54–77, and Marousek, "The Indian Child Welfare Act of 1978," esp. 102, 107, 110, 113; McCartney, "The American Indian Child-Welfare Crisis," 551 (Tonasket).

58. Enid Nemy, "Adopted Children Who Wonder, 'What Was Mother Like?,' " *New York Times*, 25 July 1972: 22.

59. Wayne Carp, "The Sealed Adoption Records Controversy in Historical Perspective," *Journal of Sociology and Social Welfare* 19 (June 1992): 27–42; Lincoln Caplan, *An Open Adoption* (Boston: Houghton Mifflin, 1990), 38 (stat. and qtn.).

60. Carp, "The Sealed Adoption Records Controversy," 43–51; Caplan, *An Open Adoption*, 41 (Paton).

61. Nemy, "Adopted Children Who Wonder," *New York Times* (25 July 1972) re Fisher; Lucinda Franks, "The War for Baby Clausen," *New Yorker* (22 March 1993): 58 (CUB); Bartholet, *Family Bonds*, 54–60.

62. Siegel, *A Death in White Bear Lake* (qtn., 508–09).

63. Ibid., 418 (qtn.).

64. See, e.g., Pleck, *Domestic Tyranny*, 171.

65. Pelton, *For Reasons of Poverty*, 27–28 (handbook); Joan Kaufman and Edward Zigler, "Do Abused Children Become Abusive Parents?" *American Journal of Orthopsychiatry* 57 (April 1987): 186–92 (qtns., 187, 190).

66. Wexler, *Wounded Innocents*, 54–55.

67. For criticism of the medical model, see, e.g., ibid., 56–57; Pelton, *For Reasons of Poverty*, 37–42 (Mondale qtn., 37); Pleck, *Domestic Tyranny*, 171–75; Nanette Schorr, "Foster Care and the Politics of Compassion," 7 *Tikkun* (May/June 1992): 19, 21–22.

68. Johnson, "Symbolic Salvations," 301.

69. On *Ingraham v. Wright*, see Philip Greven, *Spare the Child: The Religious Roots of Punishment and the Psychological Impact of Physical Abuse* (New York: Knopf, 1991), 98–108.

70. Robert J. Lifton and Charles B. Strozier, "Waiting for Armageddon," *New York Times Book Review* (12 August 1990): 24; Greven, *Spare the Child*, 60–81; Letty C. Pogrebin, "Do Americans Hate Children?" *Ms.* (November 1983): 48 ("lib"). The similarities between Puritan attitudes on childrearing and the ideas of Dobson and others are clear, as Greven shows.
71. *Esquire* (March 1974); Pogrebin, "Do Americans Hate Children?," 47–50, 126 (qtns.).
72. Curt Suplee, "Obsessed with Children Possessed," *Washington Post*, 21 July 1977: D1, 4 (industry); Joyce Maynard, "The Monster Children," *Newsweek* (26 July 1976): 10–11; Pogrebin, "Do Americans Hate Children?," 47 (qtn.), 49.
73. David Hechler, *The Battle and the Backlash: The Child Sexual Abuse War* (Lexington, Mass.: Heath, 1988), 3 (qtns.).

Chapter 8

1. Larry Lipman, "Code Blue," *Lewiston Tribune*, 8 June 1990 (re: code blue): 1; Duncan Lindsey, *The Welfare of Children* (New York: Oxford University Press, 1994), 4–5.
2. Stats. in Lindsey, *The Welfare of Children*, 93.
3. *People* (7–14 March 1994): 170–71; CBS, 6 April 1990.
4. Ed Penhale, "House OKs Child-Abuse Bill Despite Flaws," *Seattle Post-Intelligencer*, 16 April 1987: D1, 4.
5. See Joyce Johnson, *What Lisa Knew: The Truth and Lies of the Steinberg Case* (New York: G. P. Putnam's Sons, 1990), 17 (qtn.); Robert Coles, "The Death of a Child," *New York Times Book Review* (8 April 1990): 7 (stat.), 30–31; Nat Hentoff, "How the Press Fails All the Lisa Steinbergs," *Village Voice* (26 Jan. 1988): 17 (TV); Vincent J. Fontana and Valerie Moolman, *Save the Family, Save the Child* (New York: Dutton, 1991), 136–37 (training). Officially, some 1,200 children died of abuse in 1987, but experts believed that many "accidental" deaths were in fact murder.
6. Richard Wexler, *Wounded Innocents: The Real Victims of the War Against Child Abuse* (Buffalo: Prometheus Books, 1990), 267.
7. *Newsweek* (23 November 1987): 70 (Schene); Wexler, *Wounded Innocents*, 245.
8. Wexler, *Wounded Innocents*, 12, 14, 21, 78–94, 119–20, 132, 251.
9. Richard Wexler, "Invasion of the Child Savers," *The Progressive* (September 1985): 19–22; also cover.
10. Wexler, *Wounded Innocents*, 296.
11. Walter Olson, "The Hand That Rocks the Cradle," *National Review* (11 May 1992): 34; Mary Pride, *The Child Abuse Industry* (Westchester, Ill.: Crossway Books, 1986), esp. x, 24, 32, 56, 123, 142.

12. Pride, *The Child Abuse Industry*, 130, 145; Philip Greven, *Spare the Child: The Religious Roots of Punishment and the Psychological Impact of Physical Abuse* (New York: Knopf, 1990), 69, 79.

13. Murray A. Straus, *Beating the Devil Out of Them: Corporal Punishment in American Families* (Lexington, Mass.: Lexington Books, 1994), 1 (qtn.); stats., 23–24, 32, 149; 182–86. Between 1979 and 1989, five countries made spanking children illegal: Sweden, Finland, Denmark, Norway, Austria (170).

14. Ibid., 110–11, 171–73; 23 June 1993 progress report of EPOCH-USA (End Physical Punishment of Children), re: the hearings, in author's possession.

15. Straus, *Beating the Devil Out of Them*, 178; Greven, *Spare the Child*, 222.

16. Straus, *Beating the Devil Out of Them*, 5 (Texas), 173 (qtn.).

17. Debbie Nathan, "The Making of a Modern Witch Trial," *Village Voice* (29 September 1987): 22 (stat.).

18. Marjie Lundstrom and Rochelle Sharpe, "Getting Away with Murder," *Public Welfare* 49 (Summer 1991): 19–24.

19. Ibid., 20–21, 23–24.

20. Ibid., 20–21, 27–28.

21. Joel Best, *Threatened Children: Rhetoric and Concern about Child-Victims* (Chicago: University of Chicago Press, 1990), 96 (Snow); Christina Crawford, *No Safe Place: The Legacy of Family Violence* (Barrytown, N.Y.: Station Hill Press, 1994), 160.

22. Paula Hawkins, *Children at Risk: My Fight Against Child Abuse* (Bethesda, Md.: Adler and Adler, 1986), 1, 72 (qtns.).

23. John Engstrom, "Actor Emerges Reborn from Abyss of Childhood Horrors," *Seattle Post-Intelligencer*, 13 January 1993: C11 (Blake); Lenore Terr, *Unchained Memories: True Stories of Traumatic Memories, Lost and Found* (New York: Basic Books, 1994), 121–24 (Van Derbur).

24. Suzanne Somers, ed., *Wednesday's Children: Adult Survivors of Abuse Speak Out* (1992; paperbound ed., New York: Jove Books, 1993), 27–28 (qtns.).

25. Richard Rhodes, *A Hole in the World: An American Boyhood* (New York: Simon & Schuster, 1990), 88, 117, 160 (qtns.).

26. Crawford, *No Safe Place*, 1–10.

27. Russ Rymer, *Genie: An Abused Child's Flight from Silence* (New York: HarperCollins, 1993), 8 (qtn.); Andrew Vachss, "A Murderer Rocked the Cradle," *New York Times Book Review* (15 July 1990): 13.

28. Pride, *The Child Abuse Industry*, 32; Ellen Goodman, "Don't Pull Plug on Families Just Yet," *Spokesman-Review*, 23 November 1994.

29. Hentoff, "How the Press Fails All the Lisa Steinbergs," 23.

30. Maria Laurino and Rick Hornung, "Nobody Knows Their Names," *Village Voice* (26 January 1988): 20; Hentoff, "How the Press Fails All the Lisa Steinbergs," 21.

31. Re: the dilemmas, see Ellen Goodman, "Who Can Protect a Joshua DeShaney?" *Washington Post*, 28 February 1989: A23.

32. See, e.g., ibid.; "The Battered Child," *The New Republic* (20 March 1989): 7.

33. Al Kamen, "State Absolved in Rights Case," *Washington Post*, 23 February 1989: A6; "Saving Joshua and Others," ibid., 24 February 1989; Linda Greenhouse, "Court Says Intervention in Child Abuse Isn't Mandated," *New York Times*, 23 February 1989: A1, B7; Laura Mansnerus, "Limits to the Duty to Rescue," *New York Times*, 28 February 1989; Amy Sinden, "In Search of Affirmative Duties toward Children under a Post-*DeShaney* Constitution," in *Child, Parent, & State: Law and Policy Reader*, ed. S. Randall Humm et al. (Philadelphia: Temple University Press, 1994), 141–75.

34. Kamen, "State Absolved in Rights Case" (Blackmun); Mansnerus, "Limits to the Duty to Rescue" (Brennan); Sinden, "In Search of Affirmative Duties," 148.

35. Goodman, "Who Can Protect a Joshua DeShaney?"

36. On Adam Mann and his brothers, see PBS *Frontline* documentary, "Who Killed Adam Mann," 3 December 1991; Celia M. Dugger, "7 Deaths in 1990 Point Up Failings of Child Protection System," *New York Times*, 23 January 1992: B1, 5.

37. "The Battered Child," *New Republic* (20 March 1989): 7 (Dallas); Wexler, *Wounded Innocents*, 22, 241; Laurino and Hornung, "Nobody Knows Their Names," 20; John Crewdson, *By Silence Betrayed: Sexual Abuse of Children in America* (1988; paperbound ed., New York: Harper & Row, 1989), 178 (L.A.).

38. "Report: Child Abuse Huge Threat to Social Fabric," *Lewiston Tribune*, 15 September 1991: 2A (panel); Ron Word, "Child's Ghastly Life on Conscience of Parent, Agency That Failed Her," *Spokesman-Review*, 5 June 1994 (Shipley).

39. Crewdson, *By Silence Betrayed*, 21 (stat.); Leroy Pelton, *For Reasons of Poverty* (Westport, Conn.: Greenwood, 1989), 42 (percentages).

40. David Hechler, *The Battle and the Backlash: The Child Sexual Abuse War* (Lexington, Mass.: Heath, 1988), 4.

41. Crewdson, *By Silence Betrayed*, 1–19; Hechler, *The Battle and the Backlash*, 111–16.

42. Crewdson, *By Silence Betrayed*, 21 (Maine), 132–59; *Newsweek* (20 August 1984): 44.

43. Wexler, *Wounded Innocents*, 148. In 1995 Home Box Office produced the Emmy Award–winning movie, "Indictment: The McMartin Trial."

44. Ruth Shalit, "Witch Hunt," *New Republic* (19 June 1995): 14–16; Lawrence Wright, "Child-Care Demons," *The New Yorker* (3 October 1994): 5–6; Nancy Hass, "Margaret Kelly Michaels Wants Her Inno-

cence Back," *New York Times Magazine* (10 September 1995): 37–41; Anna Quindlen, "When Children Allege Sex Abuse, Truth Can Be Maddeningly Elusive," *Spokesman-Review,* 1 April 1993. See also Debbie Nathan and Michael Snedeker, *Satan's Silence: Ritual Abuse and the Making of a Modern American Witch Hunt* (New York: Basic Books, 1995), which describes "a crusade whose enemies were phantoms, but whose casualties were all too real" (253).

45. Walter Reich, "The Monster in the Mists," *New York Times Book Review* (15 May 1994): 1, 33, 37; *Time* (23 May 1994): 51 (Ramona); *Newsweek* (19 April 1993): 54; ibid. (15 July 1996): 64 (overturned conviction).

46. See, e.g., Reich, "The Monster in the Mists," 38; unidentified clipping in author's possession (Montgomery).

47. Anne Gearan, "The 'Abuse Excuse' Is All the Legal Rage," *Lewiston Tribune,* 27 February 1994; John White, "Parent Killer Convicted of Manslaughter," *Spokesman-Review,* 31 August 1992 (WA); "Mother of Drowned Boys Said Stepfather Molested Her," ibid., 27 November 1994 (Smith); Rowland Nethaway, "Abuse—A Trendy, All-Purpose Excuse and Major Growth Industry," ibid., 12 August 1993.

48. Hechler, *The Battle and the Backlash,* 118; Crewdson, *By Silence Betrayed,* 22; Paul and Shirley Eberle, *The Politics of Child Abuse* (Secaucus, N.J.: Lyle Stuart, 1986), 129, 283; John M. Johnson, "Symbolic Salvation: The Changing Meanings of the Child Maltreatment Movement," *Studies in Symbolic Interaction* 6 (1985): 300 (PAPS); James Cronin, "False Memory," *Z Magazine* (April 1994): 31 (FMSF). See also *The Backlash: Child Protection Under Fire,* ed. John E. B. Myers (Thousand Oaks, Calif.: Sage Publications, Inc., 1994), esp. Myers's essays, "Definition and Origins of the Backlash Against Child Protection," 17–30, and "The Literature of the Backlash," 86–103.

49. Johnson, "Symbolic Salvation," 300, 302 (qtn.).

50. Hechler, *The Battle and the Backlash,* 125–26, 152–53.

51. Lundstrom and Sharpe, "Getting Away with Murder," 25–27.

52. Ibid., 29; Hechler, *The Battle and the Backlash,* 150–51 (Vachss).

53. Shalit, "Witch Hunt," 16 (Ofshe); Hechler, *The Battle and the Backlash,* 220 (hamburger).

54. Wexler, *Wounded Innocents,* 79.

55. Debbie Nathan, "Sex, the Devil, and Day Care," *Village Voice* (29 September 1987): 23, 26; Wright, "Child-Care Demons," 6. See also Nathan and Snedeker, *Satan's Silence,* esp. 29–50, a fascinating discussion of subversion myths, urban legends, and cult fears, and Marilyn Ivy, "Memory, Silence and Satan," *The Nation* (25 December 1995): 832–36.

56. Best, *Threatened Children,* 182–83.

57. Lindsey, *The Welfare of Children*, 157.

58. Elizabeth Pleck, *Domestic Tyranny: The Making of American Social Policy against Family Violence from Colonial Times to the Present* (New York: Oxford University Press, 1987), 197–98; Cronin, "False Memory," 36 (platform).

59. Lou Cannon, *President Reagan: The Role of a Lifetime* (New York: Simon & Schuster, 1991), 517–19; Joan Gittens, *Poor Relations: The Children of the State in Illinois, 1818–1990* (Urbana: University of Illinois Press, 1994), 65 (Ill.); Sheila B. Kamerman and Alfred J. Kahn, *Starting Right: How America Neglects Its Youngest Children and What We Can Do About It* (New York: Oxford University Press, 1995), 65 (nat'l); David S. Broder, "How to Rescue Our Children," *Washington Post National Weekly Edition* (11–17 March 1991): 4 (1989 figure). See also Robert Kuttner, "Punishing the Poor," ibid. (8–14 May 1995): 5.

60. "The Politics of Adoption," *Newsweek* (21 March 1994): 64–65.

61. "Adoption Country," *New Yorker* (10 May 1993): 8; Lincoln Caplan, *An Open Adoption* (Boston: Houghton Mifflin, 1990), 87–91 (qtn., 89).

62. Ibid., 81; Betty J. Lifton, *Journey of the Adopted Self: A Quest for Wholeness* (New York: Basic Books, 1994), 92, 103, 315.

63. Lifton, *Journey of the Adopted Self*, 92; Caplan, *An Open Adoption*, 50, 80–82, 92–94 (qtn., 94).

64. Kathy Dobie, "Nobody's Child: The Battle Over Interracial Adoption," *Village Voice* (8 Aug. 1989):18 ff.

65. Lynne Duke, "Drawing the Best Family Circle for an Adoptive Child," *Washington Post National Weekly Edition* (18–24 May 1992): 33.

66. "All in the Family," *The New Republic* (24 January 1994): 6–7.

67. "The Politics of Adoption," 65; Randall Kennedy, "Orphans of Separatism: The Painful Politics of Transracial Adoption," *The American Prospect* (Spring 1994): 38–45.

68. Tom Diemer, "Adoption Law Misunderstood, Metzenbaum Says," *The [Cleveland] Plain Dealer* (27 April 1995): 6A.

69. Barbara Vobejda, "GOP Plan Revives Adoption Battle," *Washington Post* (13 April 1995): A6.

70. "Tribe, Adoptive Parents Fight for Custody of Boy," *Spokesman-Review*, 20 August 1993: B4 and "Court: Couple Can't Adopt Sioux Boy," 5 October 1993: B6. In July 1996 the House narrowly passed an amendment that would reduce the role of tribal courts in adoption proceedings. The fate of the bill, sponsored by Rep. Deborah Pryce, an Ohio Republican, depended on a House-Senate conference committee. See Coleman McCarthy, "Protecting the Tribe's Interest in the Child," *Liberal Opinion Week* (22 July 1996): 3.

71. Judy Daubenmier, "The Crying Game," *Lewiston Tribune*, 3 August 1993: A1, 4; Lucinda Franks, "The War for Baby Clausen," *New Yorker* (22 March 1993): 56–73.

72. Joan Beck, "Bitter Adoption Case Sends Warning," *Spokesman-Review*, 4 April 1993, and Ellen Goodman, "Slow, Inept System Serves Children, Prospective Adoptive Parents Badly," 4 August 1993; *Lewiston Tribune*, 4 August 1993 (cartoon). See also "Standing Up for Fathers," *Newsweek* (3 May 1993): 52–53.

73. "Child Taken to New Family," *Spokesman Review*, 1 May 1995: A1, 5.

74. "Adoption Country," 8; ABC Evening News, 16 June 1994 (Ariz.); "Compromise Settlement in Custody Case," *Spokesman-Review*, 29 August 1993 (Vt.).

75. "DeBoers Adopt Again After Losing Jessica," *Spokesman-Review*, 12 June 1994 and "Baby Richard Interacts with Biological Parents," ibid., 2 May 1995; *Newsweek* (21 March 1994); "Learning to Live Without Jessi," *Newsweek* (21 March 1994): 63.

76. "The Limits of Tolerance?" *Newsweek* (14 February 1994): 47; Neil Modie, "Seattle Gay Couple's Adoption of Boy Approved," *Spokesman-Review*, 25 December 1994: B6.

77. Modie, "Seattle Gay Couple's Adoption of Boy Approved."

78. Katha Pollitt, "Adoption Fantasy," *The Nation* (8 July 1996): 9; "Family-Value Rhetoric and Reality," *Washington Post National Weekly Edition* (13–19 May 1996): 25.

79. Pollitt, "Adoption Fantasy," 9; Jeff Barnard, " 'Celebration Family' Stands Accused," *Lewiston Tribune*, 31 August 1992, 7A; "Witness Tells of Mistreatment," ibid., 29 December 1994: 6C.

80. Ron Harris, "Adult Drug Abuse Often Turns Children into Victims," *St. Paul Pioneer Press*, 14 May 1990: 7A ('80s stats.). Michael Massing, "The Welfare Blues," *New York Review of Books* (24 March 1994): 45 ('94 stats.); Hal Spencer, "Foster Parents Seek More Money for 'A System That Runs on Love,' " *Lewiston Tribune*, 25 April 1991 (qtn.); Patricia Gabbett Snow, "No More Shelter Hopscotch," *Albuquerque Journal*, 23 October 1994: A1, 12.

81. Jim Lynch, "State Enlists Local Teams to Help Kids," *Spokesman-Review*, 13 August 1995: A7 (qtn.); *Public Welfare* 48 (Winter 1990) focused on the theme, "Child Protective Services: A System Under Stress."

82. "Children Lost in the Quagmire," *Newsweek* (13 May 1991): 64.

83. Gittens, *Poor Relations*, 84–85; "The Storm Over Orphanages," *Time* (12 December 1994): 60; Richard J. Gelles, *The Book of David: How Preserving Families Can Cost Children's Lives* (New York: Basic Books, 1996), esp. 94, 115–43, 148–52.

84. Lois G. Forer, *Unequal Protection: Women, Children, and the Elderly in Court* (New York: Norton, 1991), 147, 194, 241n6.

85. Penelope Lemov, "The Return of the Orphanage," *Governing* (May 1991): 31–35; "The Storm Over Orphanages," pp. 60–61 (Ill.). See

also, Joyce Ladner, "Bring Back the Orphanages," *Washington Post* (29 October 1989).

86. Massing, "The Welfare Blues," 45.

87. Qtns. in "Critics Told to Go See 'Boys' Town' " *Spokesman-Review*, 5 December 1994: A1, and "The Return of the Orphanage," 58; *Newsweek* (12 December 1994).

88. Kay Sunstein Hymowitz, "Reproduced and Abandoned: Hollywood's New Orphans," *Tikkun* 7 (January/February 1992): 89–92.

89. Ruth Wallen, "Memory Politics," *Tikkun* 9 (November/December 1994): 35–40; Crewdson, *By Silence Betrayed*, 24–25 (poll).

Epilogue

1. "Abandoned to Her Fate," *Time* (11 December 1995): 32–36; also, "The Death of Little Elisa," *Newsweek* (11 December 1995): 42, 45.

2. Katha Pollitt, "The Violence of Ordinary Life," *Nation* (1 January 1996): 9; Shalala qtn., Jill Smolowe, "Making the Tough Calls," *Time* (11 December 1995): 41.

3. See Lela B. Costin, Howard J. Karger, and David Stoesz, *The Politics of Child Abuse in America* (New York: Oxford University Press, 1996), 145–51, for an excellent recent summary of the class-based nature of child abuse.

4. Ibid., 117–29.

5. On family preservation, see ibid., 119–22, 124, 131, 155–57 (re: recycled friendly visiting). For a skeptic's worries, see Richard J. Gelles, *The Book of David: How Preserving Families Can Cost Children's Lives* (New York: Basic Books, 1996).

6. Murray Kempton, "Child Welfare Agency Assumes Tragic Proportions for Giuliani," *Liberal Opinion Week* (29 January 1996): 12.

7. Margot Hornblower, "Fixing the System," *Newsweek* (11 December 1995): 45 (Los Angeles boy).

8. "Clinton Signs Welfare Reform Bill," *Spokesman-Review*, 23 August 1996: A8 (demonstration, Edelman); Clarence Page, "Poor Children: The Guinea Pigs of Welfare Reform," *Liberal Opinion Week* (19 August 1996): 13 (Moynihan). In 1996, as journalist Vanessa Gallman indicated, "about 14 million people, 9 million of them children, receive AFDC benefits." Gallman, "Clinton Says He'll Sign," *Spokesman-Review*, 1 August 1996: 1.

9. "Clinton Signs Welfare Reform Bill," 1A (Shaw, half-century); Bob Herbert, "The Mouths of Babes," *Liberal Opinion Week* (29 July 1996): 5 (Shaw re: rescue); Mickey Kaus, "Day of Reckoning," ibid. (5 August 1996): 8; Molly Ivins, "Children Will Pay the Price for Welfare Reform," ibid.: 1 (Gingrich); Donald Kaul, "Where's Charles Dickens

When You Need Him?" ibid. (19 August 1996): 10 (Gramm); Jonathan Alter, "Washington Washes Its Hands," *Newsweek* (12 August 1996): 42–44 (Clinton qtn., 43). See also Mickey Kaus, "Clinton's Welfare Endgame," ibid. (5 August 1996): 65.

10. "Poor Children: The Guinea Pigs of Welfare Reform," 13 (Moynihan, fearsome); "Study Says Reform Bill Hurts Kids," *Spokesman-Review,* 26 July 1996 (million); Victor Volland, "Current Push to End Welfare Not the First, Historian Says," *St. Louis Post-Dispatch,* 18 August 1996: 13D (Reconstruction); Daniel Patrick Moynihan, "Congress Builds a Coffin," *New York Review of Books* (11 January 1996): 33 (deception); Bob Herbert, "Welfare Stampede," *Liberal Opinion Week,* 27 November 1995: 6 (obscene); Carl Rowan, "We'll Rue the Results of This Welfare Reform," ibid. (12 August 1996): 4 (Lewis); Robert Sheer, "Welfare Mother the Target of Opportunity," ibid.: 7 (scapegoating); Herbert, "Welfare Hysteria" (percentage) ibid., 6; Norman Solomon, "Cherishing Kids . . . While Neglecting Them," ibid. (27 May 1996): 5; David T. Ellwood, "Welfare Reform As I Knew It," *The American Prospect* (May-June 1996): 22 (Moynihan re: failure).

11. Ruth Sidel, "The Welfare Scam," *The Nation* (12 December 1994): 712 (qtn. and 1993); "Clinton Signs Welfare Reform Bill," *Spokesman-Review,* 23 August 1996: A8 (Romer); David Broder in *Lewiston Tribune,* 2 October 1995 (study); Children's Defense Fund, *The State of America's Children* (Wash. D.C.: Children's Defense Fund, 1995), 13; Murray Kempton, "Welfare Aid Cuts Are Legislative Version of Child Abuse," *Liberal Opinion Week* (8 January 1996): 19.

12. "The Return of the Orphanage," 58–59; "The Orphanage," *Newsweek* (12 December 1994): 31 (Rothman). Costs in Barbara Vobejda, "Are There No Orphanages?" *The Washington Post National Weekly Edition* (26 December 1994–1 January 1995): 32; Duncan Lindsey, *The Welfare of Children* (New York: Oxford University Press, 1994), 58; "The Orphanage," 30; Ronald Feldman, "Please Sir, I'll Need More," *Spokesman-Review,* 18 December 1994: A17. For a positive assessment of life in an orphanage in the 1950s, see Richard McKenzie, *Home: A Memoir of Growing Up in an Orphanage* (New York: Basic Books, 1996). McKenzie's survey of several hundred alumni from his and several other orphanages discovered that the former residents have done exceptionally well, socially, professionally, and psychologically (pp. 4–6). For another defense of institutional care, see Mary-Lou Weisman, "When Parents Are Not in the Best Interests of the Child," *The Atlantic Monthly* (July 1994): 43–63, but Weisman makes clear how expensive well-run institutions are.

13. Katha Pollitt, "Subject to Debate," *The Nation* (12 December 1994): 171.

14. "Child-Care Issues Haunt Society," *Spokesman-Review*, 11 March 1995; "Children of a Lesser Country," *The New Yorker* (15 January 1996): 24 (Edelman).
15. Ellen Goodman, "Who Will Win Custody of the Kids?" *Spokesman-Review*, 26 July 1995; Joel Best, *Threatened Children Rhetoric and Concern about Child-Victims* (Chicago: University of Chicago Press, 1990), 23–24, 190n4 (missing).
16. Children's Defense Fund, *The State of America's Children*, 18–19, 72–73; Barbara Vobejda, "Unto the Next Generation," *The Washington Post National Weekly Edition* (11–17 April 1994): 37, and Ted Conover, "The Hand-Off," *New York Times Magazine* (8 May 1994): 30 (AIDS).
17. On criminalizing child abuse, see Costin, Karger, and Stoesz, *The Politics of Child Abuse in America*, 142–43, 165, 182, and Lindsey, *The Welfare of Children*, esp. 165; Michael Costello, "The Big Leftist Lie about Domestic Violence," *Lewiston Tribune*, 27 January 1996 (qtn.); "Bill would Ease State Definition of Child Abuse," *Spokesman-Review*, 26 January 1996: B1, 4; "Child Abuse Bill Denounced at Public Hearing," ibid., 27 January 1996: B3.

Bibliographic Essay

On the history of dependent, neglected, and abused children in the United States, there are several invaluable collections of primary materials, laced with scholarly commentary. Most prominent is Robert H. Bremner, ed., *Children and Youth in America: A Documentary History*, 3 vols. (Cambridge, Mass.: Harvard University Press, 1970–74). Also important are Edith Abbott, *The Child and the State*, 2 vols. (Chicago: University of Chicago Press, 1938), and Henry W. Thurston, *The Dependent Child* (New York: Columbia University Press, 1930). Robert H. Bremner, ed., *Care of Dependent Children in the Late Nineteenth and Early Twentieth Centuries* (New York: Arno Press, 1974), is a small collection of reprinted essays by well-known child savers such as Hastings Hart and Homer Folks.

Joseph M. Hawes and N. Ray Hiner's *American Childhood: A Research Guide and Historical Handbook* (Westport, Conn.: Greenwood Press, 1985) is an important reference work and guide to the historical literature on American children. Hawes and Hiner have also edited a fine anthology of recent historical essays, *Growing Up in America: Children in Historical Perspective* (Urbana, Ill.: University of Illinois Press, 1985). Harvey Graff, ed., *Growing Up in America: Historical Experience* (Detroit: Wayne State University Press, 1987), is a similarly useful collection.

Dependent, neglected, and abused children have been conspicuous figures in the history of American welfare. Histories of social welfare in the United States that include considerable information about children are Walter I. Trattner, *From Poor Law to Welfare State: A History of Social Welfare in America*, 2d ed. (New York: Free Press, 1979); Michael B. Katz, *In the Shadow of the Poorhouse: A Social History of Welfare in America* (New York: Basic Books, 1987); and Mimi Abramovitz, *Regulating the Lives of Women: Social Welfare Policy from Colonial Times to the Present* (Boston: South End Press, 1988). Theda Skocpol's *Protecting Soldiers and Mothers: The Political Origins of Social Policy in the United States* (Cambridge, Mass.: Harvard University Press, 1992) is a sweeping synthesis of the concept of a maternalist welfare state; Skocpol argues that the welfare state's origins can be found in the pensions for veterans and mothers. See also Linda Gordon, "The New Feminist Scholarship on the Welfare State," in Gordon, ed., *Women, the State, and Welfare* (Madison: University of Wisconsin Press, 1990). *Unto the Least of These: Social Services for Children* (New York: Appleton-Century-Crofts, Inc., 1947), by Emma O. Lundberg, still contains useful information about the history of child welfare services, as do *Children of the Storm: Black Children and American Child Welfare* (New York: Harcourt Brace Jovanovich, 1972), by Andrew Billingsley and Jeanne M. Giovannoni, and Jan Mason's "An Historical Policy Analysis of United States Child Welfare Policy" (Ph.D. diss., University of New South Wales, 1986).

The history of children is, of course, interwoven with that of the family, a subject that has spawned a rich and abundant literature. Good starting points are Steven Mintz and Susan Kellogg, *Domestic Revolutions: A Social History of American Family Life* (New York: Free Press, 1988); Stephanie Coontz, *The Way We Never Were: American Families and the Nostalgia Trap* (New York: BasicBooks, 1992); Arlene Skolnick, *Embattled Paradise: The American Family in an Age of Uncertainty* (New York: BasicBooks, 1991); Mary F. Berry, *The Politics of Parenthood: Child Care, Women's Rights, and the Myth of the Good Mother* (New York: Viking, 1993); and Steven Mintz, "Regulating the American Family," *Journal of Family History* 14, no. 4 (1989): 387–408. See also Bruce Bellingham, "The History of Childhood Since the 'Invention of Childhood': Some Issues in the Eighties," *Journal of Family History* 13, no. 2 (1988): 347–58.

For studies of the shifting historical perceptions of children, so fundamental to the changing awareness of children's issues, see Peter Slater, *Children in the New England Mind in Death and Life* (Hamden, Conn.: Archon Books, 1977); Bernard Wishy, *The Child and the Republic: The Dawn of Modern American Child Nurture* (Philadelphia: University of Pennsylvania Press, 1968); Joseph Kett, *Rites of Passage: Adolescence in America* (New York: BasicBooks, 1977); Karin Calvert, *Children in the House: The Material Culture of Early Childhood, 1600–1900* (Boston: Northeastern University Press, 1992); John R. Sutton, *Stubborn Children: Controlling Delinquency in the United States, 1640–1981* (Berkeley, Calif., University of California Press, 1988); and Viviana A. Zelizer, *Pricing the Priceless Child: The Changing Social Value of Children* (New York: Basic Books, 1985), which focuses mainly on the period between the 1870s and 1930s. Ann Douglas, *The Feminization of American Culture* (New York: Knopf, 1977), is also good on the sentimentalization of childhood. Articles concerning changing perceptions of children include William McLoughlin's influential essay, "Evangelical Child-rearing in the Age of Jackson: Francis Wayland's Views on When and How to Subdue the Willfulness of Children," *Journal of Social History* 9 (Fall 1975): 20–43; Anne M. Boylan, "Sunday Schools and Changing Evangelical Views of Children in the 1820s," *Church History* 48 (September 1979):

320–33; and Ruby Takanishi, "Childhood as a Social Issue: Historical Roots of Contemporary Child Advocacy Movements," *Journal of Social Issues* 34, no. 2 (1978): 8–28.

Thoughtful studies that place particular children's issues against the shifting social, cultural, and legal backdrop are Mary Ann Mason, *From Father's Property to Children's Rights: The History of Child Custody in the United States* (New York: Columbia University Press, 1994), and Michael Grossberg, "Children's Legal Rights? A Historical Look at a Legal Paradox," in Roberta Wollons, ed., *Children at Risk in America: History, Concepts, and Public Policy* (Albany, NY: State University of New York, 1993), 111–40, which examines the evolving language of the law. Joseph M. Hawes's *The Children's Rights Movement: A History of Advocacy and Protection* (Boston: Twayne, 1991) is a fine, brief overview of its subject, but see also Hamilton Cravens, "Child Saving in Modern America 1870s–1990s," in Wollons, ed., *Children at Risk in America*, 3–31. Joan Gittens's *Poor Relations: The Children of the State in Illinois, 1818–1990* (Urbana: University of Illinois Press, 1994) is an admirable state study that provides insights into national trends and pays substantial attention to dependent children. Gittens's conclusion that Illinois has historically "underfunded, underbuilt and undertaxed in regards to children's needs, with the result that its programs are often so inadequate as to constitute downright neglect" applies all too aptly to the entire history of children's welfare in the United States. Tim Hacsi's "From Indenture to Family Foster Care: A Brief History of Child Placing," *Child Welfare* 74 (January/February 1995): 162–80 is a solid, succinct overview.

A number of studies shed light on issues of child dependency, neglect, and abuse during particular eras. For the colonial and revolutionary period, "The Child in Seventeenth-Century America," by Ross W. Beales Jr., in Hawes and Hiner, *American Childhood*, 15–56, and Constance B. Schulz's "Children and Childhood in the Eighteenth Century," 57–109, are good starting points. On the colonial family, see especially Carole Shammas, "Anglo-American Household Government in Comparative Perspective," *The William and Mary Quarterly* 52 (January 1995): 104–44; Edmund S. Morgan, *The Puritan Family*, rev. ed. (New York: Harper & Row, 1966); John Demos, *A Little Commonwealth: Family Life in Plymouth Colony* (New York: Oxford University Press, 1970); Darrett B. and Anita H. Rutman, *A Place in Time: Middlesex County, Virginia, 1650–1750* (New York: Norton, 1984); and Philip Greven, *The Protestant Temperament: Patterns of Child-Rearing, Religious Experience, and the Self in Early America* (New York: Alfred A. Knopf, 1977). On orphans particularly, see Lois Green Carr, "The Development of the Maryland Orphans' Court, 1654–1715," in Aubrey C. Land et al., *Law, Society, and Politics in Colonial Maryland* (Baltimore: Johns Hopkins University Press, 1977), 41–62, and Alan D. Watson, "Orphanage in Colonial North Carolina: Edgecombe County as a Case Study," *North Carolina Historical Review* 52 (April 1975): 105–19. On indenture, see Marcus

W. Jernegan, *Laboring and Dependent Classes in Colonial America, 1607–1783* (Chicago: University of Chicago Press, 1931), and Lawrence W. Towner, "The Indentures of Boston's Poor Apprentices: 1734–1805," *Proceedings of the Colonial Society of Massachusetts* 43 (1962): 417–34. On the landmark Body of Liberties and "stubborn child" law in colonial Massachusetts, see Sutton, *Stubborn Children.*

For the nineteenth century, David J. Rothman's pioneering work, *The Discovery of the Asylum: Social Order and Disorder in the New Republic* (Boston: Little, Brown, and Co., 1971), includes much regarding houses of refuge and the emerging orphanages. Notable case studies include Priscilla F. Clement, *Welfare and the Poor in the Nineteenth-Century City: Philadelphia, 1800–1854* (Rutherford, N.J.: Fairleigh Dickinson University Press, 1985), and Eric C. Schneider, *In the Web of Class: Delinquents and Reformers in Boston, 1810s-1930s* (New York: New York University Press, 1992). A strength of Peter C. Holloran's *Boston's Wayward Children: Social Services for Homeless Children, 1830–1930* (Rutherford, N.J.: Fairleigh Dickinson University Press, 1989) is that it not only is loaded with information but also is attentive to issues of religion, race, ethnicity, and gender. Ruth Shackelford's "To Shield Them from Temptation: 'Child-Saving' Institutions and the Children of the Underclass in San Francisco, 1850–1910" (Ph.D. diss., Harvard University, 1991) is far more expansive than the title suggests; the first half of this prodigiously researched study is a sweeping overview of child-saving efforts in the United States until the late 1800s; the second half focuses mainly on the San Francisco Boys and Girls Aid Society. Richard A. Meckel effectively notes the sources of state intervention in behalf of children in the late 1800s in "Protecting the Innocents: Age Segregation and the Early Child Welfare Movement," *Social Service Review* (September 1985): 455–75.

Ronald D. Cohen's "Child-Saving and Progressivism, 1885–1915," in Hawes and Hiner, eds., *American Childhood*, 273–309, and Susan Tiffin's *In Whose Best Interest? Child Welfare Reform in the Progressive Era* (Westport, Conn.: Greenwood Press, 1982) emphasize the importance of children within the Progressive Era reform agenda. Anthony M. Platt's *The Child Savers: The Invention of Delinquency* (Chicago: University of Chicago Press, 1969) is an influential study but overemphasizes the theme of social control. More balanced is Steven Schlossman's *Love and the American Delinquent: The Theory and Practice of "Progressive" Juvenile Justice, 1825–1920* (Chicago: University of Chicago Press, 1977). Jack M. Holl's *Juvenile Reform in the Progressive Era: William R. George and the Junior Republic Movement* (Ithaca, N.Y.: Cornell University Press, 1971) is illuminating on the junior republic idea.

On the progressive reformers' efforts in behalf of dependent children, *The Care of Destitute, Neglected and Delinquent Children* (New York: Macmillan, 1902), by Homer Folks, is still valuable. For a more recent analysis, see LeRoy Ashby, *Saving the Waifs: Reformers and Dependent Children, 1890–1917* (Philadelphia: Temple University Press, 1984). Sandra M. Stehno's "Foster

Care for Dependent Black Children in Chicago, 1899–1934" (Ph.D. diss., University of Chicago, 1985) and Sandra M. O'Donnell's "The Care of Dependent African-American Children in Chicago: The Struggle Between Black Self-Help and Professionalism," *Journal of Social History* 27 (Summer 1994): 763–76, treat the issue of race and dependency. On the mothers' pension movement, Molly Ladd-Taylor's *Mother-Work: Women, Child Welfare, and the State, 1890–1930* (Urbana, Ill.: University of Illinois Press, 1994) is excellent, but see also Mark H. Leff, "Consensus for Reform: The Mothers' Pension Movement in the Progressive Era," *Social Service Review* 47 (September 1973): 397–417; Joanne Goodwin, "An Experiment in Paid Motherhood: The Implementation of Mothers' Pensions in Early Twentieth Century Chicago," *Gender and History* 4 (Autumn 1992): 323–42; and Ann Vandepol, "Dependent Children, Child Custody and the Mothers' Pensions: The Transformation of State-Family Relations in the Early 20th Century," *Social Problems* 29 (February 1982): 221–35.

The shift from mothers' pensions to Aid for Dependent Children (ADC) receives insightful treatment in Linda Gordon's laudable *Pitied But Not Entitled: Single Mothers and the History of Welfare* (New York: Free Press, 1994). Also useful is Christopher Howard's "Sowing the Seeds of 'Welfare': The Transformation of Mothers' Pensions, 1900–1940," *Journal of Policy History* 4, no. 2 (1992): 188–227. Winfred Bell's *Aid to Dependent Children* (New York: Columbia University Press, 1965) is a basic study. Invaluable works on ADC, and the later Aid to Families of Dependent Children (AFDC), within the larger context of debates over welfare, are James T. Patterson, *America's Struggle Against Poverty, 1900–1980* (Cambridge, Mass.: Harvard University Press, 1981), and Blanche D. Coll, *Safety Net: Welfare and Social Security, 1929–1979* (New Brunswick, N.J.: Rutgers University Press, 1995). Frances Fox Piven and Richard A. Cloward's *Regulating the Poor: The Functions of Public Welfare* (New York: Random House, 1971) includes useful information about AFDC during the 1960s, but see also Guida West, *The National Welfare Rights Movement: The Social Protest of Poor Women* (New York: Praeger, 1981).

Important works that focus on recent child welfare policies bearing upon dependency, neglect, and abuse are Leroy H. Pelton, *For Reasons of Poverty: A Critical Analysis of the Public Child Welfare System in the United States* (New York: Praeger, 1989), and Duncan Lindsey, *The Welfare of Children* (New York: Oxford University Press, 1994). Both fault the child welfare system for not confronting issues of poverty. Historically, according to Pelton, social welfare agencies have pursued incompatible roles, trying to investigate as well as to help families. Lindsey regrets that agencies have been caught up in protecting criminally assaulted children (the job of law enforcement agencies) rather than working to aid those who are impoverished.

In recent years, orphanages have begun to receive careful attention. Timothy A. Hacsi's " 'A Plain and Solemn Duty': A History of Orphan Asylums in

America" (Ph.D. diss., University of Pennsylvania, 1993) is a commendable overview. "Institutions for Dependent and Delinquent Children: Histories, Nineteenth-century Statistics, and Recurrent Goals," by Rachel Marks, in Donnell P. Pappenfort et al., eds., *Child Caring: Social Policy and the Institution* (Chicago: Aldine, 1973), and Alfred Kadushin's "Institutions for Dependent and Neglected Children," 145–76, have much information.

Susan L. Porter's "The Benevolent Asylum—Image and Reality: The Care and Training of Female Orphans in Boston, 1800–1840" (Ph.D. diss., Boston University, 1984) is an excellent case study of the early years of the Boston Female Asylum. Another case study, Judith A. Dulberger's "Refuge or Repressor: The Role of the Orphan Asylum in the Lives of Poor Children and Their Families in Late-Nineteenth-Century America" (D.A. diss., Carnegie-Mellon University, 1988), examines the transformation of the Albany Orphan Asylum. Using correspondence from superintendents, parents, and children, Dulberger shows how orphanages sometimes provided relief to poor families in crisis—an interpretation that other studies, particularly Nurith Zmora's solid work, *Orphanages Reconsidered: Child Care Institutions in Progressive Era Baltimore* (Philadelphia: Temple University Press, 1994), and Dulberger's *"Mother Donit Fore the Best": Correspondence of a Nineteenth-Century Orphan Asylum* (Syracuse: Syracuse University Press, 1996), a marvelous collection of letters and commentary, have helped to document. Three perceptive studies examine the history of various Jewish orphanages: Gary E. Polster, *Inside Looking Out: The Cleveland Jewish Orphan Asylum, 1868–1924* (Kent, Ohio: Kent State University Press, 1990); Hyman Bogen, *The Luckiest Orphans: A History of the Hebrew Orphan Asylum of New York* (Urbana, Ill.: University of Illinois Press, 1992); and Reena S. Friedman, *These Are Our Children: Jewish Orphanages in the United States, 1880–1925* (Hanover, N.H.: Brandeis University Press, 1994). For a model history that shows how the study of an institution can illuminate many themes, see Kenneth Cmiel, *A Home of Another Kind: One Chicago Orphanage and the Tangle of Child Welfare* (Chicago: University of Chicago Press, 1996).

Briefer studies of particular orphanages include Clyde Buckingham's "Early American Orphanages: Ebenezer and Bethesda," *Social Forces* 26 (March 1948): 311–21, which sketches out the history of those initial institutions. Elizabeth Glidden's *The Baby Fold: An Investment in Humanity* (Normal, Ill.: The Baby Fold, 1992) shows how one orphanage has adjusted over almost a century to changing policies and funding. See also Patricia Clement, "Children and Charity: Orphanages in New Orleans, 1817–1914," *Louisiana History* 27 (Fall 1986): 337–51; Marian J. Morton, "Homes for Poverty's Children: Cleveland's Orphanages, 1851–1933," *Ohio History* 10 (Winter-Spring 1989): 5–22; Jeanne Abrams, " 'For a Child's Sake': The Denver Sheltering Home for Jewish Children in the Progressive Era," *American Jewish History* 79 (Winter 1989/90): 181–202; Cecile P. Frey, "The House of Refuge for Colored Children," *The Journal of Negro History* 66 (Spring

1981): 10–25; R. S. Patterson and Patricia Rooke, "The Delicate Duty of Child Saving: Coldwater, Michigan, 1871–1896," *Michigan History* 61 (Fall 1977): 195–219; Priscilla F. Clement, "With Wise and Benevolent Purpose: Poor Children and the State Public School at Owatonna, 1885–1915," *Minnesota History* 49 (Spring 1984): 3–13; and Arthur E. Fink, "Changing Philosophies and Practices in North Carolina Orphanages," *North Carolina Historical Review* 48 (October 1971): 333–58. An examination of the St. Louis Protestant Orphan Asylum by Susan Whitelaw Downs and Michael W. Sherraden, "The Orphan Asylum in the Nineteenth Century," *Social Service Review* 57 (June 1983): 272–90, argues that changing labor market conditions required institutions to house children who were no longer part of the labor force. Kathleen Garrett's "The Cherokee Orphan Asylum," *Bulletin of the Oklahoma Agricultural and Mechanical College* 50 (1953): 3–38, is a short chronicle.

Especially good on the plight of orphan asylums during the Great Depression is Marshall B. Jones, "Crisis of the American Orphanage, 1931–1940," *Social Service Review* 63 (December 1989): 613–29. On the renewed popularity of orphanages by the 1990s, see Penelope Lemov, "The Return of the Orphanage," *Governing* (May 1991): 30–35. Eve P. Smith's "Bring Back the Orphanages? What Policymakers of Today Can Learn from the Past," *Child Welfare* 74 (January/February 1995): 115–42, is a cautionary tale.

Although Charles Loring Brace's famous book, *The Dangerous Classes of New York, and Twenty Years' Work Among Them* (New York: Wynkoop & Hallenbeck, 1872), has long been familiar, careful assessments of Brace himself, of "placing out," and of the orphan trains have only recently been made. Miriam Z. Langsam's *Children West: A History of the Placing-Out System of the New York Children's Aid Society 1853–1890* (Madison, Wis.: The State Historical Society of Wisconsin, 1964) helped to point the way. Then came a series of brilliantly provocative interpretations of Brace that underlined his contributions to nineteenth-century reform: R. Richard Wohl, "The 'Country Boy' Myth and Its Place in American Urban Culture: The Nineteenth-Century Contribution," *Perspectives in American History* 3 (1969): 77–156; Thomas Bender, *Toward an Urban Vision: Ideas and Institutions in Nineteenth Century America* (Lexington: University Press of Kentucky, 1974); and Paul Boyer, *Urban Masses and Moral Order in America, 1820–1920* (Cambridge: Harvard University Press, 1978).

Kristine E. Nelson's "The Best Asylum: Charles Loring Brace and Foster Family Care" (D.S.W. diss., University of California, Berkeley, 1980) is an outstanding work, especially regarding the ideology of Brace's movement, which "legitimated and explained fostering," and its blending of the old and the new. In " 'Little Wanderers': A Socio-Historical Study of the Nineteenth Century Origins of Child Fostering and Adoption Reform, Based on Early Records" (Ph.D. diss., University of Pennsylvania, 1984), Bruce Bellingham uses the New York Children's Aid Society records during its formative months to establish a profile of the children and to distinguish between the agency's rhetoric and practice. Several published essays contain the key arguments of Bellingham's dissertation: "Waifs and Strays: Child Abandonment, Foster Care, and Families in Mid-Nineteenth-Century New York," in Peter Mandler, ed., *The Uses of Charity: The Poor on Relief in the 19th-Century Metropolis* (Philadelphia: University of Pennsylvania Press, 1990): 123–60; "The 'Unspeakable Blessing': Street Children, Reform Rhetoric, and Misery in Early Industrial Capitalism," *Politics and Society* 12, no. 3 (1983): 303–30; and "Institution and Family: An Alternative View of Nineteenth-Century Child Saving," *Social Problems* (December 1986): S33-57.

Other notable interpretations of Brace and his agency appear in the following works: Christine Stansell, *City of Women: Sex and Class in New York, 1789–1869* (Urbana, Ill.: University of Illinois Press, 1987); Jeanne F. Cook, "A History of Placing-Out: The Orphan Trains," *Child Welfare* 74 (January/February 1995): 181–97; Shackelford, "To Shield Them from Temptation"; and especially Marilyn I. Holt, *The Orphan Trains: Placing Out in America* (Lincoln, Neb.: University of Nebraska Press, 1992). Holt's fine book, drawing on a wide variety of sources, provides a comprehensive history of the orphan trains. For a popularly written account, see Leslie Wheeler, "The Orphan Trains," *American History Illustrated* 18 (December 1983): 10–23. And for the recollections of an orphan whom the NYCAS sent to Kansas in 1899, see Harry Colwell, "A New York Orphan Comes to Kansas," *Kansas History* 8 (Summer 1985): 110–23. The one-hour *American Experience* television segment "The Orphan Trains" (first shown on 27 November 1995) includes information from recently discovered agency letters and a number of interviews. A. Blake Brophy's *Foundlings on the Frontier: Racial and Religious Conflict in Arizona Territory, 1904–1905* (Tucson: University of Arizona Press, 1972) is a revealing treatment of the fate of some children placed by the New York Foundling Hospital.

On the history of adoption in the United States, see especially Joseph Ben-Or, "The Law of Adoption in the United States: Its Massachusetts Origins and the Statute of 1851," *The New England Historical and Genealogical Register* 130 (October 1976): 259–72; Stephen B. Presser, "The Historical Background of the American Law of Adoption," *Journal of Family Law* 11 (1971): 443–516; and Jamil S. Zainaldin, "The Emergence of a Modern American Family Law: Child Custody, Adoption, and the Courts, 1796–1851," *Northwestern University Law Review* 73 (1979): 1038–89. E. Wayne Carp's important work on the history of openness and secrecy in adoption (forthcoming from Harvard University Press) has already yielded some fruitful essays: "The Sealed Adoption Records Controversy in Historical Perspective: The Case of the Children's Home Society of Washington, 1895–1988," *Journal of Sociology and Social Welfare* 19 (June 1992): 27–57; "Professional Social Workers, Adoption, and the Problem of Illegitimacy,

1915–1945," *Journal of Policy History* 6, no. 3 (1994): 161–84; "Adoption and Disclosure of Family Information: A Historical Perspective," *Child Welfare* 74 (January/February 1995): 217–39. Rickie Solinger, *Wake Up Little Susie: Single Pregnancy and Race Before* Roe v. Wade (New York: Routledge, 1992), is insightful on "the postwar white adoption mandate." In "Problem Adoptions," *The Atlantic Monthly* (September 1992): 37–69, Katharine Davis Fishman concludes that "not all children thrive in traditional nuclear families, and an honest view of adoption difficulties dictates that we now explore other options."

Lincoln Caplan's *An Open Adoption* (Boston: Houghton Mifflin, 1990) provides a brief history and a case study of that controversial issue. Psychologist Betty Jean Lifton has been a leading advocate of open adoption reform; see especially her *Twice Born: Memoirs of an Adopted Daughter* (New York: McGraw-Hill, 1975), *Lost and Found: The Adoption Experience* (New York: HarperCollins, 1988), and *Journey of the Adopted Self: A Quest for Wholeness* (New York: BasicBooks, 1994). The personal accounts of Jean Paton, *Orphan Voyage* (New York: Vantage, 1968), and Florence Fisher, *The Search for Anna Fisher* (New York: Arthur Fields, 1973), are impassioned works that challenge confidential adoptions and provide rallying points for an open process. For a popular guide to open adoption, see Lois R. Melina and Sharon K. Roszia, *The Open Adoption Experience* (New York: HarperCollins, 1993).

On the controversies surrounding transracial adoption, the main sources include Rita J. Simon and Howard Alstein, *Transracial Adoption* (New York: John Wiley & Sons, 1977); Elizabeth Bartholet, *Family Bonds: Adoption and the Politics of Parenting* (Boston: Houghton Mifflin, 1993); J. Douglas Bates, *Gift Children: A Story of Race, Family, and Adoption in a Divided America* (New York: Ticknor and Fields, 1993); and Randall Kennedy, "Orphans of Separatism: The Painful Politics of Transracial Adoption," *The American Prospect* (Spring 1984): 38–45. Kathy Dobie's "Nobody's Child: The Battle Over Interracial Adoption," *Village Voice* (8 August 1989), 18 ff., is a poignant essay focusing on the San Francisco area in the 1980s. David Rosner and Gerald Markowitz, in "Race and Foster Care," *Dissent* (Spring 1993): 233–37, provide a sad reminder of the larger historical context in which "the current suffering of America's dependent minority children" has unfolded. See also Patricia M. Collmeyer, "From 'Operation Brown Baby' to 'Opportunity': The Placement of Children of Color at the Boys and Girls Aid Society of Oregon," *Child Welfare*, 74 (January/February, 1995): 242–63.

On child abuse and neglect, Beatrice J. Kalisch's huge *Child Abuse and Neglect: An Annotated Bibliography* (Westport, Conn.: Greenwood Press, 1978) is a thorough guide to the literature that existed by the late 1970s. Bertram Wyatt-Brown, "Child Abuse, Public Policy and Childrearing: An Historical Approach," in Barbara L. Finkelstein, ed., *Governing the Young: Working Papers No. 2* (College Park, Md.: University of Maryland College of

Education, 1981): 1–34, discusses common generalizations about the causes of child abuse, criticizes social control interpretations, and warns against interpretations that homogenize family experience and simplify childrearing patterns. Useful essays regarding legislation and the changing scholarly literature on the subject of children at risk are contained in Robert T. Ammerman and Michael Hersen, eds., *Children at Risk: An Evaluation of Factors Contributing to Child Abuse and Neglect* (New York: Plenum Press, 1990). E. Wayne Carp, "Family History, Family Violence: A Review Essay," *Journal of Policy History*, 3, no. 2 (1991): 203–23, is thoughtful on the larger context of family violence in American history.

Indispensable on the various "discoveries" of abuse are Barbara Nelson, *Making an Issue of Child Abuse: Political Agenda Setting* (Chicago: University of Chicago Press, 1984); Lela B. Costin, Howard J. Karger, and David Stoesz, *The Politics of Child Abuse in America* (New York: Oxford University Press, 1996); Joel Best, *Threatened Children: Rhetoric and Concern about Child-Victims* (Chicago: University of Chicago Press, 1990); John M. Johnson, "Symbolic Salvation: The Changing Meanings of the Child Maltreatment Movement," *Studies in Symbolic Interaction* 6 (1985): 289–305, and "Horror Stories and the Construction of Child Abuse," in Joel Best, ed., *Images of Issues: Typifying Contemporary Social Problems* (New York: Aldine De Gruyter, 1989), 5–19; and Stephen J. Pfohl, "The 'Discovery' of Child Abuse," *Social Problems*, 24 (February 1977): 310–23.

Exceptionally fine histories of family violence that have much material on children are Elizabeth Pleck, *Domestic Tyranny: The Making of American Social Policy against Family Violence from Colonial Times to the Present* (New York: Oxford University Press, 1987), and Linda Gordon, *Heroes of Their Own Lives: The Politics of Family Violence* (New York: Penguin Books, 1988). Mason P. Thomas Jr.'s "Child Abuse and Neglect, Part I: Historical Overview, Legal Matrix, and Social Perspectives," *The North Carolina Law Review* 50 (February 1972): 293–349, is a useful essay that covers much legal and social ground.

For additional, significant information on the late-nineteenth-century movement to end cruelty to children, see Sherri Broder, "Informing the 'Cruelty': The Monitoring of Respectability in Philadelphia's Working-Class Neighborhoods in the Late Nineteenth Century," *Radical America* 21 (July-August, 1987): 34–47, and Lela B. Costin, "Unraveling the Mary Ellen Legend: Origins of the 'Cruelty' Movement," *Social Service Review* 65 (June 1991): 203–23. Mary Ellen Connolly's life and the lives of her children are traced in Stephen Lazoritz, "Whatever Happened to Mary Ellen?" *Child Abuse and Neglect* 14 (1990): 143–49. Instructive, too, is Catherine J. Ross's "The Lessons of the Past: Defining and Controlling Child Abuse in the United States," in George Gerbner et al., eds., *Child Abuse: An Agenda for Action* (New York: Oxford University Press, 1980), 63–81.

Critical analyses of the physical abuse of children include Philip Greven's *Spare the Child: The Religious Roots of Punishment and the Psychological*

Impact of Physical Abuse (New York: Knopf, 1991), which examines the impact of the apocalyptic impulse in American Protestantism on childrearing. "The American family is often a most dangerous place to be," writes Greven, fusing history with an appeal for an end to "violence that begets further violence." David Gil's *Violence Against Children: Physical Abuse in the United States* (Cambridge: Harvard University Press, 1970) is a pioneering study. *Intimate Violence* (New York: Simon & Schuster, 1988), by Richard J. Gelles and Murray A. Straus, is the product of two leading scholars of family violence. For their more recent statements, see Straus, *Beating the Devil Out of Them: Corporal Punishment in American Families* (New York: Lexington Books, 1994), which includes useful surveys of family violence, and Gelles's *The Book of David: How Preserving Families Can Cost Children's Lives* (New York: Basic Books, 1996), in which he shifts from his earlier enthusiasm for family preservation programs.

Vincent J. Fontana's *Somewhere a Child Is Crying: Maltreatment—Causes and Prevention* (New York: Macmillan, 1973) and *Save the Family, Save the Child* (New York: Dutton, 1991) are eloquent works by another authority. Also important are the major anthologies by Ray E. Helfer and Ruth S. Kempe, eds., *The Battered Child* (Chicago: University of Chicago Press, 1968), which has gone through subsequent editions, and Leroy H. Pelton, ed., *The Social Context of Child Abuse and Neglect* (New York: Human Sciences Press, 1981). *Defining Child Abuse* (New York: Free Press, 1979), by Jeanne M. Giovannoni and Rosina M. Becerra, wrestles with the problem of definitions and includes a historical chapter on child mistreatment. Naomi F. Chase's *A Child Is Being Beaten: Violence Against Children, An American Tragedy* (New York: McGraw-Hill, 1975) is a readable account that discusses many topics, including the Roxanne Felumero case, institutional abuse, and family courts. N. Ray Hiner's "Children's Rights, Corporal Punishment, and Child Abuse: Changing American Attitudes, 1870–1920," *Bulletin of the Menninger Clinic* 43 (1979): 233–48, and John Demos's "Child Abuse in Context: An Historian's Perspective," in Demos, *Past, Present, and Personal: The Family and the Life Course in American History* (New York: Oxford University Press, 1986), are fine historical essays. Poignant case studies include Joyce Johnson, *What Lisa Knew: The Truth and Lies of the Steinberg Case* (New York: G. P. Putnam's, 1990); Barry Siegel, *A Death in White Bear Lake* (New York: Bantam, 1990); and Russ Rymer, *Genie: An Abused Child's Flight from Silence* (New York: HarperCollins, 1993).

Recently, the sexual abuse of children has generated a considerable literature. Journalistic studies that are particularly informative and balanced are John Crewdson's *By Silence Betrayed: Sexual Abuse of Children in America* (Boston: Little, Brown, 1988) and David Hechler's *The Battle and the Backlash: The Child Abuse Sexual War* (Lexington, Mass: Lexington Books, 1988), both of which show the injustices of cases such as the one in Jordan, Minnesota, but also emphasize the harsh realities of child abuse. Debby Nathan is among the more perceptive students of the ritual abuse panic of the 1980s and 1990s; see, for example, "The Making of a Modern Witch Trial," and "Sex, the Devil, and Day Care," *Village Voice* (29 September 1987). *Satan's Silence: Ritual Abuse and the Making of a Modern American Witch Hunt* (New York: BasicBooks, 1995), by Nathan and Michael Snedeker, is a superior work that places the panic in the context of a troubled society's search for scapegoats during an era of unsettlingly rapid change. Also relevant in that regard is Lawrence Wright's "Child-Care Demons," *New Yorker* (3 October 1994): 5–6.

The role of recovered memories in sexual abuse cases has unleashed a storm of debate. Lawrence Wright's *Remembering Satan* (New York: Knopf, 1994) is a gripping account of a case in Olympia, Washington. Ellen Bass and Laura Davis's *The Courage to Heal: A Guide for Women Survivors of Child Abuse* (New York: Harper & Row, 1988), a best-selling self-help book, stirred up controversy by asserting that even women who could not remember being abused were possibly victims. *Unchained Memories: True Stories of Traumatic Memories, Lost and Found* (New York: BasicBooks, 1994), by Lenore Terr, presents eight case studies, including that of Marilyn Van Derbur. For skeptical views, see Michael D. Yapko, *Suggestions of Abuse: True and False Memories of Childhood Sexual Trama* (New York: Simon & Schuster, 1994), and Frederick Crews, *The Memory Wars: Freud's Legacy in Dispute* (New York: New York Review, 1995). According to his article "False Memory," *Z Magazine* (April 1994): 31–37, James Cronin believes the controversy over false memories is a "contrived" and regrettable diversion from the terrible realities of abuse—a diversion whose fundamental purpose is to turn attention from family violence.

First-person accounts of child abuse have grown in number. Buster Keaton's *My Wonderful World of Slapstick* (Garden City, N.Y.: Doubleday, 1960) is an early example, but Christina Crawford's *Mommie Dearest* (New York: William Morrow, 1978) was pivotal in broadening public perceptions of how extensive child abuse has been. Suzanne Somers's *Wednesday's Children: Adult Survivors of Abuse Speak Out* (New York: Healing Vision, 1992) features essays by 22 well-known entertainers and writers who suffered either emotional, physical, or sexual abuse. Memoirs with searing renditions of abuse include Richard Rhodes, *A Hole in the World: An American Boyhood* (New York: Simon & Schuster, 1990); Anthony G. Johnson, *A Rock and a Hard Place* (New York: Crown, 1993); and Ruthie Bolton, *Gal: A True Life* (New York: Harcourt, Brace, 1994). Brief personal stories may be found in Ellen Bass and Louise Thornton, eds., *I Never Told Anyone: Writings by Women Survivors of Child Sexual Abuse* (New York: Harper & Row, 1983), and Mike Lew, *Victims No Longer: Men Recovering from Incest and Other Sexual Child Abuse* (New York: HarperCollins, 1988, 1990).

For firsthand accounts of experiences in orphanages and/or foster care, see Richard McKenzie, *The Home: A Memoir of Growing Up in an Orphanage*

(New York: BasicBooks, 1996), a poignant and mostly favorable recollection, and Art Buchwald's less nostalgic but witty *Leaving Home: A Memoir* (New York: Fawcett Columbine, 1993). *Tender Mercies: Inside the World of a Child Abuse Investigator* (Chicago: The Noble Press, 1992), by Keith Richards, is a moving discussion of the travails and conditions that caseworkers face. For the reflections of a trial judge who dealt often with the cases of dependent, neglected, and abused children, see Lois G. Forer, *Unequal Protection: Women, Children, and the Elderly in Court* (New York: Norton, 1991).

Child protection agencies have faced swelling criticism in recent years. Among the most formidable critics is Richard Wexler, whose wide-ranging *Wounded Innocents: The Real Victims of the War Against Child Abuse* (Buffalo: Prometheus Books, 1990), is an unsparing attack on "the child-protective empire." Wexler argues scathingly that child saving from the nineteenth century until the present has been compulsively interventionist, unsympathetic and insensitive to poor people, and overly reliant on the foster care system. He argues for family preservation, but in terms of society's obligations to help families; and he combines criticism with a long list of recommendations to improve the system and make it more protective of children.

A number of vociferous critics on the right share Wexler's dislike of the child protective agencies but, unlike him, focus mainly on the rights of parents, rather than of children. Among the most prominent is Mary Pride's *The Child Abuse Industry* (Westchester, Ill.: Crossway Books, 1986). Paul and Shirley Eberle's *The Politics of Child Abuse* (Secaucus, N.J.: Lyle Stuart, 1986) presents the views of organizations such as Victims of Child Abuse Laws (VOCAL). John E. B. Myers, *The Backlash: Child Protection Under Fire* (Thousand Oaks, Calif.: Sage Publications, Inc., 1994), contains essays from the perspectives of VOCAL as well as from critics of the backlash.

As a counterbalance to polemical treatments of interventionism, the commendably nuanced historical interpretations of Gordon's *Heroes of Their Own Lives* and Broder's "Informing the 'Cruelty' " are refreshing. Although both scholars agree that the anticruelty movements were often condescending toward poor people, they reject simplistic social control theories and show that working-class people often favored reforms and looked to the middle- and upper-class child savers for help. For additional essays that stress historical complexities, see Broder, "Child Care or Child Neglect? Baby Farming in Late-Nineteenth-Century Philadelphia," *Gender and Society* 2 (June 1988): 128–48, and Gordon, "Child Abuse, Gender, and the Myth of Family Independence: A Historical Critique," *Child Welfare* 64 (May-June 1985): 213–24.

Among the many sources that discuss major court cases, as well as changing laws and policies concerning children, Michael Grossberg's *Governing the Hearth: Law and the Family in Nineteenth-Century America* (Chapel Hill, NC: University of North Carolina Press, 1985) and *A Judgment for Solomon: The D'Hauteville Case and Legal Experience in Antebellum America* (Cambridge: Cambridge University Press, 1996), and Peter W. Bardaglio's "Families, Sex, and the Law: The Legal Transformation of the Nineteenth-Century Southern Household" (Ph.D. diss., Stanford University, 1987) are impressive. *Child, Parent, and State: Law and Policy Reader* (Philadelphia: Temple University Press, 1994), by S. Randall Humm et al., is a fine anthology that includes informative essays on the *DeShaney* case as well as foster care. Monrad G. Paulsen's "The Legal Framework for Child Protection," *Columbia Law Review* 66 (April 1966): 679–717, is also good.

Very useful on particular laws are Mary A. Jimenez, "Permanency Planning and the Child Abuse Prevention and Treatment Act: The Paradox of Child Welfare Policy," *Journal of Sociology and Social Welfare* 17 (September 1990): 55–72; Marc Mannes, "Factors and Events Leading to the Passage of the Indian Child Welfare Act," *Child Welfare* 64 (January/February 1995): 264–82; Manuel P. Guerrero, "Indian Child Welfare Act of 1978: A Response to the Threat to Indian Culture Caused by Foster and Adoptive Placements of Indian Children," *American Indian Law Review* 7 (1979): 51–77; and Richard Holodny, "Reforming Foster Care: A History of New York's [1979] Child Welfare Reform Act" (D.S.W. diss., Yeshiva University, 1993). An extremely valuable insider's account ot the 1996 welfare legislation that ended AFDC is David T. Ellwood, "Welfare Reform As I Knew It," *The American Prospect* (May-June 1996): 22–29. Also useful on changing policies is Ruth A. Mattingly's "The Legal Development of Child Dependency Policy: A Case Study of Federal and Pennsylvania State Policies from 1900 to the Present" (D.S.W. diss., Bryn Mawr, 1985).

Index

Abbott, Edith, 81, 96, 98, 114
Abbott, Grace, 81, 114, 116
Abbott, Jacob, 58
abortion, 66, 166
abuse: and animals, 56, 57, 58, 59; and wives, 58, 184. *See also* child abuse
"abuse excuse," 163
Act to Provide for the Adoption of Children (Mass., 1851), 43
Addams, Jane, 80, 81, 83
"adopted child syndrome," 168
Adoptees Liberty Association, 144
American Spectator, 164
adoption, 16, 125; and antebellum courts, 42–43; and "best interests of the child," 42; championing in 1990s, 167; colonial precedents for, 42; crisis in, 169–73; debates over, 5, 145; and English common law, 42; federal tax credit for, 173; and gay couples, 172–73; haphazard procedures of, 106–7, 147, 168; increase in, 120, 122–23, 144; legislative formalization of, 43; and Massachusetts Act, 43; and New England Home for Little Wander-

ers, 43; and openness issue, 145, 167–68, 172; "placing out" movement's impact on, 42–44; "postwar mandate" for, 122–23; problems of, 106–7, 175, 181; and race, 73, 122–23, 167, 168–71; rights movement of, 145, 172; and sealed records, 144–45, 167; Senate hearings on, 124; underground market of, 123–24. *See also* Children's Home Societies; Indian Child Welfare Act
Adoption Assistance and Child Welfare Act (1980), 140, 174, 180–81, 221n. 49
Adoptive Parents Committee, 144
adults, as determiners of children's needs, 1–7, 115, 132, 149
African Americans, 122, 125–26, 131; and Aid to Dependent Children, 116, 121; and antebellum institutions, 32–33; and apprenticeship laws, 76; and child abuse in slavery, 13–14; informal child-care system of, 85; and mothers' pensions, 97, 112; and "placing out" movement,

The Author

LeRoy Ashby is the Claudius and Mary Johnson Distinguished Professor of History at Washington State University. His other works include *The Spearless Leader: Senator Borah and the Progressive Movement in the 1920s* (1972), *Saving the Waifs: Reformers and Dependent Children, 1890–1917* (1984), *William Jennings Bryan: Champion of Democracy* (1987), and, with Rod Gramer, *Fighting the Odds: The Life of Senator Frank Church* (1994), winner of the 1994 Evans Biography Award. Ashby has twice been named the state of Washington's Professor of the Year by the Council for the Advancement and Support of Education.

The Editors

Joseph M. Hawes is Professor of History at the University of Memphis. His most recent book is *The Children's Rights Movement: A History of Advocacy and Protection* (Twayne, 1991). He is also the author of the forthcoming *American Children Between the Wars, 1920–1940* (Twayne).

N. Ray Hiner is Chancellors' Club Teaching Professor of History and Education at the University of Kansas. He has published widely on the history of children and education in the United States and is coeditor (with Joseph M. Hawes) of *Growing up in America* (1985), *American Childhood* (1985), and *Children in Historical Perspective* (1991). He is currently writing a book on children in the life and thought of Cotton Mather.